AUSTRALIAN CRIME

AUSTRALIAN CRIME

Edited by Malcolm Brown

CHILLING TALES OF OUR TIME

LANSDOWNE

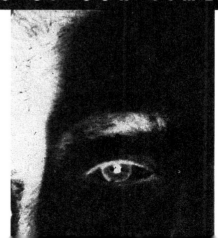

Published by Lansdowne Australia Pty Limited
Level 5, 70 George Street, Sydney NSW 2000, Australia

First published 1993

© Copyright: Lansdowne Australia Pty Limited
© Copyright design: Lansdowne Australia Pty Limited

Designer: Stan Lamond, Lamond Art & Design
Cover design: Judy Hungerford
Managing Director: Jane Curry
Production Manager: Sally Stokes

Typeset in Palatino
Printed in Singapore by Toppan Printing Co (Pte) Ltd

National Library of Australia Cataloguing-in-Publication data

Brown, Malcolm, 1947-
Australian crime: chilling tales of our time.

Includes index.
ISBN 1 86302 312 7

1. Crime—Australia—History. 2. Crime—Australia—Case studies.
I. Title
364.994

All effort has been made to contact owners of copyright.

For

BASIL SWEENEY

CEDRIC CULBERT

BILL ARCHIBALD

*and all the other hardworking,
old-style police reporters of
Australian journalism.*

CONTENTS

from settlement to the 1920s

CRIMINAL AUSTRALIA: A VIOLENT HISTORY

Terror in Van Diemen's Land   *16*
Bushrangers hold the colony to ransom

The Bank of Australia Robbery   *26*
Daring thieves tunnel into a bank vault

The Rainbird and Other Murders   *36*
Cold-blooded killings and legal executions

The Life and Times of Thunderbolt   *46*
Fred Ward, Australia's most wanted man

Squizzy Taylor, Gangster   *56*
The crime wars of 1920s Melbourne

1960s

KIDNAPPINGS, NIGHTCLUBS AND THE MAFIOSI

The Plight of the Defenceless   *70*
Abduction and murder of children

Eric Cooke, Random Killer   *80*
Death on the streets of Perth by night

Abe Saffron   *90*
The many sides of the man and his money

Domenico Italiano, Australian "Godfather"   *100*
The workings of the mafia in Victoria

The Hunt for Larry Boy   *109*
Stalking a killer across the Outback

The Pressler Case   *118*
Double murder and double-dealing

1970s

MADNESS, MURDER AND INTIMIDATION

The Croation Bombings   *132*
International terrorism in Australia

The Dark Side of Adelaide   *141*
Sex, fear, perversion and a serial killer

The Whiskey au Go Go Outrage   *151*
Fifteen die in a nightclub inferno

The Great Bookie Robbery   *161*
Australia's answer to the Great Train Robbery

Battle for the Waterfront   *170*
Violence and death in a Melbourne union

The Truro Murders   *179*
Seven bodies, one madman

1980 and beyond

DRUGS, GANGSTERS AND GRANNIES

The Murder of Donald Mackay   *192*
His death changed the drug world

Barlow and Chambers   *202*
Two Perth-based drug traffickers hang

The Walsh Street Shootings   *212*
The police versus the Melbourne underworld

Neddy Smith in the Spotlight   *222*
Thug, thief, rapist, murderer, informant

The Granny Killer   *232*
The man who preyed on elderly women

CRIMINAL AUSTRALIA: A VIOLENT HISTORY

Australia might or might not become a Republic. At the time of writing, the issue was up for debate and many words were likely to be spoken before it was resolved. But one suggestion came quietly, at a Sydney seminar in April 1993, organised by a social conscience group, Christian Forums for Justice. Professor Stuart Rees, Professor of Social Work at Sydney University, said in a paper, "Denial as the Means of Supporting Violence", that if Australians were fair dinkum about creating a Republic, they should look to some of the more unpalatable truths about themselves.

"A precondition of Australia becoming a Republic could be a willingness to be more open about the violence which led to the creation of a colony over 200 years ago", he said. "The creation of a Republic provides an opportunity to repudiate that violence, to ... say that we will no longer pretend that violence did not occur and is not embedded in this culture. To do otherwise is to perpetuate the processes of denial which place vulnerable men and women and children at the mercy of those stronger and often more privileged people to whom they are exposed".

Rees asks whether the time might not be right to face the reality that we have a violent past.

We differentiate between "direct" and "indirect" violence. Direct violence we define as a wilful, hostile act (or acts) causing physical injury to a person or property. Theft or damage to property is, in the eyes of law, so close to physical assault that aggravated damage is labelled "malicious injury". The use of force during law enforcement and military operations comes within the definition, although most of this is legally justifiable.

Indirect violence is the injustice which can arise in social and economic systems. We do not concentrate on this subject, though it is implicit in the background circumstances of so much direct violence. Attitudes towards Aborigines have for long been part of that background. These sank to their lowest level in Tasmania and in subsequent history they have never been satisfactory. Attempts have been made to achieve some sort of compromise in the operation of the law as it applies to our indigenous people. But the white man's law is still applied, as our chapter on Larry Boy Janba and his flight from white justice in northern Australia illustrates.

Professor Rees says that in any review of Australia's violent past, we must look for the hidden victims—women beaten by their husbands, children abused by family members, men set upon by bullies—people who have been overlooked in the past in the various sanitised accounts of Australia's history and society. As our chapter on child abuse makes clear, some cases involving children have received national, and justifiable, prominence but there is without doubt a hidden tragedy throughout our history. And for that matter, what of the abuse of the elderly, whose vulnerability was so brutally exposed when pie salesman John Wayne Glover went on his rampage?

The reader of this history will be taken through or referred to more than 170 violent deaths, as well as an assortment of thefts, robberies, bashings and rapes. By taking violence from some of its earliest incidents in the aftermath of white colonisation, we ask whether Australia, for all the progress that has been made in so many ways, has ever really improved.

A suitable gauge is Sydney's George Street, referred to by R. Therry Esq in *Thirty Years of Residence in New South Wales and Victoria* when he described an Englishwoman's discovery, in 1825, of a gold comb that had been snatched from her hair in London. Therry said the comb was on display in a George Street jeweller's shop, part of a traffic in stolen goods between the two countries.

"George Street—the principal [street] in the town—was brilliant with jewellers' shops", he said. "I soon ascertained that Sydney had been remarkable, even at an earlier period, for the same phenomenon—for it could seem to [be] no less acquainted with the reason. This display of splendour was, after all, but a very natural result of the convict element in town."

It was in George Street in 1828 that a gang of convicts and ticket-of-leavers committed Australia's first significant bank raid by tunnelling into the vault of the Bank of Australia. Their haul, some £14,500, was enormous by the standards of the day. It sent the unfortunate bank on a downward spiral from which it did not recover. Then in 1988, thieves did a nifty bit of excavating in George Street, through walls that should have kept them out, and raided the vaults of the Haymarket branch of the National Australia Bank. It was our biggest bank robbery. Rupert Murdoch's *Australian* said: "The gang grabbed an estimated $20 million over the New Year when they smashed open 80 deposit boxes after blasting their way with gelignite into the inner vault".

Yet again, in the southern extension of George Street, the Broadway branch of the ANZ Bank was hit by a succession of robberies. The available parking, getaway routes and crowds that surrounded the building suited the criminal purpose.

The newspapers of the early nineteenth century, in particular the (non-Murdoch) *Australian* and the *Sydney Gazette*, carry an almost monotonous account of punishments—hangings, floggings, gaolings—as the most effective way of maintaining law and order in the colony. Just as punishment is varied, so are the reactions of the criminals. Some have reformed, many have not, yet others have discovered ways to beat the system.

William Blackstone, who helped rob the Bank of Australia in 1828, decided that turning informer was the best way to get off Norfolk Island. At the time of writing, 165 years later, the NSW Independent Commission Against Corruption is inquiring into allegations by Arthur Stanley "Neddy" Smith, criminal, standover man and convicted murderer, who has also decided his best way of getting out of the confines of the State's prison system is to turn informer. One of the incidents on which he informed concerned an assault he allegedly bribed his way out of—at the City of Sydney RSL Club, George Street, so close to where Blackstone's most serious problems began.

Away from the urban centre of Sydney, we can still see the threads from past to present—the lure of the wilderness to escape detection. Last century, Thunderbolt preferred fast horses to confrontations with troopers but they were not always avoidable, even in the open country. This newsbrief from the *Sydney Morning Herald* in May 1993, does not read that differently from our accounts of the bushranger except that these criminals were less equipped for the rough.

> *A bank robber involved in a shoot-out with police yesterday morning escaped into bushland in the upper Hunter Valley, police said last night. A search would resume for the man this morning. Another man was arrested shortly after the shoot-out, which followed a bank robbery at Willow Tree about 11 am.*

An interesting aspect throughout our criminal history has been the ambivalence of public attitudes towards criminals, especially when nobody is hurt. The bushrangers, who evolved from the first convicts who skipped away from work parties, had the tacit support of many in the population because they had the courage to stand up to the system. Our first chapter goes to where, affected by the confinements of geography and the acute sense of isolation, the violence and the suffering were worst: Van Diemen's Land. The major villains were all hunted down but managed to achieve such grudging admiration that the last of the big operators, Martin Cash, was actually saved from the noose.

This admiration of criminal pluck and daring has continued through Australia's history. It can be found in the career of Thunderbolt and in the public reaction to Squizzy Taylor in the early twentieth century, who toyed with the police and played to the public gallery. It carried over into public admiration for one-time master escapologist Darcy Dugan, an armed robber who was spectacularly unsuccessful (he spent 42 years in prison) but found a ready audience when he chose to speak out. Dugan, as his biographer Rod Hay records in *Catch Me If You Can*, received help from time to time from people in his own working class milieu during his scrambling escapes from police.

Big, bold and lucrative criminal raids have always snared our attention, and the reaction has always been mixed. Just as the Bank of Australia raid of 1828 captured the public imagination, so did the Great Bookie Robbery in 1976, even if ultimately most of the Great Bookie robbers did no better in life than the bank robbers of the previous century.

Of course there have been crimes from the earliest days of the colony which gained no public approval—beastly murders like those we detail in our chapter on the Rainbird and other killings in South Australia in the last century, and other crimes which went tragically wrong, as did the Whiskey au Go Go nightclub bombing in Brisbane in 1973. As the chapter on the Pressler case of the late 50s and early 60s demonstrates, domestic murders or those of neighbours will always be with us. And looking at the painters and dockers and Walsh Street sagas of Victoria, we see that the gangland tradition is very much part of our society.

There is now much greater opportunity for those with strong malice to do harm. Firearms are more efficient, movement is fast and easy, and in huge metropolitan areas like Sydney and Melbourne or even Adelaide killers can disappear into the passing crowd. The present century, with its increased pace of life and intensification of pressures along with the saturation publicity given to sensational crimes and all their attendant suggestiveness to deranged minds, has given rise to the phenomenon of the Clifton Hill massacre, the serial killer and the sex murders of Adelaide in the 1970s.

It has produced such horrors as the already widely documented murder of Anita Cobby at Prospect in Sydney's outer west in 1986, when a gang of hoodlums happened upon a hapless 26-year-old nurse walking alone. When her body was found, the head had been almost severed from her body by the ferociousness of the cuts to her throat.

Modern media communication has changed the nature of crime in other ways. It has brought justified outrage from the public and given timely information to the police—as demonstrated by the success of such television programs as *Australia's Most Wanted*. This has occasionally backfired as with the Chamberlain case which began with the disappearance of Azaria Chamberlain in August 1980. It is widely believed that mass publicity added a political dimension to the case—such intense debate as to whether a crime had even occurred—and so poisoned the atmosphere against Michael and Lindy Chamberlain that it limited their chances of ever receiving a fair trial.

The global communications network and new ease of movement have also brought to Australia ethnically related terrorist violence, the international drug scene and criminal organisations with international roots—such as the mafia.

At the time of writing, a coroner's inquest was being conducted in Melbourne into the murder of a reputed mafiosi, Alfonso Muratore, in August 1992. The same names that feature in that case are present in this book's chapter on the Market Murders in Melbourne in the 1960s. Alfonso was a boy of about 12 when his father, Vincenzo, was shot dead in January 1964. Father and son died within a kilometre of each other in the northern Melbourne suburbs.

A sad feature of the late twentieth century is that old-style crime, where criminals took their chances using stealth or strength, demonstrated courage and gave the forces of law and order a reasonable chance, has given way to the ruthlessness of the narcotics trade. As Rod Hay observed in his biography of Dugan, towards the end of the criminal's life crime and prison had ceased to be a world that he knew. The majority of prisoners were in for narcotics offences. And narcotics, with huge rewards for those who are successful, knows no codes of ethics, even among criminals.

We have devoted a chapter to Abraham Gilbert Saffron, whose ambition in life was to make money. He did it through nightclubs, particularly at Kings Cross, but inevitably, because of the world in which he moved, was dragged into the controversy surrounding such ugly and mysterious events as the abduction, and murder, of Mark Foys heiress Juanita Nielsen. Much adverse comment has been made about Saffron, little established, but he does represent both a world in which nasty things happened, and an era. It was an era associated with nightclubs and sauciness, and offences often accompanied by a wink and a nod, like sly-grogging. The association did not include narcotics. Drugs have now certainly made an entry although Saffron has denied any involvement. But the sickness of the narcotics trade, as in New York's Broadway and other nightlife centres through the western world, has slowly spread its stain and taken crime out of the era of the bobbies and bushies, where, however unwelcome, it kept within broad parameters and lent itself to legend.

MALCOLM BROWN
May 1993

TERROR IN VAN DIEMEN'S LAND

BUSHRANGERS HOLD THE COLONY TO RANSOM

The colonisation of Van Diemen's Land in September 1803 and its use as a prison for the worst convicts had several predictable results. The local Aborigines who, unlike their mainland counterparts, had no vast reaches of country into which they could retreat, would be completely decimated. The wolf-like thylacine, which had an unrealised appetite for sheep, would be wiped out. And the convicts would take to the bush in large numbers to create mischief.

As with the main settlement, at Sydney Cove, the colony had been founded with poor forward planning. Within a year its food supplies had dwindled and it was necessary to go hunting for wildlife. Firearms were distributed. Some of the best shots were convicts. Inevitably, convicts absconded with the weapons and the bushranging menace began.

Living in the wilderness of Van Diemen's Land, which to those from the bricked alleyways of London or the fields of Surrey must have been the end of the earth, was unrelentingly harsh. The mountains and thick forests gave protection. But it could also be bitterly cold. Bushrangers dressed in animal skins, lived in caves and hollow logs, and were wildly bearded.

These bushrangers were able to gain concessions from convicts and former convicts. "They were free: their daring seemed like heroism to those in bondage", wrote an editor, John West. Simple freemen in outlying regions realised their best chances of survival lay in compromise. Stock-keepers traded with the bushrangers and warned them of pursuit.

Some crimes were of the nuisance variety. In 1806 the chatty Hobart diarist, Rev Robert Knopwood, complained: "My bitch

Miss is stolen ... by Fossett, one of the bushrangers". In a colony where criminals outnumbered free citizens, the problem grew rapidly beyond the odd missing dog. John West wrote: "Towards the close of 1813, the daring and sanguinary violence of bushrangers reduced the colony to utmost distress".

West saw that a formidable system of loosely organised crime had developed. Much of the criminal fraternity's attention was directed against the government—symbol of oppression and guarantor of a swift end for many of them. By May 1814, it was officially recognised by the colonial administration in Sydney that Van Diemen's Land was facing nothing less than an armed insurrection. Law and order depended on the ill-prepared and slow-moving "lobsterbacks", the platoons of red-coated military. The bushrangers believed it was open to themselves to take over.

The administration adopted a hard line, which was in itself not remarkable, given the circumstances that had brought most of the population there. A man could be hanged for stealing a sheep. The trouble was that in order to execute criminals it was first necessary to apprehend them.

In a change of tack the government invited all the "banditti", as it called them, to come in from the bush and be forgiven. In Sydney Town, Governor Lachlan Macquarie, whose jurisdiction included Van Diemen's Land, offered an amnesty for all crimes excluding murder. It was to last six months, till 1 December 1814.

The amnesty was a spectacular failure. All it did was give the bushrangers months to ravage the countryside before coming in, just short of the deadline, to have their records cleared. After that, and perhaps a brief rest, they were off again.

Inevitably, a criminal emerged who rose above the rest in terms of skill, daring and notoriety. He was Michael Howe.

One look at his record would quickly indicate that Howe, set loose in Van Diemen's Land, would go in only one direction. A seaman in the British merchant navy, which he deserted, Howe had been convicted in 1811 in York of highway robbery, and would have been hanged but for a technicality. Sentenced to seven years transportation, he arrived in Van Diemen's Land and went into service to a farmer on the Derwent River. He chose to move on, boasting that having once served the King in the navy he would be no man's slave.

Howe is recorded as having cynically taken advantage of the

1814 amnesty. Within weeks he rejoined the bushrangers, in what was probably the largest gang roaming the colony. The gang grew to eight members. Settlers 20 kilometres up the Derwent on the plains at New Norfolk soon felt their heat. In early 1815 the New Norfolk Settlers' Arms was pilfered. Near Hobart, precious wheat stacks, barley and peas were burned. Within a week the gang was back at New Norfolk. They had two skirmishes. In one a settler was killed and five others wounded; in the second, the gang lost its leader, Whitehead, mortally wounded.

The authorities' rising fear of bushrangers was no less ghastly to see than what the bushrangers got up to. The authorities had the body of Whitehead, decapitated after death, hung from a gibbet at Hunter Island at the centre of Hobart's docks, and it remained there for public viewing for weeks. It was joined by the remains of another bushranger, McGuire, who was caught, summarily tried and hanged within a week.

Howe became undisputed leader of his gang. Little is known of his personality, though it appears to have been complex. A knapsack he once dumped in a hurry was said to hold a crude notebook made of kangaroo skin. In the notebook he used blood to record nightmares in which he was visited by people from his past. There was also a list of vegetables, fruit and flowers with which he dreamed of adorning a peaceful future home.

It was to remain a dream. The reality was the eastern foothills of the island's alpine central plateau. Howe's gang grew to 15. He marshalled them in military fashion during a three-year run as the self-styled governor of the ranges. Howe imposed discipline. Members were bound by oaths to obey and suffered whippings and other penalties if they transgressed. He ordered his followers to listen while he read them the Scriptures. The gang roamed over hundreds of kilometres from Launceston in the north to the fringes of Hobart.

The Lieutenant Governor, Thomas Davey, was most disturbed. Even his farm was not safe. Twice in 1816, including Christmas Day, Howe's gang raided it for food and clothes. With no higher court established in Van Diemen's Land, Davey said in a martial law declaration that he intended to stem the distressing calamities caused by "banditties of runaway felons". He was to be overruled by Governor Macquarie—but not before two more were sent to the gallows.

In the meantime, Howe was only ever a few steps beyond the forces of the law. Any encumbrance, such as sickness or infirmity, or a distraction, was enough to put him in dire peril. His taking up with an Aboriginal woman, named Black Mary, became an encumbrance at a critical moment. Surprised by a detachment of infantry, he shot at them and managed to hit Black Mary. Convinced the shooting was deliberate, Black Mary assisted the military in tracking Howe. Howe was forced to bargain with the incoming governor, William Sorell, for his life.

The awkwardness of this association did not go unnoticed. West wrote: "Society must have been on the verge of dissolution, when letters and messages passed between the government and an outlaw". But, through a middleman, Howe and Sorell struck a deal. Howe could come in on a conditional pardon if he would inform on others. In the winter of 1817, Howe, in keeping with the bargain, gave information. He rocked Hobart by naming Rev Knopwood as a man mixed up in bushrangers' business. In reply, Knopwood admitted to acting as a go-between in one bush-ranger's case, but said he was acting on the authority of the previous lieutenant governor. After the charge was dismissed, the indignant Knopwood exclaimed: "My business with what Howe the bushranger had said against me to traduce my character was entirely confuted..."

Howe was spared the noose but went to gaol, in loose custody, on the understanding he would get a pardon. But his gang kept maurauding. Settlers, numbering about 2,000 across the island, were still desperately isolated. The richer of them retreated to towns. Van Diemen's Land could never be developed like this. Sorell realised he would have to contain the menace. He began a concerted campaign, visiting towns and talking to the bush-rangers' likely confederates, such as convict stock-keepers. He posted more guards, rewarded informers, established a muster and a pass system and provided free search rights for constables to hunt convicts in houses.

Howe heard that his pardon might be in doubt. He escaped, evaded one attempt by a former gang member to take him in, and with a £200 reward on his head took to the mountains of the Upper Shannon district, northwest of Hobart. Living in a honeysuckle-covered hut on a rise above a stream he was about as close to nature as anyone could be, his hair wild and unruly, black-bearded, dressed in skins. He knew reward-hunters were after him and used his bush skill to elude them. But inevitably he was to meet his fate. Enticed to a hut by the promise of supplies, he was surprised by two armed men. After an exchange of shots, Howe ran off "like a wolf" and had nearly reached cover when he fell on rough ground on a creek bank.

His pursuer, the whiskered Jack Worrall, claimed Howe turned and shouted: "Blackbeard against Greybeard, for a million!". The two fired. Howe was wounded, then beaten to death. "At 9 am Private William Pugh, a private of HM 48th Regt and Robt [sic] Woberton brought in the head of Michael Howe, the notorious murderer and bushranger", Knopwood recorded. "A great many people went to see the head".

With Howe's departure the colony appeared to be moving into a more sedate phase, with more material riches. But Sorell, who had had some success at containing the bushrangers, moved on. There was still ample scope for outlaw activity, and in 1824 another criminal arrived to take full advantage of it. He was Matthew Brady, who was to become known as "the Prince of Bushrangers".

Transported for theft in 1820, Brady was sent to Van Diemen's Land. He was caught committing petty crime and was sent to a prison within a prison, the notorious Macquarie Harbour penal settlement on the island's isolated west coast. Brady wanted out. With 13 others he seized a small boat on 9 June 1824. They rowed out of the harbour and made their way around the hazardous, gale-ridden southern coast to land safely on the shores of Storm Bay at the mouth of the east coast's Derwent River. Nine days later, a settler there was bashed.

Word went out that the gang was active. When they made their next move, there was a reception committee. Five gang members were captured, found guilty and ordered for execution by the newly installed Judge Pedder. About eight others, including Brady, got away. Lieutenant Governor George Arthur wanted them. He issued a proclamation calling upon all settlers as their "positive duty" to help apprehend the gang. But the loyalty of convict servants undoubtedly lay with Brady. For those who wavered, there was an additional incentive not to try turning him in. It was said that Brady had laid down rules that his men must not harm the defenceless, nor molest women. But they could kill traitors, revenge injuries, and carry away all that was useful.

Mounted on horses and well armed, Brady's gang quickly spread alarm through the island. Exposed settlers retreated behind rifle loopholes. Some hired bands of armed constables drawn from the ranks of ex-convicts. The odds were tightening against Brady. But he had more mayhem to create. Late in 1824, Knopwood wrote breathlessly: "We were informed that six of the Macquarie Harbour bushrangers had made their way into Hobart Town. Parties of gents on horseback and military constables went out in every direction".

Brady consolidated his hit-and-run tactics on settlers' houses through the summer, earning himself and another bushranger, McCabe, a £25 price on their heads. Also offered, courtesy of Lieutenant Governor Arthur, was a free pardon. Diligent country constables who helped arrest the two were offered other incentives. Brady had sufficient cheek to pin on an inn door a reply to Arthur: "It has caused Matthew Brady much concern that such a person known as Sir George Arthur is at large. Twenty gallons of rum will be given to any person that will deliver his person unto me..."

There was a certain romance about Brady. "His countenance was open, good-tempered, but determined", wrote the author James Bonwick. "Tall, robust and handsome, capable of the most withering sneer or winning smile, he was formed by nature for the control of man and the conquest of woman".

The Brady gang's bravado reached a height in 1825 with a raid on the village of Sorell. First they occupied a country house, taking the owner and his servants prisoner. Next evening they attacked the gaol. Marching a total of 18 people before them, the eight bushrangers arrived just as the soldiers were cleaning their guns, after a day in the field looking for those very bushrangers. The gaoler escaped and warned an officer and local magistrate who went to the scene. One was disarmed by the bushrangers, the other shot and wounded. The cocky bushrangers locked the prisoners in the gaol, then rode off, leaving a log at the door dressed up as a sentry.

The reward was doubled. Not only was Brady creating havoc but he was encouraging others to take up the bushranging life. Arthur decided it was time to make plain what the situation was: the bushrangers were terrorising settlers with immunity. "If all only unite in circulating information of the movements of the banditti, it is quite impossible that they can long escape the hands of justice", he said in his proclamation. McCabe was captured. Brady had a brush with soldiers and was briefly taken prisoner. But he escaped and grew even more daring.

Repeating the Sorell escapade, Brady's gang attacked a house outside Launceston, held the family, then moved on to the town gaol. Brady cheekily notified the commandant beforehand what he was going to do. When the gang arrived there was resistance. Shots were exchanged and the attack was successfully repulsed. Brady escaped.

By October 1825, Knopwood estimated the number of Van Diemen's Land bushrangers at about 100, in a colonial population of nearly 14,000 (half of them prisoners). Brady's gang numbered up to 26. They appeared to be out there beckoning to others to join them. Townspeople in Hobart worried that there was so little security there might be a mass breakout from prison. The military searched constantly for lawbreakers. Throughout the month, Knopwood wrote of the "general alarm". The highways were thought to be riddled with bushrangers. Travellers were bailed up and sometimes shot. Or they were beaten or forcibly made drunk so they could not foil a getaway. Brady took continuing care of his image, treating womenfolk chivalrously. But he knew that would not help much if he was caught.

Colonial justice responded to Brady's brand of lawlessness with the rope. Many of the 103 people hanged in 1825–26 were bushrangers. "One is carried by imagination to the … French Revolution at this condition in society", wrote Bonwick. "This frightful thirst of blood in hunters and their victims". The government offered a 300 guinea reward and a free pardon to any prisoner who helped capture any bushranger.

With the heat intensifying, the Brady gang began to scatter. Brady was alone in the rugged Western Tiers and limping through a gully with a wounded foot when John Batman, later to be the founder of Melbourne, caught up with him. Taken without a fight, Brady was taken to Hobart where he became an instant sensation. Despite his notoriety, he was besieged by well-wishers. His cell was heaped with fruit, flowers and sweets. Petitions were gathered to deliver him from death. They failed. "May 4 1826. Ascension Day", remarked Knopwood without noting any irony.

"I got up early this morn and attended at the gaol. At 8 o'clock the following persons were executed for murder ... such a scene never before witnessed five men for different murders and God knows the number they have committed. It is dreadful to think of the horrid deeds ... Matthew Brady for murder, the leader of the bushrangers".

The last of the three major players in the Van Diemen's Land bushranging era was an Irishman, Martin Cash. Transported at the age of 18 for attempted murder, Cash served out his seven-year sentence in New South Wales, was out of trouble for four years, and was then accused of branding knowingly stolen cattle. Cash and a woman, known as "Mrs Cash", made for Van Diemen's Land, arriving in 1837. Within a year Cash was charged with theft, convicted and sent to penal work outside Hobart. He escaped and moved with his wife to a new district, staying for a year untroubled. Arrested once more, he was sent to the penal settlement of Port Arthur where he made one unsuccessful escape attempt, swimming to get past a line of guard dogs.

In a second attempt, he decided to take with him two others: Lawrence Kavanagh and George Jones. "I reflected that I was now in a measure pledged to two desperate men, who had been under arms in the bush in New South Wales", Cash was to write sombrely. On Boxing Day 1842, they sprang out of their work gangs and into the scrub. Once clear, they made their choice: "Kavanagh here put the question as to what was to be done when Jones answered without a moment's deliberation that we should take up arms and stand no repairs", Cash explained. "To this Kavanagh agreed, and of course, I consented also".

According to Cash's later record, he and his companions made their way across country, breaking into cottages, huts and public houses, and "levying" food, clothes and money. Several weeks later the trio took on, and repelled, a party of constables in an exchange of fire at the Woolpack Inn, New Norfolk. In an eight-month running battle, Cash and his company ranged the length of Tasmania's midlands and south, raiding houses and bailing up travellers, skirmishing with the military and jousting with the government.

Cash wrote later: "We now resolved that we would give the district of Hamilton an opportunity of contributing towards our support". He and his comrades raided a homestead, "Dunrobin", home of the Kerr family. First taking prisoner the shepherds, the bushrangers learned the lie of the land. At dusk, Cash said, they approached the house where a young woman exclaimed "Here's the bushrangers!" and fainted. Assuring the women of their safety, Cash tied up all the men except Mr Kerr, whom he ordered to write a letter to the Governor. In the letter the trio demanded the release of Cash's wife, who had been arrested for receiving their stolen goods, threatening the Governor with a flogging otherwise. Soon after, they left. "Our exactions were not heavy in this house, owing to the good feeling evinced by the family...", Cash said.

Jaunty though Cash made his escapades sound, the populace again feared that their community would be ruled by the outlaws. Military parties were sent out to reinforce badly hit districts. In the prospering midlands, gentlemen farmers talked of forming their own yeomanry corps but were dissuaded by the government. Sizeable rewards of £150 were put on the head of each bushranger. "The colony is in a dreadful state owing to the bushrangers", Rev Knopwood said. "Almost all the military out and a great number of prisoners. The town at night is being defended by patrols of the inhabitants".

When Kavanagh's gun accidentally discharged, it marked the beginning of the end for Cash's bushranging career. Seriously injured in the arm, Kavanagh decided to give himself up. Jones and Cash fell into dispute. Cash decided to go into Hobart to make contact with Mrs Cash. He was recognised, chased through the city streets, and caught after fatally wounding a pursuing constable. He was put on trial for his life and should not have had any real expectations of leniency.

Then something happened. There was a mystical element. The night before the court pronounced his death sentence, he dreamed that he successfully fought off an attack by a large black snake. "I augured favourably from this dream, which caused me to think for the first time since my incarceration that my life might be spared", he said. Two days before the execution date, the prison chaplain told Cash he was going to live. It was a more pleasant encounter than the previous one that day, when he had brushed past the hangman, Solomon Blay, in a corridor. Cash was reprieved, apparently due to Robert Murray, a Hobart newspaper proprietor who held sway with the government.

Fifteen months later Cash was sent to Norfolk Island, the end of the line as far as convicts were concerned. He survived and eventually became a constable. When Norfolk Island penal settlement was shut down, Cash returned to Van Diemen's Land. He retired to an apple orchard near Hobart. His memoirs were published in 1870, when he was 60. Dressed rigidly in a stiff-collared shirt and necktie, he stared out through the "new" medium of photography with all the worldweariness of a small-time politician. Cash died peacefully seven years later, "known to all, and enjoying the good will of all".

The story of the three—Howe, Brady and Cash—illustrates in its own way the transition of Van Diemen's Land as a prison for brutalised humanity (Howe was shot and beaten to death), which struggled to impose its system of law enforcement and justice (Brady was hanged) to the stage where a man, like Cash, starting with nothing, could finally grasp that he was not an exile but resident in a new land which promised a new beginning.

The dream of Howe, written in blood on a piece of kangaroo skin, of adorning his own home with the goods of the earth, were in Cash's life translated into some sort of reality.

THE BANK OF AUSTRALIA ROBBERY

DARING THIEVES TUNNEL INTO A BANK VAULT

Sydney in 1828 was still, in essence, a gaol. In the post-Macquarie era there had been an increased influx of free immigrants, but a big portion of the population was still under sentence or barely removed from it. That year, the colony's first full-scale census calculated a total white population of 36,598 that included 15,728 convicts.

It was a harsh place. The draconian system of punishments, that had brought most of the population there, continued. The *Australian* reported on 12 July 1826 that one Thomas Devlin had been charged with stealing a handkerchief, valued at 10 pence, and three silver dollars. He received two years in a chain gang!

Also reported in that issue: "Fourteen men received corporal punishment at Parramatta on the 3rd instant; some 25 lashes, and some fifty. On Monday last, fifteen men received some fifty and some twenty-five lashes each..."

Convict George Farrell, soon to feature in Australia's first bank robbery—the looting of the Bank of Australia—got a mention that same day: "Edward Murphy, George Farrell, and Isaac Allen, all prisoners of the Crown, all charged yesterday with robbing a man, whom they had inveigled in their company, on the previous evening, of some silver monies—sentenced to work in irons for the space of three months".

The system was not slow to summon the hangman. It was a measure designed both to despatch and to warn. On 12 July 1826, the *Australian* said: "The native black who is suspected to have been an active agent in the murder of Taylor, the stock-keeper, remains still in confinement in the Gaol—he was among the other prisoners who were drawn up to witness the execution of two unhappy criminals, on Monday last".

A man could be hanged for stealing cattle and sheep. "The drop" was introduced in the 1820s to make executions more expeditious. In the late 20s they were running at an average of 36 a year. Those escaping the gallows might have looked forward to terms at places like Port Macquarie, Moreton Bay and Norfolk Island. Norfolk Island, reoccupied by the British Government in 1824, had been dedicated as a place for "the most dissolute and depraved convicts".

Yet despite all that, there was always a willingness among many in the convict fraternity to have another go, to defy the system and commit crime. The police, referred to as "watchmen", had evolved only slowly into anything resembling a proper force. The quality of manpower was at best suspect. The equipment was poor. Sydney was not to get gas lighting till 1841. The attitude of the populace to the police was at best ambivalent.

In 1826, against such a background of degradation, merchants and pastoralists welcomed the establishment of the Bank of Australia. Its board of directors were highly respected colonists. The prestigous new bank, dubbed "the gentlemen's bank", was quickly contrasted with "the people's bank", the Bank of New South Wales that had been established almost a decade earlier. The Bank of Australia's premises were solidly constructed of thick sandstone in George Street, almost opposite the present Grosvenor Square. The premises doubled as the residence of the managing director, Thomas McVitie. It was an early forerunner—or should have been, had its foundations been more solidly and wisely constructed—of corporate Australia.

On one side of the bank was a private house, unfinished and belonging to a Mr Underwood. On the other was a public house with a sign, "Don't Go Beyond Your Compass", meaning not to get drunk or go beyond your capacity.

Well-heeled business people entered the bank's portals. The bank appeared to prosper. On 19 October 1827, it was announced that at a special meeting of proprietors it had been decided that, on 23 October, the ""discount" (interest) on bills and promissory notes should be charged at 10 percent a year".

But the wretchedness outside was readily apparent. On the day the bank announced its decision, the *Australian* said: "On Monday half a dozen ragged creatures belonging to the government gangs at Newcastle, were brought to the police-office there, charged with having absented themselves from divine service the previous day. They rested their defence chiefly on the state of their clothing, if clothing it could be called, alleging that they were ashamed to go into the church in the condition they were in. This excuse did not avail them, and a cell was allotted to each of them, to enable them coolly to reflect on their offences".

That day, the *Australian* also reported a court appearance of Thomas Turner, a man had worked on the construction of the bank. Turner had been charged with receiving a quantity of stolen soap. The man accused of stealing it had been seen going towards Turner's home. Turner had a good defence. The evidence was that Turner's home was used as a thoroughfare for workers going into the factory. It was also stated that Turner had in fact gone to bed before the theft. Turner, helped by testimony as to his good character, was acquitted.

Some time in 1828, James Dingle, a former convict who had obtained his Certificate of Freedom in January 1827, dropped to it that there might be more ways into the Bank of Australia than through the door. He knew of a drain under George Street that flowed into the Tank Stream, passing beneath Underwood's house and close to the bank's foundations. He conceived the idea of tunnelling into the vault. At some time, probably in August 1828, he put the idea to George Farrell. Farrell agreed to become part of the plan.

Turner gave expert information on the bank's construction. He said the brickwork in the foundations was held together by inferior mortar. The gang agreed with Dingle that a tunnelling operation was feasible. For the tools they needed they went to William Blackstone, who had reputedly been a safebreaker in London known as "Sudden Solomon".

Blackstone, recorded in the *Sydney Gazette* in January 1820 as being an absconder from penal servitude, appears to have still been a convict. He worked at the establishment of blacksmith Thomas Seeny near York Street and lived in Seeny's house in Cumberland Street.

At 8 pm one night, Blackstone was woken when Dingle and Farrell threw a stone on to the roof shingles. He knew the two. They told him their plan. He asked for time to consider. The next night he said he would join in. All three recognised it would be a difficult task, physically laborious, in danger of discovery, and hampered by restrictions on their activities.

Farrell, still a convict, and Blackstone were obliged to attend church muster on Sundays. The three decided digging should be done on Saturday nights and that it should take about three nights. Dingle told Blackstone he would need to provide the team with two joisters and a crowbar.

On Saturday 30 August, Dingle, Farrell, Blackstone and Turner went to the bank, carrying the tools Blackstone had provided. They measured distances on the surface, went down into the drain through a manhole on the east side of George Street, at "Thornton's paddock", near George Thornton's Union Hotel, and carefully measured distances there to correspond.

"Farrell assisted Dingle to take out the bricks of the drain and I distributed them about", Blackstone said later. "We worked all day Saturday [night] and came out at 7 o'clock".

Turner pulled out of the scheme. He believed that, because he had worked on the construction of the bank, he would have been a natural suspect. His decision was respected. He was promised a share of the loot.

The gang needed another worker. They recruited a man named Clayton, who was at the time living at Farrell's house. Little is known to identify who this man was. Blackstone apparently knew him as "Creighton, alias Walford". The team were to resume work the following Saturday, 7 September. When they went down to Thornton's paddock a man accosted them, asking what they were doing. The gang were immediately on the defensive. Blackstone and Clayton went into the drain to continue digging. Dingle and Farrell remained at the top as lookout.

They returned the next Saturday, 14 September. Blackstone and Clayton again went into the drain, with Dingle and Farrell again keeping watch. After the day's work the four went to relax in a hotel, but got into a brawl and barely escaped being arrested.

Inside the bank, as the *Gazette* was soon to record, staff finalised business and left at 10 pm on Saturday with everything intact. The robbers were anxious to finish their job. They decided the bank would have to be relieved of its wealth that weekend. They decided they had no option but to work through Sunday.

The problem was that Farrell and Blackstone were obliged to attend church muster. So while they and Clayton went back to digging, Dingle approached the clerk in the convict supervision office, James Wood, and obtained permission for both Farrell and Blackstone to be absent. He dispatched another convict, Val Rook, to inform them of the fact. The sudden appearance of Rook in the drain did not impress the three. It meant they would have to cut him into the share of the loot.

"We went to work and in the course of the day just at the time the drums beat for church we took out the corner stone nearest the street", Blackstone said later. "We determined to take it [the loot] out immediately and sent Farrell in, him being the smallest man. Farrell went in and came out with two locked boxes".

Opening the boxes, the gang realised straight away their efforts were not in vain. After they had gone through the whole vault the gang's haul, listed later, was: 800 pieces of silver coin, half crowns, valued at £100; 8,000 shillings valued at £400; 1,200 sixpences valued at £300; 100 x £50 notes; 200 x £20 notes; 400 x £10 notes; 400 x £5 notes; 500 x £2 notes; 1,000 x £1 notes; 1,000 dollar coins valued at £360; 3,000 pieces of paper valued at £30; seven boxes at seven shillings; four canopy bags at four shillings. The total cash taken was given later as £14,500.

The gang stayed in the drain till 7 pm on the Sunday. They emerged through Thornton's paddock and went to Dingle's home. Blackstone went home for a few hours sleep. At midnight the gang woke him. They returned to the drain and continued looting. They spared nothing. They even took the bank's ledgers, bills and receipts, tore them up and strew them around—the ultimate spit in the face to the bank they were ravaging. They put their booty into bags to carry it out. And almost came unstuck.

Two patrolling policemen, Constable Robert Melville and Constable Quinn, suddenly appeared. Dingle at least was not carrying anything at that moment. Thinking quickly, he feigned drunkenness while the other members of the gang disappeared into the shadows.

"I was on duty and at about half past 2 o'clock", Melville would explain later, "I and Constable Quinn met a man named Dingle on Church Hill. He was coming from the way of the place where he lived to the Bank of Australia. Quinn stopped him and asked him who he was and where he was going, he answered that he was going to get a glass of rum. I know him as he had lived in my neighbourhood for some time, I said it was strange that he was going from his house to knock any publican up at that time in the morning.

"He replied that he had been drunk overnight, had fallen asleep in the paddock just above, had just awakened, hardly knew where he was going. The night was very rainy. I observed that it was strange that his clothes should be quite dry, I be wet through; after some little pause I told him that I knew him and thought him to be an honest man and permitted him to pass".

At bank opening time later that morning, bank staff entered the strongroom and found a scene of devastation. The only item left untouched was a large chest containing silver plate. Everything else had been removed. John Wallace, a member of the bank staff, went through the hole in the wall.

The *Gazette* said: "On exploring the drain through which the entry had been effected, there were found therein, a crow bar, a sword saw, an instrument which stonemasons use called a sonunder, a tinder-box and steel, a dark lantern broken, a lamp, a bottle of oil, together with some empty rum bottles and a gill measure".

Sydney's Senior Constable, George Jilks, was called. News of the robbery spread fast among Sydney's population, officially counted at 10,815. It was an outrage, but brought titillation and mirth. McVitie called on the public to come in with the bank notes to have them marked, so as to quickly isolate the stolen notes. The *Gazette* published the serial numbers of the stolen notes. McVitie worked the whole of the Monday night striking new notes. But there was a poor public response.

Police were at a loss as to who had committed the crime. Even if people were found to have isolated stolen notes in their possession, how could it be proved they had anything to do with the robbery? A modest reward of £100 offered for information leading to the convictions of those responsible did not bring a response. The reward went up to £120. Still no response. Governor Darling offered an absolute pardon and a free passage home to England as an inducement for someone to come forward.

The gang had problems in deciding exactly what to do with the proceeds of their extraordinarily successful enterprise. The bank had announced it was on the lookout for its money. The numbers of the notes had been printed. And denominations of £5 and above would have quickly attracted attention.

They decided to use a "fence", Thomas Woodward, who had received his ticket-of-leave in May 1825, and in December that year had been sentenced to 50 lashes for assault. According to the *Gazette*, he had his ticket-of-leave taken back in July 1828, for the heinous offence of leaving his lawful wife and cohabiting with another woman. On Tuesday, 17 September, Blackstone went to Woodward's home. His visit was observed by Woodward's next-door neighbour, Ann Houseley, who noted the visit because she had not seen Blackstone for some time. She was later to give evidence to that effect.

Blackstone gave Woodward £1,133 in notes. Woodward said he would give £1,000 for it. They went together to the Bank of New South Wales where Woodward told Blackstone to wait outside to watch for police while he went in to change the money. Instead, he slipped out the side door and disappeared with the cash.

Blackstone was not left destitute by this action, but in all probability squandered the rest of his takings at the gambling table. Several months after the Bank of Australia robbery, he and an accomplice attempted to loot an illegal gambling den in Macquarie Street, Sydney—probably the place where he had lost his money. A policeman surprised them and opened fire, killing Blackstone's companion and wounding Blackstone.

Under arrest, Blackstone knew he was in serious trouble. He asked another blacksmith, David Morris, to go to Thomas Seeny and get money to retain counsel. Seeny said he had little to spare, but then the morning before the trial he came up with £2. Morris retained a Mr Rome, for a fee of £5, of which £3 was the helpful Morris's own money.

"I don't remember that he [Blackstone] ever told me that any person in Sydney had money of his", Morris said later. "I don't recollect Blackstone ever told me that Woodward had any money of his".

Blackstone was convicted and sentenced to death. The sentence was commuted to 14 years imprisonment. He was sent to Norfolk Island. He did not care for the place. In 1831 he decided to do a deal. He would become a prison informer. He would sell out his colleagues to gain a chance of freedom. And that meant real freedom—a free passage back to England. Blackstone approached the feared commander, Lieutenant Colonel Morisset, and said he had information about the bank robbery.

Taken back to Sydney, Blackstone told the whole story. Police arrested Dingle and Farrell. Both were then free, Farrell having obtained his Certificate of Freedom in May 1829. Clayton was not arrested, perhaps because Blackstone did not give his proper name. Nor was Rook. Dingle and Farrell, however, were charged as principals in breaking and entering the dwelling house of Thomas McVitie on 14 September 1828. Woodward was charged with being an accessory after the fact. He was charged with knowingly receiving: 10 x £50; 20 x £20; 40 x £10, 40 x £5; 50 x £2 and 100 x £100, and 300 pieces of paper valued at 30 shillings.

Blackstone, on the prison hulk, the *Phoenix*, was developing feelings of paranoia. He made a number of declarations claiming that Woodward had been receiving information on the evidence he was about to give and taking steps to counter it. One of Woodward's probable informants, according to Blackstone, was the convict, Joseph Irving who, being able to write, had taken down Blackstone's statements.

Dingle, Farrell and Woodward appeared before Justice James Sheen Dowling in the NSW Supreme Court on 10 June 1831. Blackstone gave evidence. Woodward's lawyer, a leading counsel, William Foster, objected strongly to Blackstone being allowed to give evidence. He pointed out that Blackstone had been convicted of a capital crime, adding: "His accumulated crimes render his testimony valueless, the sanction of an oath is of no force". Dowling said the trial should proceed and the question of the admissibility of Blackstone's evidence decided later. The three accused were convicted on Blackstone's evidence.

Whether the evidence was admissible was deliberated by Chief Justice Francis Forbes in company with Justices Dowling and Alfred Stephen on 23 June 1831. It was in fact an appeal against the convictions. The law in England, which was regarded as applicable in New South Wales, was that evidence of such a person as Blackstone should not be admitted. The issue before the judges was whether that law was in fact applicable in a jurisdiction with such unique characteristics as New South Wales.

Dowling and Stephen took the view that it was not applicable. Dowling said: "To all intents and purposes it [the colony] has been treated and regarded as an extensive gaol and most, if not all, the laws and regulations for its government have been founded on that footing. In no sense of the word has it been nor can it have been considered as a free Settlement and Colony of Englishmen. In this respect it has been in the lowest grade in which a society of English subjects could be placed to form a community, and differed from every other Colony under the dominion of the British Crown".

Dowling, with Stephen concurring, said the law would have to be applied differently in New South Wales and that Blackstone's evidence, which was backed up in many respects by other evidence, should be accepted. Forbes dissented, saying the law had to be applied as it stood and the courts should not take it on themselves to be legislators. The decision went with the majority.

Woodward's lawyer, Foster, backed by two other defence counsel, said he would appeal to the King-in-Council. He asked the court to defer sentencing until that was done. The judges declined to grant leave to appeal. Dowling then said to the prisoners: "Of your moral guilt of the nefarious crimes of which you have been severally convicted, no reasonable person can entertain a shadow of doubt".

He pronounced the sentence of death on Dingle and Farrell. But, in deference to the position taken by the Chief Justice, he said he would decline to order that the sentence be carried out. Instead, the sentences of death would be "recorded" only. Both would receive an effective sentence of ten years hard labour. It was a decision seen at the time as too lenient.

Regarding Woodward, Dowling believed that, notwithstanding good character references, the "aggravated circumstances" of his case, merited "the extremest punishment in the eyes of the law in the case of receivers of stolen goods". He sentenced him to 14 years imprisonment.

Blackstone expected to get his passage home to England. But just before he was due to go, he was caught stealing £20 from a shop. He was convicted and sent back to Norfolk Island—for life.

The man remained controversial. Cockatoo Island in Sydney Harbour opened as a prison in 1839. Blackstone was sent there and by December 1840 was soon to be released. The *Australian* said: "We have been told ... that the most notorious and infamous scoundrel William Blaxstone [sic], celebrated for the part he took in the robbery of the Bank of Australia; a vagabond who has been twice sentenced to death for Capital offences, and was sent to Norfolk Island with a recommendation that he should never be returned ... will again be set free to commit his predatory predations upon the inhabitants of Sydney".

Blackstone did go back to Sydney life. He was not particularly reformed, although he does not appear to have done anything gross. The *Sydney Morning Herald* noted in December 1842 that he was convicted of assaulting a police constable who was arresting him on a charge of stealing shoemakers' tools. Blackstone got out of the stealing charge but was fined 40 shillings for the assault, plus costs.

Blackstone's time was running out. In 1844, his body was found in a swamp at Woolloomooloo. Blackstone well knew that he had been branded, to use modern prison parlance, as a "dog", and would have to watch over his shoulder. It was presumed someone had caught up with him.

The Bank of Australia did scarcely better. The bulk of the loot was never found. The bank never recovered from the robbery and went into decline. An English bank, the Bank of Australasia, tried to help it, but to no avail. The Bank of Australia closed its doors in 1843. In 1845, following passage of a special bill in the NSW Legislative Council, it disposed of its remaining assets by lottery.

THE RAINBIRD AND OTHER MURDERS

COLD-BLOODED KILLINGS AND LEGAL EXECUTIONS

The public's fascination in reading about crime, matched by its desire for justice, was alive and well in South Australia last century. As far back as the 1840s, newspapers informed their readers of every macabre detail of murders committed throughout the state. They faithfully printed full transcripts of ensuing court cases. There was always a ready readership. The reports sometimes had the effect of stirring up desires for`a mob retribution. Sometimes this was helped along by the editorial line taken by the newspapers.

Because the death penalty was invoked for capital crimes, there was always the added element of sensation. In the Victorian era, among the great fetishes was domestic murders, sinister whodunits and dark secrets. Even the coup de grâce of Victorian-era crime, the simple domestic poisoning, was not unknown in South Australia. But there were also murders that had none of this morbid fascination about them at all.

The episode of the Rainbird murders—involving the deaths of a mother and two children—was nasty for several reasons. It was nasty because of the brutality. It was doubly nasty because the people accused were Aboriginal, and their plight brought to the surface some of the vicious racism that has always plagued Australian society.

Kapunda, 110 kilometres north of Adelaide, was the centre of a prosperous farming and copper mining district at the beginning of the 1860s. Copper had been mined there since its discovery in 1842. It was, by all accounts, a law-abiding town where farmers and miners lived in harmony. Many Aboriginal inhabitants of the district had not moved on. There was shearing work available.

On 11 March 1861, a farmer named Rainbird left for Kapunda to pick up supplies. At the homestead were his wife, Mary, and two small children, Emma and Robert. When he returned home, Rainbird could not find his family. He searched for them with increasing urgency. He called on friends. Nothing was found. The next day, two searchers discovered the bodies about 150 metres from the house. The mother and children had been mutilated and their bodies stuffed down wombat holes.

News spread around the district. People went into shock. Police called to the property found numerous imprints of bare feet around the wombat holes. Suspicions were immediately aroused that Aborigines had committed the crime. Who else went around in bare feet? A party of Aborigines had been seen in the district the day Mary Rainbird and the children disappeared.

Panic developed. Farmers' wives, normally so easygoing like rural people anywhere, locked all doors at night and in the daytime insisted on going out with their husbands into the fields. Firearms were loaded and ready for self-defence.

A coroner's inquest found: "Mary Anne Rainbird, Emma Pickett Rainbird and Robert Rainbird were murdered by some person or persons unknown, and that strong suspicion is attached to the natives who have lately been seen in the neighbourhood".

Police identified the Aboriginal men they regarded as prime suspects. They believed the group had split up and scattered. It was necessary to track them down. Within a few weeks, they had arrested five men and charged them with murder. Community outrage was at such a level that there were real fears for the safety of the detainees. Sergeant Major James Hall escorted the men, handcuffed and manacled, through Kapunda to the railway station, where they were placed on a train for Adelaide.

The five suspects went on trial. One, Jacky Pyke, decided to turn Queen's evidence and testify against the others. He said that several days prior to the murders, there had been a fight among Aborigines near Kapunda. A young boy had been knocked on the head and died from the injury. There had been a ceremonial burial not far from the Rainbird home. On their way home they had called at that homestead and had asked Mary Rainbird for some water. When they discovered she was alone, save for her two small children, they had taken advantage of her.

Mary Rainbird had been assaulted. She was raped by one of the men. She escaped and got outside the house but was caught and bashed with an iron coupling of a wooden harrow. The two children had been killed to stop them screaming. The bodies had been put where they were found.

The four men who were the subjects of Pyke's testimony were found guilty and hanged at Adelaide Gaol on 7 June 1861. That in itself was not quite enough for people seeking retribution. There were complaints that the hangings should have been made public. The *Northern Star* made its feelings clear:

The cannibals who murdered Mrs Rainbird and her two innocent children were choked yesterday morning outside Adelaide Gaol.
This is what we have heard from the lips of Mr Patrick Kingston, MP, who saw them dancing upon nothing as the train conveyed His Highness to another reunion, the Burra and Clare election dinner.

We do not think that, considering the circumstances of this case, Tommy Reynolds [Premier of South Australia at the time] has done justice to the Colony—to the district of Light in particular. The fellows should have hanged up here or they should have been placed at the rifle target for volunteers to shoot at, so that they would have had a lingering death. Lots of centres and no whites. We have been cheated. Tommy Reynolds must never stand for this district.

It was not long before the issue of community demands for vengeance was to rise again. But here we must retrace our steps to look at the history of Malachi Martin, who had a starring role.

Martin, who came from the Coorong region of South Australia, had a long history of violence. He came to the notice of police in a big way in 1856. A man named Robinson was found with his throat cut in bushland near Martin's hotel. The knife that had inflicted the fatal wound was in Robinson's right hand.

It appeared at first sight to be a case of suicide. Then it was found that Robinson had been left-handed, and there were no bloodstains on the right hand, which must inevitably have been present had he inflicted the wound on himself. Local Aboriginal men showed police the track of a man who had walked from Robinson's body to the edge of a lagoon. The signs suggested the person making the tracks had squatted down to wash his hands. The Aborigines pointed to two sets of horse tracks near the body.

Robinson's wife told police that Martin had been very amorous towards her. An Aboriginal police officer said: "Me see Malachi and Mrs Robinson plenty play about when Robinson alive". Police confronted Martin with their belief that he had killed Robinson. Martin denied the allegations but was charged with murder. There was not enough evidence, however, to convict him and he was set free. He married Mrs Robinson on 23 June 1858.

Several years passed before Martin came to police attention again. The body of a young woman, Jane Macmenimen, was discovered in a flour bag which had been stuffed down a wombat hole near a water course called Salt Creek. (These wombats!) The woman had been murdered in February 1862 but the body remained undiscovered for months. On 7 May 1862, Police Officer William Rollison received information on the "mysterious disappearance of a servant girl named Jane Macmenimen who lived lately at Malachi Martin's of Salt Creek at the Coorong". Later that month, Macmenimen's body was discovered. Police did a search of Martin's hotel. They found various articles of her clothing. There were blood stains on several walls. Martin had built a cupboard in front of the worst stains. On 1 June 1862, Martin was charged with the murder of Macmenimen.

It appeared that another man had also been involved—William Wilsen, a German migrant who had started working on a nearby Coorong property in 1861. Apparently he and the victim had become closely acquainted. Police received information that Wilsen had made an admission to another stockman that he and Martin had raped and killed Macmenimen. Wilsen had been observed at that time with scratch marks on his face. Both Martin and Wilsen were charged with murder and committed for trial. The case received saturation publicity. There were screams for public executions.

Chief Justice Sir Richard Davies was not persuaded that the evidence was sufficiently strong against Wilsen and set the murder charge aside, though Wilsen remained on trial for related offences. But he had no doubts about Martin and damned him in his summing-up. After a 55-minute deliberation, the jury pronounced Martin guilty. Sir Richard sentenced Martin to death and Wilsen to four years' imprisonment with hard labour for being an accessory to murder. Martin refused to accept the verdict and unsuccessfully petitioned the Governor for clemency. He was hanged at Adelaide Gaol on 24 December 1862.

The next person to stir up both the passion and the pen in the community's quest for justice was Elizabeth Woolcock.

We must mention here that the poor befuddled wombat played a role in her story as well, even if in a most indirect way. Wombats had been scratching burrows for themselves east of Moonta on the Eyre Peninsula 180 kilometres from Adelaide. An illiterate shepherd discovered traces of copper in the diggings, recognised them for what they were, and formed a partnership with Captain Walter Hughes, later Sir Walter Hughes. The two took out extensive leases. The site turned out to be the richest of all copper mines ever developed in South Australia. The lodes proved so rich and the yield of ore so heavy the proprietors did not have to contribute capital. The mines, which became world famous, had the distinction of being the first Australian mining venture to pay its shareholders £1 million in dividends. At their height, the Moonta mines employed some 1,700 people. Hundreds continued to flock to the district in the hope of making their fortunes. And it was those mines that attracted the attention of Thomas Woolcock, a widower with two young sons.

Elizabeth, unlike the shepherd who discovered the copper at Moonta, was not blessed by circumstances and was not to have much luck in life.

Her parents migrated from England in 1842 and settled at Burra, in the midnorth of South Australia. Her father worked in the Burra copper mines. Then news came through of the riches to be gained at the Victorian gold fields. Elizabeth's mother decided that was the place to go. But she complicated things no end by deserting her family and going to Victoria with a lover. Elizabeth's father stayed on with his young children. Then he died. At nine years of age Elizabeth was forced to go to work as a kitchen hand. Her employer continually abused and raped her.

Some time after that Elizabeth appears to have discovered that her mother had returned to Adelaide with a new husband. Elizabeth got in touch with her and the mother asked her to come and stay with them. Elizabeth agreed. It was in Adelaide that Thomas Woolcock came onto the scene. He liked Elizabeth and began courting her although Elizabeth's mother disapproved. She counselled Elizabeth against marrying him. Elizabeth married him anyway, saying later it was to spite those opposing it. Thomas and Elizabeth moved to Moonta.

But if the mining promised prosperity, for Elizabeth married life did not turn out to be pleasant at all. Thomas was mean with money. The couple took in a boarder. Thomas accused her of having an affair with him. It seems that at some point Elizabeth decided enough was enough and resolved to put an end to the misery of her marriage.

One day, Thomas Woolcock called at the police station and reported that someone had poisoned his dog. Soon afterwards, he became ill himself and died. A post-mortem examination revealed that Woolcock had died of mercury poisoning. Police investigated. They confirmed that mercury was available from the local chemist. They also discovered that Elizabeth had sent her young stepson to the chemist to buy some of it, and that she had told him to say his mother's name was "Mary Edwards". The police charged Elizabeth with murder. She appeared on trial on 4 December 1873. It was of short duration. The jury took 25 minutes to decide she was guilty.

The drama of the occasion was faithfully captured by the *South Australian Register*. According to the report the trial judge, who apparently was considerably affected by what had transpired, said in his pre-sentence address:

> *Elizabeth Woolcock, you have been found guilty after a lengthy and most careful inquiry, of the awful crime of murder. It is no part of my duty and still less of my inclination to add to your sorrow by any lengthy observations.*
>
> *Everyone must feel satisfied that the verdict is a proper one and you yourself must have felt that great patience has been shown throughout the proceedings and every consideration given to you.*
>
> *I must say I entirely concur in the verdict at which the jury has arrived. It is now my duty to pass sentence on you. The jury have recommended to you mercy on account of your youth, and it will be my duty to forward that recommendation to His Excellency the Governor in whose hands the prerogative of mercy is reposed by our Most Gracious Sovereign the Queen.*
>
> *I have now only the solemn duty to perform of pronouncing the sentence of the court, which is that you be taken from the place from which you are brought and there hanged by the neck until you are dead.*

Twenty-one days later, Elizabeth Woolcock, aged 26, became the first and last woman to be hanged in South Australia. The

Register was around to see that everybody would be acquainted with the event. It reported:

> *The extreme penalty of the law was carried out at the criminal sessions for the murder of her husband Thomas Woolcock by poison. The convicted had been attended since her conviction by the Rev J Pickford and after his visit manifested great penitence and seemed perfectly resigned to the fact which she knew awaited her.*
>
> *In a spare leaf of her Bible between the Old Testament and the New, it was found she had inscribed a few words to her memory, writing her age, her name and the date of her death. She also in writing made a full confession of her guilt, stating that she had not been well treated, and had been tempted by Satan to carry out the act.*

Execution time was set for 8 am. The *Register* said: "When the hour neared, she was taken from her cell by the Gaol Governor and Rev Pickford having completed a prayer as the rope was adjusted and after the usual formalities the bolt was drawn. Death did not immediately ensue. Fully five minutes elapsed before the convulsions of the body ceased, but it was afterwards ascertained that dislocation was produced with the drop of the bolt".

Over the next decade there would be a further eight hangings in South Australia, all for murder. Nineteen-year-old William Ridgeway was hanged on 1 January 1874 after confessing to murdering a man on an outback sheep station six months previously. Dutchman Charles Streitman was hanged on 24 July 1877 for the murder of a court bailiff. Hugh Fagan was hanged on 16 April 1878 for the horrific murder of his best friend, Patrick Bannon, which included dismembering him with an axe. William Burns was hanged on 18 January 1883 for the murder of a seaman on board a ship off the South Australian coast.

Among the victims of crime were police officers. Although South Australia did not have convict origins, and hence no early shiploads of confirmed criminals, it was still a wild place. It was a harsh country, desert for the most part, with the continual movement of prospectors and miners breaking up established social patterns. It bred harsh people. Often, police assigned to keep order in the wilderness had to take their chances. By the turn of the century about a dozen South Australian police officers were to die in the line of duty.

In May 1881, Trooper Constable Harry Edmond Pearce set out

on the trail of a man named Robert Johnson, a notorious horse thief wanted in connection with the illicit supply of alcohol to Aborigines. Pearce apprehended Johnson and was taking him to Kingston, in the southeast of the state.

According to the account Pearce gave later, he and Johnson were about six kilometres short of the destination when Johnson told Pearce he could go no further. Pearce threatened to handcuff Johnson if he did not continue his journey quietly. Pearce turned his back to untie his horse from a log. Johnson attacked him with a knife that had been concealed in his clothing. He stabbed Pearce 14 times, in the back, stomach and hands. Johnson unsaddled Pearce's horse and set it loose. He took Pearce's revolver and emptied it. "You can die there", he cursed, before riding off.

A man later riding a horse along the same track found his horse shying at an object in the bushes. Investigating, he found Pearce, alive but badly wounded. The rider contacted police at Kingston. Weak from loss of blood, Pearce was still able to tell his superior, Sergeant Robert Morris, what had happened.

Morris arranged for Pearce to be returned to Kingston for treatment, then set out in company to track down Johnson. Five kilometres away the pursuers found horse tracks. Then three kilometres further on, they found Johnson. A search of Johnson revealed a bloodied sheaf knife in his clothing. There was blood on his trousers. Morris returned Johnson to Kingston tied around the midriff of a horse. Johnson was paraded in front of Pearce who said: "That's the man who stabbed me and that's the knife".

It was about the last thing Pearce was ever to say. He died that night. Johnson was found guilty by a jury following a short trial several weeks later, and was hanged at Mt Gambier Gaol on 18 November 1881.

The hanging of Chinese immigrant Mah Poo was still to come, and it aroused the greatest interest.

Poo's contribution to society was to shoot shopkeeper Tommy Ah Fook in the head in Hindley Street, one of Adelaide's main thoroughfares. He got rid of the body by hiding it in one of Hindley Street's cesspits.

Fook was soon missed. Many of his associates believed he had absconded to avoid creditors. One creditor, Way Lee, questioned Poo's associates about the disappearance. Eventually Willie Yung mentioned that he had seen blood spots on the floor at the rear of

Fook's shop. That initially had not seemed significant because it was thought Fook had fled. The discovery had not been brought to police notice, though Fook's disappearance had been. Then Fook's body was found. Some items were missing from his possessions. His ornamental breast pin had been removed. So had his watch and chain. Fook was known to have had a lot of money. Had robbery been the motive?

A coroner's inquest was held. Poo and Yung were arrested. Poo was charged with murder, Yung with being an accessory after the fact. The charge against Yung was later dropped.

Poo's trial started on 9 October 1883. Police had not been idle. They had plenty of evidence against Poo. The main flaw in the Crown case was lack of motive. Although Fook was reputed to be wealthy, none of his money could be found among Poo's possessions. The trial took a new turn when one of Poo's defence counsel was placed in the witness box. He said he had received a blank bank order from Poo to enable him to withdraw cash from a bank account. The bank order was signed "J. Bing". It was then proved that Poo had deposited cash in the name of Bing.

There was a hiccup in the progress of justice. The trial had to be aborted after one of the jurors went off the rails. A new trial, with the same evidence, produced the expected verdict. In fact the jury reached it in a lightening 12 minutes. Poo was sentenced to death by hanging.

Back in his cell, Poo was kept under constant observation. He went on sporadic hunger strikes and feigned ailments in his legs so he did not have to wear irons. None of these devices served any purpose in changing his destiny.

Three days before his scheduled hanging, Poo admitted to the murder to two Chinese missionaries. "As I am about to suffer the extreme penalty of the law, I sincerely and solemnly declare that I murdered Tommy Fook", he wrote in his confession. "He was always cursing and swearing at me and finding fault in everything I did. My temper was such that I would not control it. I fired the shot that killed Tommy at five or six yards distance, and he fell mortally wounded. I threw him down the closet. After taking his money I broke the breast pin up in small pieces and threw them away. I know nothing of his watch and chain. He was not wearing it when I killed him. No other person assisted me. I did it all myself".

On the appointed day, 10 November 1883, Poo walked up the steps of the scaffold, resigned to his imminent fate, and said the words: "Love save men, Lord save me". The noose was adjusted, the bolt pulled, and Poo dropped two metres to his death.

THE LIFE AND TIMES OF THUNDERBOLT

People loved the handsome outlaw,
People loved him far and wide,
Tried to guard him from the troopers
When he roamed the countryside!
Housewives used to hang a blanket
As a signal on the line,
Red ones said, "Look out for troopers!"
White ones asked him to dine!

—From a song, Thunderbolt, *by Pannifex and Cumming,*
winner of the Grenfell Henry Lawson Song Award 1963

The truth is somewhat different to the song. Fred Ward, alias "Thunderbolt" or "Captain Thunderbolt", was an outlaw, marginally nicer than the rest of his ilk. Though he exchanged many shots with police, his long-term policy was to flee rather than stand, and he made generous gestures from time to time to appease public opinion.

The terrain Ward chose was expansive—about a quarter the size of England. The Kelly gang, whose day in the spotlight was to come later, operated in more settled country and took advantage of a close-knit circle of family and friends.

Ward was more self-reliant. The northwest, with its huge distances between population centres, its bush, plains and ranges, gave him scope to strike and retreat. Police forces did not have the resources to contain him. In 1867, at the peak of his career, the entire New England region had just 22 mounted and eight foot policemen, dispersed in 11 centres of population. They were not as well-mounted, lacking the advantage Ward had of being able to steal racehorses. There was a wide variation in their training and quality.

Ward might have got some help from members of the public, though only a couple of shepherds were ever proved to have harboured him. He was never betrayed, like Johnny Gilbert and John Dunn, nor like the Kelly gang.

A lot of romantic nonsense has been written about Thunderbolt over the years. Annie Rixon, in her book, *Captain Thunderbolt*, portrays him this way:

"Thunderbolt emerged from the mouth of the cave and stood in rapt admiration, gazing at the splendour of the early morn. He was stripped to the waist, his feet bare ... His muscles rippled in the sunlight. Suddenly his splendid body skimmed the air like a swallow, and with hardly a splash hit the water ... Once again he pulled himself up on the surface of the rock, and with flesh glowing a warm pink, stood and gazed on this wonderful world with fearless eyes. Nature's beautiful playground was his best garb".

It was in fact a dreadful life. Always on the run, nowhere to settle, facing death time and again, Ward could only count on a short career. He had nowhere to retreat to, nowhere he could store his ill-gotten gains, not even a roof over his head most of the time, though he chanced an occasional night in an inn. There was no doctor when he got sick. On the two occasions he was shot, he had to fend for himself.

A police description years later is undoubtedly more accurate than Annie Rixon's romanticized portrait. It said: "Dressed in a cabbage-tree hat, crimean shirt, striped moleskin trousers, and long boots, his person ... was found to be dirty like the commonest type of bush labourer".

For all that, Fred Ward was spirited. He was daring, skilful with horses, courageous and intelligent. His talents enabled him to last six years as a bushranger where contemporaries in the golden bushranging era of the 1860s lasted only three or four. He did not kill anyone. The worst injury he inflicted was a hole through a policeman's hand. The official government attitude was that Ward was to be caught. But the highest reward the government offered, on 12 October 1868, was £400, compared with the £1,000 offered for information on Morgan.

Newspapers had no liking for Ward. But in the minds of the public there was always ambivalence. During his career, Ward managed to relieve honest, hard-working citizens of a sum-total of £40,000 of their money at a time when a stockman's annual wage was £40. When he was ultimately shot dead, people queued in Uralla for a chance to view his body. Women clamoured for a lock of his hair.

Fred Ward was born in 1835 or 1836 in the Windsor area north of Sydney. He was possibly the son of an ex-convict. He had little formal education. As soon as he was old enough he worked as a horsebreaker and groom. But he did not care for hard work, and horse-stealing was an easy start for a scoundrel. Frank Gardiner, born about five years earlier than Ward, started that way.

By the age of 20, Ward was a member of a horse-stealing gang. He took about 75 horses that had been stolen by gang members in the Hunter Valley and helped drove them to Windsor for sale. Arrested, he appeared before Maitland Quarter Sessions on 13 August 1856, and got ten years gaol with hard labour.

Ward was a prisoner on Cockatoo Island in Sydney Harbour where convicts quarried sandstone and worked on ships. The island was reasonably close to shore, but the water—allegedly shark-infested—was forbidding. The company in gaol was less than inspiring. Bushranger Frank Gardiner had been sent there, sentenced to seven years for horse stealing. There would have been much talk of bushranging. In all probability, word got through to the Cockatoo Island prisoners about the Eugowra Mail Escort robbery of 15 June 1862, where a gang, later found to include Johnny Gilbert and Ben Hall, took a haul of £14,000 in gold and bank notes.

Released in 1860 on a ticket of leave, Ward went to Mudgee to work on a station. It was there that he met Mary Ann, a half-caste Aboriginal girl, product of a union between another ex-convict and an Aboriginal woman.

Mary Ann, born 7 May 1834, was taken from her family at the age of three, the policy for Aboriginal children. She was brought up in the Orphan School in Sydney, had been taught to read, write and perform domestic tasks. She had many sterling qualities, including an astonishing self-reliance and a total loyalty to Ward. It was her devotion to him during Ward's bushranging career that lifts his story from the common mould.

At the age of 14, Mary Ann left Sydney and returned to the Gloucester area, the homeland of her mother's tribe. Though she had spent much time in white society, her Aboriginality remained intact. She had retained much of what her mother taught her. Mary Ann was briefly married to a shepherd and had a child by him but he appears to have died by the time Mary Ann met up with Ward. The two obviously got on, and stayed together. They went to Dungog in central western New South Wales. In September 1861, Ward was charged again with horse stealing and was sent back to Cockatoo Island to serve the remaining six years of his sentence plus another three. He had to leave Mary Ann, who was by then heavily pregnant with his child.

Ward undoubtedly had Mary Ann on his mind, as well as her own child and the unborn baby. There was no joy for him at Cockatoo. Conditions were so harsh that they had provoked a revolt in January of that year. At one time, 88 men were crammed into a ward 18 metres long and six metres in breadth, with one large window and five small ones. A government committee recommended improvements. Ward was not prepared to wait. He is supposed to have tried to escape and failed a few times. At least once he was placed in solitary confinement in a dungeon scooped from rock and sealed with a flagstone.

Mary Ann gave birth in October 1861. By some accounts, she took a domestic job in Balmain, within sight of Cockatoo Island, and worked out a way of assisting Ward. She is supposed to have swum across on three successive nights with a file for Ward to use to saw through shackles he was meant to have had on him (but almost certainly didn't), and to have succeeded on the third night. Whatever the truth, Ward did, in company with another prisoner, Frederick Britten, escape on 11 September 1863, swam to shore and from there, almost certainly with Mary Ann in tow, made it to the New England region on stolen horses.

Ward and Britten arrived in the Uralla area, got to an isolated station and robbed a widow of a rifle and a ham. They decided to rob the mail coming out of Uralla and, to prepare for it, sat on Split Rock, an outcrop that still exists beside the New England Highway and since named "Thunderbolt's Rock". The driver on his way into Uralla saw them and alerted police. On the return journey, the coach was accompanied by one Sergeant Grainger and Constables Reynolds and Mulhall.

The police opened fire. Ward and Britten fled. The *Armidale Express* said Grainger saw Ward take shelter behind a tree, aim, and fire hitting Ward in the knee. "The bushranger then gave a bound about two yards to the right and Grainger jumped onto his horse to rush upon him, but the horse immediately sank to his girths in the [marshy] soil", the paper said.

Ward escaped on foot and limped across country till he came upon a sawyers' camp between Uralla and Bendemeer. The timber workers helped him. Ward was to carry the scar for the rest of his life. From then on his policy was to avoid confrontations with police, relying instead on fast horses. Britten went south to Victoria, where he continued his criminal career but otherwise disappeared into obscurity.

Ward was destined never to be obscure. Soon local newspapers such as the *Singleton Times* were carrying accounts of his holdups of mails and inns. The police, usually not well-mounted and hopelessly undermanned, were nevertheless on his tail. On 22 December 1863, the *Sydney Empire* said: "A bushranger stuck up the toll-bar, the Spread Eagle Hotel and several people at Maitland this morning [21 December 1963]. Some policemen got close to the bushranger and fired three shots at him, but he escaped to the mountains. The police are now in pursuit".

Ward, now being referred to as "Thunderbolt", hid in mountain ranges with Mary Ann and the two children. Mary Ann was an extraordinary woman. Having the care of two infants, and not even the most rudimentary support, she coped. She supplied the family with yams and other bush fruits and proved adept at nobbling and slaughtering livestock. When the family moved, the children went on horseback. As babies, they went in the saddlebags. She was no slouch when it came to helping Ward earn his living. She accompanied him on his robberies, dressed as a man. She also spied for him in towns and villages.

An anonymous balladeer wrote of her:

> *There was a laughing, nut-brown maid, her name was Mary Ann.*
> *She lived with a sister and an Uncle, a well known drover man.*
> *Like two bright starts her brown eyes shone, her head was a mass of curls,*
> *She laughed, and danced, and sang, her teeth were as white as pearls ...*

There is a real question as to how long Ward would have lasted without her.

Ward made criminal sorties into the Gloucester, Muswellbrook and Maitland areas. A Dungog correspondent told the *Maitland Mercury* that if police did not act, settlers would take the law into their own hands.

In February 1984, Ward and Mary Ann were spotted in the Stroud district. Police arrived a day after them. Ward decided the area was too "hot". He shifted his operations entirely to the far west, in the Bourke area where his brother William had a property. The family settled in a camp near the Culgoa River.

Ward successively recruited three boys to help him commit robberies. They provided lookouts for him and sometimes did robberies under his supervision. But it was not the life for boys. They were not tough or skilful enough. Two were captured, one shot in the process. Various adult accomplices Ward picked up from time to time were more useful, but did not stay. Ward never had a gang.

A news report described the robbery of a hawker, George Davis, at Culgoa by two men, one of whom was named as "Ward alias Thunderbolt". The hawker was tied to a tree and robbed of £150 and "a quantity of women's wearing apparel". The *NSW Police Gazette* of 8 February 1865 reported: "The first offender is supposed to be Frederick Ward, alias Captain Thunderbolt, described as 30 years of age, five feet 8 inches high, pale sallow complexion, dark hazel eyes".

The western plains of New South Wales were not, however, the place for bushranging. The *Police Gazette* of 8 February said: "Sergeant Cleary and a black tracker pursued three offenders for 200 miles, came upon their camp in thick scrub on the borders of Queensland, and recovered a greater portion of Davis' property ... A half-caste woman at the camp stated she was the wife of the offender Ward".

Mary Ann was pregnant again. She and the children were taken to a station while police continued their search for Ward. Ward eluded them, went to the station, picked up his family and moved to the Manilla–Barraba region. On 24 April 1865, he decided to rob Walford's Inn at Millie, unaware that police had been tracking him from Barraba, 110 kilometres away.

Just as Ward and his boy John Thomson arrived to announce

themselves, the police, accompanied by a blacktracker, came into sight. The *Sydney Empire* reported a skirmish between three constables and Ward and Thomson. The police expended 40 rounds. Thomson was hit, fell off his horse, and was captured.

Ward retreated north, to Queensland, and laid low. Then he returned and set up a camp near Wallabadah. In May he stole a racehorse, Eucalyptus, and held up Cook's Inn at Quirindi. In June he abducted a woman to be midwife and support for Mary Ann, and kept her with him and his family.

In August 1865 Ward was attacking mail coaches and inns. He had several companions off and on, including an Irishman, Patrick John Kelly. On 27 December 1865, Ward and his gang robbed Earl's public house near Collarenebri and commanded the men and women there to dance. Some time later, in a chase by Port Macquarie police, Ward was shot in the thigh.

In March 1866, the abducted woman got away and alerted police as to Ward's whereabouts. Maitland police surprised Ward and Mary Ann at Pignabarney Creek, about 50 kilometres from Nundle, in the act of cutting up a carcass. Ward, under fire, got back to his camp, mounted his thoroughbred and escaped.

Mary Ann, now pregnant with her third child, was charged with vagrancy and gaoled. Political controversy erupted over the appropriateness of the conviction. She was released on 19 April 1866, after 16 days imprisonment. The *Maitland Mercury*, which like other newspapers had no truck with Ward, sneeringly referred to her as "Mrs Captain Thunderbolt". She returned to Ward. In January 1867, police surprised Ward in the Lower Paterson area. He escaped. He took on another boy apprentice, a local lad of 13 years, Will Monckton.

On 3 February 1867, Ward and Monckton held up a mail coach, an individual and an inn. Surprised by three police, Ward, half-intoxicated, escaped. So did Monckton. A certain Constable Norris made a halfhearted attempt to catch Ward. Monckton tired of the life and went to work in a shearing shed, though he was afterwards tempted back into crime and was arrested.

With another apprentice, Thomas Mason, Ward visited Denison Diggings mining camp on 25 February. The *Armidale Express* carried a correspondent's report on Ward's visit. "It would appear that he commenced operations today by sticking up Mr Cook, storekeeper, from whom he took about £70, principally in cheques", the paper said. "He then proceeded to Mr Simpson's, innkeeper, where he bailed them all up, and sent a boy named Mason (who joined him a few days ago) to look for cash; the search I am informed was pretty successful, but I have not heard the exact amount".

In August, police surprised Ward at his camp in the act of putting on his boots. He escaped under fire. Police got his horses and his boot. Mason, separated from Ward, was captured. In October, a constable lying in wait for him opened fire. Ward managed to turn round and gallop off, though his pack horse was wounded in the confrontation.

Ward had other concerns. Mary Ann was quickly failing. She had advanced consumption. Ward turned up at a station near the Goulburn River, west of Muswellbrook, on 11 November, asking for help, telling a kindly woman where Mary Ann was. Mary Ann was found, but died. Newspaper reports reported the death of Louisa Mason (a name Mary Ann used) or of "Yellow Long", a nickname given Mary Ann because of her sallow complexion.

Of her death, the balladeer wrote:

> *To Mary Ann, dear Mary Ann, we miss you so, now you have gone.*
> *Noone to read our letters now, noone to read or teach us how.*
> *When will you come back, dear Mary Ann? Wherever did you go? ...*

Despite the loss, Ward continued. The *NSW Police Gazette* of February 1868, said: "On January 30 1868, the Tamworth Mail was stopped, about six miles from Bendemeer, by two armed men, supposed to be Ward and Kelly, and robbed of mail bags; one passenger also robbed of £1 and a single barrelled gun".

Ward needed a continual supply of fast horses. When the Tenterfield races were held on 17 and 18 March 1868, he might well have been in the crowd. After the races he robbed a mailman and bailed up three German bandsmen. He robbed one Nicholas Hart, who was taking home £105 he had won. Ward would have got Hart's prize racehorse Minstrel too, except that the groom rode off with it.

On or about 6 May, an Inspector Brown and a trooper stayed the night at Abington Station, near Bundarra, leaving their horses tethered in the stables. During the night Ward sneaked in, took the inspector's horses and left his own, which were knocked up.

On 10 October 1868, he held up an inn at Wellingrove and was told the hotel was kept by a poor widow. He declared he would not rob it. At Maude's store nearby he said he would not frighten Mrs Maude, declaring: "I never molest a woman. I never beg, but I do rob. I was driven to it". He held up another inn at Oban; he stripped the Chinese miners of their earnings.

In 1869, Ward's activities were declining. He too was suffering from consumption. The strain of the life was telling. It was only time before a policeman would happen by who was a little more skilful and determined than the rest.

Such a man was Alexander Binne Walker, born at Oldenbury, near Berrima, in 1847. Walker joined the police force while still a teenager and was sent to the Northern Police District on 4 March 1867. In 1870, he was stationed at Uralla.

In May 1870, Ward, having left his knocked-up racehorse Combo at a station, was in the New England area looking for another horse. He is said to have attended the Uralla races on 23 May and to have been drinking in Uralla's Court House Hotel. On 25 May, Ward was apparently mildly affected by drink. He decided to go to hold up an inn run by John and Eliza Blanch, about eight kilometres south of Uralla.

Told at the inn that the Blanches had gone to town, he waited for them a few hundred metres north of the inn. Arnold Goode, a farmer who with his brother today owns the property on which Blanch's Inn stood—and is virtually a world authority on the last days of Thunderbolt—said Ward was doing silly things. He could have waited at the inn for them, and kept out of sight. Ward was losing his edge.

Ward held the Blanches. Mrs Blanch gave him money. He asked them to go back to their hotel and he would buy them drinks. Then he saw a boy riding north with a grey horse and a pack horse. Ward liked the look of the grey. A hawker came by, named Giovanni Cappusotto, who had been travelling New South Wales country areas with a horse and cart. Ward robbed him of £3/13/6, a small gold nugget and some jewellery. Ward told him he could go, but to the south, away from Uralla. Ward entered the inn.

Blanch was to say later: "He remonstrated with me about not letting him have a quart of rum a few evenings before; he asked me if I remembered an occasion some seven years ago with

Thunderbolt at the Rocks and remarked, "I am the man; I got shot in the knee"".

Out of eyesight, Cappusotto unharnessed his carthorse and rode it through bush back to Uralla. At about 4 pm he told Senior Constable Mulhall and Constable Walker what had happened. The two policemen rode to Blanches' and saw Ward trying to steal the horse from the boy. Mulhall and Ward exchanged shots.

Walker chased Ward five kilometres to Kentucky Creek. The grey was not up to racehorse standard. Walker stayed with him, cutting him off as he tried to double back along the creek. Ward abandoned his horse and leapt into the creek to get to the other side. Ward had one charge left in his revolver but it misfired. He stood there, confronting a determined policeman, waving the revolver and blustering. Walker shot the grey. After an exchange of words, Ward said he would die rather than surrender. Walker said: "It's you and I for it", and plunged into the water. His horse stumbled, Ward tried to pull the bridle, trying to unseat Walker and take the horse. Walker shot him dead.

Ward, after his escape from Cockatoo Island, had been at large for six years, five months and 23 days. Little of what he stole was ever to be found. Newspapers hailed his demise. The *Warwick Examiner and Times* said: "We have great pleasure in being able to announce that the pest of the northern districts for many years, Frederick Ward, alias Thunderbolt, has at last been got rid of ... "

Ward, laid to rest in Uralla cemetery, was about 35 years of age when he died. In 1970, on the centenary of Ward's death, a plaque was unveiled at Uralla to commemorate the bravery of Walker. In 1988, a bronze statue of Thunderbolt was unveiled nearby, far more prominent, clearly overshadowing the plaque.

SQUIZZY TAYLOR, GANGSTER

THE CRIME WARS OF 1920s MELBOURNE

Joseph Leslie Theodore "Squizzy" Taylor, a flamboyant, entertaining but otherwise vicious hoodlum who lived to the age of 39, provided plenty of work for Melbourne's police establishment as he moved between theft, burglary, gambling, armed robbery, sly grog, jury rigging, murder and probably cocaine-trafficking and blackmail. But he had a tranquil enough start to life.

Taylor was born in 1888, second youngest of five children of a coachbuilder in Brighton, then a coastal town south of Melbourne. Although the family soon moved—victims of the depression of the 1890s—and Taylor came under the influence of inner Melbourne street life, there does not appear to have been anything in his family that pushed him onto the path he chose. Taylor started his working life in a racing stables. But like so many before him and so many afterwards, he did not care for the grind of daily work. He took to crime.

That might have been the beginning and end of an account of "Squizzy" Taylor.

But Taylor had a special quality which was to lift him above the legions who raise eyebrows through some outrageous act or other and are then punished and forgotten. Like Sydney's Darcy Dugan, another slightly built, snappily dressed and cocksure individual who was to start his criminal career a generation afterwards, Taylor took on an extra dimension. He courted publicity, relished the notoriety, and made himself a folk hero of sorts by cocking a snook at authority.

As a juvenile, Taylor got up to mischief. He came to police notice at the age of 11, and spent time in a boys' home. He continued to commit offences, taking to picking pockets, other theft and street thuggery. He spent much of his time at the top end of Melbourne's Bourke Street, which at the turn of the century was a thriving area for hotels, clubs and pubs—with more than 30 bars concentrated in a small area—but was also a haunt of criminals.

Taylor became a member of a gang called the "Bourke Street Rats", specialising in robbing drunks, bashing them if they offered resistance. One man, who came in from the country for the 1907 Royal Show, was set upon by the gang and had his skull fractured and jaw broken in two places.

In 1916, while vast numbers of young men were engaged at the war, Taylor moved into a bigger league. In February that year, he and a companion apparently decided to rob a bank employee who was known to regularly travel a certain road at Bulleen, outside Melbourne, to a newly opened branch of the bank. Usually, on those journeys, the bank man carried £400 in cash.

The two would-be robbers, using a false name, hired a taxi driven by William Haines, 22. They told him they wanted "a drive in the country". They took with them suitcases, disguises and false number plates. Apparently the two planned to tell Haines where to stop, then get out, don their disguises and wait for the bank man. Haines apparently objected to being party to the plan. He was shot, probably by Taylor. The two criminals were seen by witnesses near a waterhole.

Whatever the actual course of events, the robbery did not come off. The taxi was later found in Bulleen Road, near Doncaster Road. Haines was found inside, covered by a blanket, with six shillings in his pocket. Police found the disguises and false number plates discarded in suitcases in the waterhole nearby. They also found a partly dug grave. The scenario they drew up was that Taylor and his associate had planned to rob and then kill the bank employee. Perhaps the plan was to kill the taxi driver also. The plan had apparently come unstuck when Haines raised an immediate objection.

Taylor and his associate were arrested, charged and committed to trial for murder. At the trial, in April 1916, several witnesses were presented who had seen Taylor and his accomplice in the taxi. Others were presented who had seen them at the waterhole. But, in court, the witnesses demonstrated an astonishing loss of memory. What later became known was that Taylor had developed the practice of intimidating witnesses. He apparently did so on this occasion. Taylor was also able to produce alibi evidence. He was found not guilty. On a second charge, of vagrancy, he was convicted and sent to prison for 12 months. He smiled as he was led away. He had beaten the murder charge.

Taylor served his sentence but was soon arrested again, for breaking into a Richmond warehouse. He was gaoled for a month.

There have been some who have argued that Taylor was already very lucky, and that he had been involved in more than the Haines murder. In *Power Without Glory*, author Frank Hardy, who deliberately put a thin veil over the real-life characters he was portraying, created a "Snoopy Tanner", a Melbourne gangster with striking resemblances to Taylor. In the book, Tanner was behind a shooting at the Trades Hall in Melbourne during which a policeman was shot dead.

In real life, such a shooting did take place at a robbery of the Melbourne Trades Hall in 1915. Constable David McGrath was killed. Contemporary Melbourne journalist Hugh Buggy, who followed the career of Taylor, said Taylor was in no way associated with the raid. So whether Hardy had hard evidence or was making a guess is unclear. But Buggy had no doubts that Taylor was guilty of the Haines murder.

Released from gaol after the warehouse conviction, Taylor quickly demonstrated that he had no wish to reform.

Instead, he did something more spectacular than ever. He organised the theft of £2,000 worth of diamond rings from a Melbourne jewellery store. The plan was deceptively simple. An accomplice bought a gift from the shop and a short time later returned saying the gift was not quite what he wanted. He asked to buy something more expensive, then paid the extra but with a bank note that required change. While the employee went to the back of the store to get change, someone snatched a tray of diamond rings. When the employee returned with the change, he saw a small man outside putting a padlock on the door. The thieves were long gone before the alarm could be raised.

By 1919, Taylor had a number of associates. They worked with him or for him. Taylor was the brains of the outfit.

One venture was the illicit sale of alcohol. The wartime measure of closing hotels at 6 pm was extended into peacetime. The market opened up for sly grog and Taylor was able to offer "protection" to illegitimate outlets. He also supplied them with alcohol stolen from legitimate vendors.

The Taylor gang clashed with rivals. A feud developed with a gang operating out of Fitzroy. One night, Dolly Grey, Taylor's wife and woman for the moment, wandered into a drinking parlour run by one of Taylor's rivals. It appeared she wanted to find out more about their operations to pass on to Taylor. She appears to have gone to sleep there, and while comatose was relieved of her jewellery and furs. Taylor was livid. His honour had been affronted. He decided to give the rival gang, and the underworld, a message they would never forget.

What followed the theft from Dolly Grey was a vicious series of shootings and bashings that became known as "The Fitzroy Vendetta". Melbournians followed almost daily newspaper accounts of the ongoing crime war. Within three weeks, five people who had been identified as the culprits of the Grey robbery had found it necessary to seek urgent medical treatment. Four had been shot and one bashed with a piece of gas piping.

Sydneysiders heard about it. There was one marked difference in crime in the two cities. Although in Sydney the Razor Gangs were dominant, in Melbourne heavy penalties for razors deterred their use. But there was no hesitation in using other tools of violence—firearms, lead pipes and boots.

By 1919, the guns on the Western Front had been silenced. But in Melbourne firearms blazed for months as the gangs struggled for supremacy. Taylor tried to end it by going to Fitzroy to meet his rivals and negotiate peace. Gunmen opened up on his car and a passer-by was shot in the neck. The war continued for nearly two years.

Then, by chance, in the city centre, a shoot-out occurred which ended the matter. It involved two criminals—Henry Stokes, who was an ally of Taylor, and the tall, powerfully built Harry Slater.

Who won the shootout was critical for the future of the underworld in Melbourne. All Taylor's cards were stacked on Stokes, who had proved his capacity to create "nice little earners". Stokes had been running the biggest and best of Melbourne's two-up schools. It was based in Richmond. He had turned two-up from a game for backyard gamblers into an event worthy of members of high society. He was also credited with introducing baccarat into Australia.

For Taylor and Stokes, Melbourne was big enough for them to share. They both took money from illegal gambling, sly grog operations, SP bookmaking and other assorted criminal activity around town. Some suggested that Taylor was in fact the front man for Stokes' operation. It appears much more likely that their relationship was a partnership, but rather a case of understanding and tolerance, built mainly on the respect they had for each other.

Slater had challenged the supremacy of Taylor and Stokes. He was allied to the Fitzroy gang, which had given such affront to Taylor and was the "other side" in the feud. A confrontation between Taylor and Stokes, on the one hand, and Slater on the other, was inevitable.

In March 1921, Stokes had just left a hotel in Little Collins Street and was walking down the hill towards Swanston Street when he saw Slater walking towards him. The meeting was apparently accidental. Slater spotted Stokes first, drew his pistol and fired two shots, which missed.

Stokes then drew his own weapon and fired back. The two exchanged shots down the hill into Swanston Street. People ran for cover. Two stray bullets hit a packed tram. Slater emptied his magazine, then quite calmly reloaded as Stokes threaded his way among screaming pedestrians. Stokes took careful aim at Slater and fired twice. The first bullet shattered Slater's elbow. The second smashed into his shoulder. Slater slumped to the ground. Stokes walked away.

Slater recovered from his injuries but he refused to name his attacker. Stokes was arrested but convicted only of discharging a firearm in a public place, receiving a six-month suspended sentence. Slater retreated to Sydney, leaving Taylor and Stokes to enjoy their continuing supremacy.

Taylor was hard to catch. Informed talk was that he had moved into the cocaine trade which had come back from World War 1 and had entered Melbourne. He was also reputed to be drawing a good income from blackmail, acting on information he picked up from good-time girls who patronised drinking establishments.

But he could not always be lucky. Soon after the shooting of Slater, Taylor was caught red-handed by a patrolling policeman in a city bond store, near a pile of fur coats worth £500. Taylor said he had seen the door open and just walked in. He later elaborated, saying he was fleeing another crime boss and had sought refuge.

Taylor was charged with breaking and entering and being unlawfully on premises. Receiving bail, with a surety of £300, he failed to turn up at court. A warrant was issued for his arrest. Taylor managed to elude police for more than a year, to their immense irritation and embarrassment. While on the run, he committed further robberies—often of successful punters—and safebreakings and burglaries.

It was the very peak of his criminal career, in bravado and notoriety. He did not leave the Melbourne region, though he was said to have gone to the then seaside village of Frankston for an occasional break. His chances of remaining at large were probably increased because he was not regarded as particularly evil.

When the Melbourne *Herald* published an article asking where he was, Taylor impishly wrote to the paper, saying: "I cannot understand what all this bull is about". He also claimed he would surrender when he had sorted out some business; then said: "I will pop into the CID knowing that I will be quite welcome, because I know I can't dodge around much longer".

The publication of the letters added to Taylor's reputation for bravado. Taylor rose to the occasion and sent more letters. In one, he said: "You always state that the elusive Pimpernel has failed to keep his word and come forward. Not at all, for I mean to come up very shortly and take whatever punishment is in store for me".

The general public was delighted. The police were furious.

Taylor moved about in disguise. He even dressed as a schoolboy, and despite being aged in his early 30s, he was small enough to get away with it. Police searched relentlessly, questioning his known associates, going to houses where he might have been. Looking through a house in which Taylor had stayed, they found a poem in his handwriting. It said:

While you live,
live in clover,
for when you're dead,
you're dead all over.

That was probably a succinct expression of what Squizzy Taylor really believed: live it up now because there are no tomorrows. One thing is certain, emerging from Taylor's career, that despite his very busy schedule of criminal activity, he accumulated little wealth. He was living for the moment.

When Taylor decided to give himself up, he did it on his terms and he made the most capital out of it that he could. He tipped off not only the police but the newspapers, and turned up dressed in his dapper best. Hugh Anderson wrote in his book on Taylor, *Larrikin Crook*:

The city newspapers lost all sense of proportion in investing his surrender with an importance equal to the threat of another war, and splashed his name and photograph over the front page. The conflict in Turkey was relegated to the inside sheets and even the eclipse of the sun hardly rated a mention.

Taylor was released on bail and gave a series of interviews in the media. He gave himself up, he said, because he was being blamed for every crime in Melbourne, his friends were continually being visited by police and his mother was ill. Taylor did have some sympathisers. Journalist Hugh Buggy complained about the exaggerated coverage some newspapers had given to Taylor's exploits. In Buggy's view, some of this was the result of "young Melbourne reporters who had become obsessed with the derring-do of the American gangsters".

Whether that was true or not, neither the majority of police (who were straight) nor the media were out to kill Taylor. If anyone from the straight community wanted to "get" him, they did it through the normal processes of justice.

But the underworld Taylor moved in observed no such rules. Several days after surrendering, he was shot in the leg; three bullets were fired by an underworld adversary. Taylor was only slightly wounded. Police charged a man with the shooting, but he was later acquitted.

Meanwhile, Taylor still had to face court on the charge which had arisen from his warehouse entry over which he skipped bail. His story about being threatened by an underworld figure was enough to convince a jury that he was innocent of the charge, and he was acquitted. At least, that is how it appeared.

Taylor was still in the business of fixing juries, by threat or the offer of money, and was similarly persuading witnesses to change their evidence. He was so successful at it that he not only fixed cases for himself, but did it for colleagues and occasionally for other parties—for a fee.

After escaping the shadow of the prison house once more, Taylor went back to big-time crime. He organised many robberies and took part in some of them, usually as the getaway driver. The

Victorian Railways was robbed of its £2,750 payroll. The two railway employees carrying the money were not only confronted with pistols but had pepper showered in their faces while the money was grabbed.

On 8 October 1923, Taylor sent two of his men to rob a bank manager, Thomas Berriman, at Hawthorn. Taylor had been tipped off by a street criminal who had observed Berriman's habits. Each Monday, Berriman walked towards Glenferrie station carrying surplus bank notes which were torn and grubby. He had taken a train to the city where he deposited the cash in the main branch of the Commercial Bank.

Walking towards the station on that particular day, carrying £1,851, Berriman was confronted by the robbers and tried to draw his pistol. One robber shot him. The robbers grabbed the cash and, chased by a passer-by, made it to the getaway car. The getaway car was believed to have been driven by Taylor.

While Berriman lay in a hospital bed, gravely wounded, police hunted for the robbers. Acting on a tip-off, they arrived at a house occupied not just by the prime suspect, a prison escapee called Angus Murray, but by Taylor as well. Murray was arrested. He was paraded before Berriman who identified him as one of the robbers, although he said it was the other robber who had fired the shot. Berriman developed blood poisoning and died. Murray was charged with murder, convicted and sentenced to death.

Two unsuccessful attempts were made to break Murray out of gaol. Taylor was said to have been behind both attempts.

On execution day, 14 April 1924, journalists who had gathered to witness the event were waiting to hear a final pronouncement by Murray implicating Taylor in the murder. They were to be disappointed. Murray said: "I have never in my life done anything to justify the extreme penalty being passed on me. I have tried to forgive all those who have acted against me. I hope that all I have injured will forgive me". As the executioner put the noose over his head, Murray said: "Pull it tight".

Taylor was charged with conspiring to break Murray out of gaol. He was tried and found not guilty. He was also charged with harbouring Murray.

A month after Murray's execution, Taylor was driving along St Kilda Road just before midnight when he hit a 22-year-old woman about to board a tram. Taylor did not stop. The woman died of her injuries. Two days later, Taylor was identified as the driver of the car by eye-witnesses. Damage to his car was consistent with the impact and police reported seeing Taylor leave a hotel minutes before the accident. Taylor was charged with manslaughter. But again he was able to intimidate witnesses, the case against him lost a lot of its force, and he was acquitted.

The court appearances and his continuing preoccupation with the charge of harbouring Murray distracted Taylor from his criminal activities. He tried a series of evasive tricks and it took three trials before he was convicted. He received a relatively heavy sentence of six months gaol.

Released, Taylor continued his criminal activities but he was in decline. He was no longer the force in the underworld that he had been. In 1925, he attempted to buy into a tobacco and hairdressing business. Once the owners found out who he was, they withdrew the share from sale. On 26 October 1927, Taylor pleaded guilty to betting in public and was fined £50. It was to be his last court appearance.

Among the many enemies Taylor had picked up during his career was John "Snowy" Cutmore, a man allied with the Fitzroy gang during the drawn-out gang war. There had never been any love lost between them.

Taylor had been keeping an eye on a friend's illicit drinking establishment in St Kilda while the friend served a gaol sentence. On the night of 26 October, Cutmore and an acquaintance arrived at the bar and drank heavily. Cutmore ended up smashing furniture, then stripped a woman working there and pushed her naked into the street. Taylor was predictably furious, and also concerned that the incident had drawn attention to the place.

The next day Cutmore was bedridden at a house in Fitzroy, suffering a heavy cold. Taylor walked in. Cutmore had had the presence of mind to keep a pistol under the sheets. Who fired first remains a mystery; both were hit. Cutmore's mother was in the room and was wounded. Cutmore took five bullets and died on the bed. Taylor was wounded in the right side. Someone took him to St Vincent's Hospital in Melbourne and dumped him outside the casualty ward.

Several scenarios were drawn up, one being that Henry Stokes wanted to get rid of Taylor and set him up, by having a companion go with Taylor and instructing the companion to ensure that both Cutmore and Taylor ended up with holes in them. Questioned by detectives, Cutmore's mother did not give details as to exactly what had happened.

Whatever the ultimate truth, Taylor's death was front-page news. And Stokes appeared to have the underworld to himself.

The final act in the Squizzy Taylor saga was the arrest in 1931 of the second robber in the Berriman case, Richard Buckley. Buckley was charged with murder, convicted and sentenced to death. The sentence was commuted to life imprisonment.

Buckley was released in 1946, aged 83, and lived to the age of 90. In his old age, Buckley might have enjoyed the accounts of the repeated escapes from custody of Darcy Dugan, who was rapidly acquiring the folk hero status that Taylor had had. Dugan was to be just as incorrigible and just as publicity conscious, if marginally less violent. But he was not nearly as cunning as Taylor. Although Dugan did live to an age where he could pass away peacefully in a nursing home, he was convicted of just about everything with which he was charged and spent a total of 42 years behind bars.

That really wouldn't have done for Squizzy.

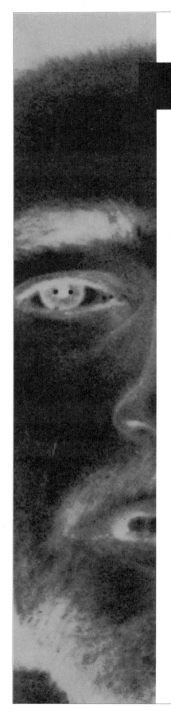

KIDNAPPINGS, NIGHTCLUBS AND THE MAFIOSI

Crime has always had its greatest focus on people most vulnerable to it. We introduce this section with an account of some of the most horrific crimes imaginable—the physical abuse, abduction, sexual assault and murder of Australian children. It is now recognised as one of our greatest hidden problems. The callousness of the overt offenders can be breathtaking. One self-acknowledged paedophile was asked by a television reporter what he saw a school as. "A smorgasbord", was his grotesque reply.

The smorgasbord can have different offerings for different people. In Australia's first kidnap for ransom, the case of Graeme Thorne, the enterprise was so badly bungled that it probably stopped forever that particular offence in this country. But the disappearance of children—as with the Beaumont youngsters in Adelaide—represents every parent's worst nightmare.

The death of a toddler in Victoria after a short, brutalised life exposes a still more persistent problem. Children, like women, are so often victims of violence by men who succumb to the pressures of the world. One quarter of all murder victims in Australia are killed by a family member. More than 40 per cent of all murders occur within a domestic context. Sociologist Professor Stuart Rees says: "The prospect of being harmed or murdered by someone who may have protested that they love you is one way of reminding ourselves of the potentially fatal dangers that lurk in the privacy of the home".

The assaults and murders that have nothing to with domestic relationships come in two forms: those with apparent reasons and those without. Muggings and robberies, which have understandable and usually financial motives, have occurred from the time of the First Fleet. The public must observe reasonable caution to avoid them. Far more terrifying are the meaningless outrages such as the random slaughter carried out by Perth's Eric Edgar Cooke and Australia's massacres of the late 80s and early 90s.

This section of the book also takes a look at the life and times of Abe Saffron, whose empire took in the nightclubs and strip joints of Sydney's Kings Cross. They satisfied demand, as did some of the area's other unsalubrious activities—prostitution and, in the latter era, drug dealing. Saffron, unlike the late George Freeman who made his money out of SP bookmaking, has shunned publicity but has emerged into public view occasionally to emphatically deny dealing in drugs. Much has been said about Saffron and he has fiercely defied the attacks that have been made by those seeking to heap odium upon him.

"The mafia"—using the term in a loose, generic sense—has had similar hangups about adverse publicity but its opponents have had far more ammunition. In Victoria, it initially established itself among people with Italian origin in the fruit and vegetable industry but inevitably branched out beyond the confines of that particular industry and community. When that world exploded in violence in Melbourne in the 1960s, Australian police encountered the frustration they have since experienced with other migrant communities—suspicion and silence.

The overwhelming majority of Italian immigrants, like those in the more recent wave from South-East Asia, are hard-working and keen to capitalise on the opportunities of a new country. The criminals who came with them are a worry, particularly when, as with the South-East Asians, they have brought with them their own brands of crime.

Larry Boy Janba raises a cultural problem of a different sort. Larry Boy knew that in killing his adulterous wife he had done the wrong thing. But his story raises the broader question of applying white man's justice to indigenous people. The problems of policing the Northern Territory are huge. At the time of the Azaria Chamberlain case in the

1980s when the Territory was receiving its widest publicity, it had a murder rate per head of population that was 4.5 times higher than the rest of Australia. The story of Larry Boy and his flight from justice is uplifted by the skill of the man himself and the perseverance of the policeman who went after him.

The concluding chapter in this section is one of murder in the canefields, the tale of twisted neighbourhood and domestic relationships which produced two deaths. It is significant in that it is an extreme form of a garden variety crime. It can happen, for any reason, at any time, in any community. Someone is killed, someone arrested, and shocked neighbours make the same comment: "I had no idea!".

THE PLIGHT OF THE DEFENCELESS

ABDUCTION AND MURDER OF CHILDREN

Abuse of children, and their abduction for sexual assault or murder, is one of the more horrifying developments in modern Australia.

When the nation was developing, when in the words of Henry Lawson "the world was wide", the loss of children who wandered off into the Australian bush was an everyday tragedy. Generations grew up with legends of missing children whose skeletons were found years afterwards, caught in undiscovered "hiding places" in the trunks of trees or in abandoned huts, burned black and buried in the drifting sands of deserts, slowly decaying in the undergrowth of the piliga or stringybark scrub, sometimes only a few tantalising metres from water.

Growing up in colonial Australia was hard. Only the best, the toughest, the quickest learning and most adaptable survived and grew stronger. An unlucky minority died from what coroners' inquiries quaintly termed "unnatural causes". Maybe.

Maybe the popular belief was wrong.

What is now certain is that, too often in modern Australia, children have not been given a fair chance to survive—to test life for themselves. Too many children have died from unnatural causes.

They have died because they have fallen prey to predators usually seeking perverse sexual gratification. The one case where the motive was financial rather than sexual was so extraordinary that it remains an exception to this day.

Children also die because, in an increasingly complex age, with greater stresses than ever before, people cannot cope with the additional stress of children. Babies and little children are bashed. Often, the offender is a man who is a boyfriend, or a de facto husband, a man not necessarily restrained by paternal feelings.

But first, the extraordinary exception—the kidnap murder of eight-year-old Scots College pupil Graeme Thorne in Sydney in 1960.

The kidnap at Bondi, in Sydney's eastern suburbs, on 7 July 1960, was the beginning of a sorry new era in Australia. It was the first known abduction of an Australian child for money. Graeme, on his way to Scots in Bellevue Hill, was lured into a car by his kidnapper and never seen alive again.

The motive for the kidnapping was immediately obvious. Five weeks earlier, Graeme's father, commercial traveller Bazil Thorne, had won the Opera House Lottery, worth the then extraordinary amount of £100,000.

On the morning the boy was taken, a man with a European accent telephoned the Thorne flat. He said to the boy's mother, Freda Thorne, "I have your son", and asked to speak to her husband. Police Sergeant Lawrence O'Shea, pretending to be Mr Thorne, took the call. The caller said: "I have your boy. I want £25,000 before five o'clock this afternoon. I am not fooling. If I don't get the money before five o'clock, I will feed him to the sharks".

Sergeant O'Shea was at the flat because Freda Thorne, always apprehensive about the size of the lottery win, had notified police as soon as she knew her son was missing. After the telephone call, police went into action. They were hunting the kidnapper, later identified as Hungarian-born Stephen Leslie Bradley, from the moment he picked up a public telephone at The Spit in Sydney's north, to deliver his ransom demand.

The intense police investigation into the kidnapping, combining traditional police footwork—collating eye-witness accounts and checking clues—with the most modern scientific techniques, has long been held up as a paradigm example of police procedure.

Sydney police, too often criticised as corrupt, worked incredibly hard, first to winnow the iridescent blue 1955 Ford Customline car used in the kidnapping from an estimated 5,000 others, then to identify Bradley as its driver. At that point the case against Bradley was not strong enough, although he had unintentionally laid a trap for himself by making a visit to the Thornes' flat before the kidnapping and being thoroughly sighted.

There was an implacable urgency about police efforts. Homicide detectives stayed on duty for weeks, even months, at a time. Rival media groups teamed as never before, or since. Police were given unprecedented help by members of the public who wrote and telephoned search headquarters in thousands, most with no thought of reward, although offers totalling many thousands of pounds were soon posted.

Members of the Sydney underworld, shocked by the realisation that it could have been one of their own children kidnapped, cooperated with police to the limit. Very early in the investigation, police knew it was not a "professional" crime. No ransom was ever paid.

On 16 August 1960, Graeme Thorne's body was found wrapped in a checkered rug in a small cave under an overhanging rock on a vacant block of land at Seaforth, 16 kilometres from Bondi and on the other side of the harbour. A silk scarf was knotted tightly around his neck. Pathologists said Graeme had died of either a fractured skull or strangulation. His body was too decomposed for a positive judgement.

The rug wrapping Graeme's body provided a smorgasbord of telltale traces for police and forensic scientists to work on. The rug carried traces of pink mortar, soil, cypress twigs and dog hairs, all of which were eventually related directly to Bradley. The scientific evidence was easy to understand, and totally convincing.

On 11 October 1960, Bradley was arrested in Colombo while fleeing Australia by ship with his family.

The trial at Sydney's Central Criminal Court in Darlinghurst in March 1961 lasted eight days. There were many moments of drama. On the very first day, Freda Thorne broke into tears when being cross-examined by Fred Vizzard, QC, for Bradley, about her identification of Bradley as the man who had called at her flat. "I don't care what you say", she said, as she pointed at Bradley in the dock. "That's the man ... "

Bradley had no answer to the massive collection of facts police had painstakingly collected against him except a flat denial and ugly allegations against detectives who had taken a statement from him which he later repudiated.

In a surprise appearance in the witness box, under oath and subject to cross-examination, Bradley said he had made a bogus confession because of police threats to implicate his wife, Magda, in the kidnapping. "I was very worried about my wife", he said. "She had been in a concentration camp. She was blind in one eye. I felt if she had to go through that ordeal [of arrest and interrogation] she will never stand it. I love my wife and family and will do anything to help them".

Bradley admitted practically nothing apart from the love he said he bore his wife and children.

He stoically accepted his speedy conviction and sentence to life imprisonment and thanked the judge and jury for a fair trial. Things might have been different, he said, if the jury had heard "the full story". He tried to tell that story. Then the verdict was announced to the crowd of 5,000 outside the court. They roared their approval. Bradley did not continue.

Bradley died of a heart attack in Goulburn Gaol eight years later, in October 1968. He was 45 years of age and had achieved some stature as a violinist in prison orchestras. He was not a pariah in prison, as had been predicted. As a criminal he had attempted "the big one", and most of the prison population eventually gave him grudging credit for it.

But, for parents, life in Australia after 7 July 1960 has never been quite the same. The kidnapping of Graeme Thorne and the memory of what probably happened—of Bradley ruthlessly gagging the terrified boy and thrusting him into the boot of the car, not caring whether he lived or not—had a profound psychological impact. One result was that, ever since, people buying lottery tickets could indicate whether or not they wanted their identity published if they won. Few people have opted for publication.

The disappearance of the three Beaumont children, Jane, 9, Arnna, 7, and Grant, 4, at Glenelg beach in South Australia on Australia Day 1966, had an additional dimension. Because no information has ever come to light as to the fate of those children, it has become a nightmare without end. Possibly it is the cruellest story of any "Mr Cruel", any child abducter, in the history of Australian crime. Certainly it is the saddest story the police and reporters involved can remember. The probability—universally accepted—is that they were kidnapped and murdered.

In all probability, the agony of the three children ended a long time ago. At worst, it was an unthinkable day or two after they were taken. The torture inflicted on the children's parents, Grant ("Jim") Beaumont and his wife, Nancy, at the time has continued every day since. No words can convey how they have suffered.

Jim and Nancy Beaumont are not "at peace". They have had few waking hours since their children disappeared when they have not paused to grieve and wonder how, and why, their family has been destroyed. When they do manage to sleep, how many nightmares do they have? How often do they wake weeping?

Jim and Nancy Beaumont were loving parents and built their lives around Jane, Arnna and Grant. They were intensely proud of their children, with good reason. Nasty things were said and suggested at the time the children disappeared, hinting that the parents might have had something to do with it. But few parents have survived intense scrutiny as well as the Beaumonts. Not many couples thrown into a blinding spotlight have been able to show they had as few secrets to hide.

The Beaumonts on the fateful day had allowed their children to leave their home at Somerton at 10 am for a swim at the beach. They took it for granted that the children would return, as they had agreed, by the noon bus. The Beaumonts had made a tragic mistake. They thought they still lived in a decent world where it was safe to let young children go to the beach alone. No responsible parents would do that now, least of all in Adelaide—the "City of Churches".

The prime suspect in the case was a tall, thin, blond young man who was seen on the day of the disappearance "frolicking" with the three children on the lawn on the foreshore of Glenelg at about 11.15 am. Witnesses later told police they had seen the children flicking the "surfie" with their towels. He was attempting to wrestle with them. A local woman said she was "vaguely troubled" by what she saw. She had not gained the impression the man was related to the children, or a particular friend.

The woman and other dependable witnesses described the "surfie" as about 185 centimetres tall with long, unkempt fair hair and a deep suntan. He was of slim build, with a thin face and a naturally fair complexion. He was "almost certainly Australian" and wearing brief blue swim trunks.

An elderly couple told police they saw the "surfie" with the Beaumont children after the game with the towels. To the couple, the children seemed to trust him completely. The man "dressed" the children by putting their shorts over their bathers. Then the man went to the changing rooms himself.

Shortly afterwards, the children bought three pasties at a milk bar near the foreshore. They used a £1 note. Mrs Beaumont had given Jane only six shillings—three florins.

Worried at the children's non-appearance, Jim and Nancy Beaumont, who knew nothing of what had happened at the beach until later, began a search for them at 3 pm. By 7 pm, they were frantic. They reported the disappearance to the Glenelg police.

Jim Beaumont, nuggety, balding, a linen salesman who drove a taxi part-time to give his wife and children a better life, asked the search headquarters at Glenelg CIB twice a day whether there was any news. Doggedly determined to be optimistic, he said he believed Jane, the "little mother", would make sure that Arrna and Grant Jr were all right. He was so proud of Jane. The children were alive, he insisted. They were being held in a hut in a remote country area by a kindly eccentric.

"I know they didn't run away, and I don't believe they were drowned or trapped in a cave-in", he said. "Their bodies would have been found by now if they had been. I think this surfie got them in by talking to them and being friendly. But they're safe, I'm sure of that".

Jim Beaumont had not quite convinced himself, however. He couldn't rest, or stand still for a moment. At Glenelg CIB, he walked ceaselessly up and down Sergeant Ron "Wingy" Blight's office. At home, he needlessly clipped the hedge at the side of the house, mowed the well-mown lawn, and made endless cups of tea for his wife.

On hooks in the hall of his house, two girls' school hats hung ready for use and, in the backyard, there were empty swings and a little boy's go-kart.

Nancy Beaumont, 38, an olive-skinned, brown-eyed woman, ate little and slept only when sedated. She could think of nothing but her children. She maintained a stubborn logic that somehow made her stronger than her husband.

"My children are dead and I know it", she said on 3 February, nine days after they had disappeared. "I mustn't think they are, but I can't be stupid. It's just been too long. I don't think they're alive any more. They can't be after eight or nine days. You can't drop your bundle, but they're just little babies huddled together".

When Jim Beaumont attempted to comfort her, she shook her head. "Oh Grant, they won't come in the front door with their skipping ropes", she said. "The poor little things are huddled up somewhere in some stupid place, and they will never find them. I haven't given up hope, but I know!

"The children all loved one another, and they'd have stuck together. If one was hurt, the others would have chipped in. That's why they're all dead together; they wouldn't have run off in different directions.

"I've said prayers. I want my children to come back. I don't want anything else. All the things I thought were important don't matter. Even our home is incidental now. I'd rather we were all together in a tent on the beach.

"I think as a mother, and I'd rather kill my children myself and get it over quickly than have them at the mercy of some bad person for so long. They could be in an old, abandoned farmhouse and no one would see them".

In a later interview, Mrs Beaumont said the police had been "wonderful". But she complained that there was always some ghoulish outsider saying: "Your children are dead—dig here".

She had reason to say that. Gerard Croiset, a Dutch clairvoyant, had flown to South Australia at the invitation and expense of an Adelaide car dealer. In Europe, Croiset had announced he had "seen" where the Beaumont children had died. They had been smothered, he said, by a sandfall in a tunnel.

At Adelaide Airport, he complained of press attention. Then he jumped on a chair and handled the crowded media conference with an aplomb any politician would have envied. Ostensibly he did not speak English. But he often answered questions while they were being interpreted. Some of the questions were from interested airport cleaners.

Croiset said the "second sight" which allegedly enabled him to find the bodies of murder and accident victims was "a gift from God". But he constantly dictated observations into a tape-recorder he carried over his shoulder. During his long tour of Glenelg, he ordered one of his companions to take 32 photographs. "To help my memory", he explained.

Croiset indicated three locations where he said the children's bodies would be found. One was beneath the cement floor of a suburban warehouse. The floor was jack-hammered to a depth of more than three feet. No bodies or traces of bodies were found. There were no better results from the other locations. Croiset lost confidence, panicked, and after three days flew to the United States.

Jim and Nancy Beaumont, who had found enough strength in each other to save their sanity, eventually sold their Somerton house, which had so many poignant memories, and separated. Jim Beaumont changed jobs and did well. Like Nancy, with whom he remained on good terms, he desperately hoped his children were still alive and that, miraculously, he would see them again.

He wondered aloud in an excruciating interview what they looked like, and whether he would recognise them. He was a heartbroken, and heart-breaking, man.

So too was Les Ratcliffe, 48, of Campbelltown, another Adelaide suburb, whose daughter Joanne, 11, was abducted with Kirsty Gordon, 4, of Hackham, during a South Australian National Football League match at Adelaide Oval on 25 August 1973. The girls had been sitting in a stand with the Ratcliffe family and Kirsty's grandmother. Just after the three-quarter time break, Joanne took Kirsty to the women's toilets at the back of the stand.

Ten minutes later, when the girls had not returned, their families began searching for them. There was no sign of them. The families asked a ground official to put a call over the public address system for them. He declined. The game had reached an exciting stage and he did not want to break people's concentration over what seemed to be just another case of lost kids. One call was allowed five minutes after the end of the game.

The information that came back was that the children had been seen being "hustled away" by a "stooped" man. The man and the children could not be found. When police got further details from eye-witnesses, the mystery man came more and more to bear a resemblance to the "surfie" in the Beaumont case.

No sign was ever seen of the little girls again.

Shortly before dying of cancer in 1981, Les Ratcliffe dictated a heart-rending letter to the people of South Australia, particularly the police. That letter, in part, read:

"Do not forget the Adelaide Oval abduction of August 1973. The man is still loose, and there are still children on the streets. As a parent, I could not wish for anyone to live through what I have had to live through.

"After Joanne disappeared it took me years to get back to three parts of what I was before we lost her. I smiled but I was crying inside. One has to go on, however difficult it is".

Life, of course, does go on, as do child abductions and murders, increasing in number, and in the publicity given them, although conflicting statistics from rival departments can confuse the issue.

One extreme and very recent example might suffice.

Early in 1993 the case of two-year-old Daniel Valerio, of Rosebud, Victoria, focused attention on child abuse as seldom before.

Daniel, born 21 April 1988, died on 8 September 1990. He was found to have had 104 bruises on and inside his tiny body. Both his collar bones had been broken. There were the marks of heavy blows on his face, stomach and groin. A pint of blood was found in his abdominal cavity. His duodenum had been ruptured. The intestines had been torn loose in several places. The pathologist who conducted the autopsy said the injuries were similar to those sustained by a road accident victim whose stomach had been crushed. The cause of death: internal bleeding.

Not only that but it was clearly evident that the boy had been starved. He weighed only 10 kilograms, less than a well-nourished toddler a quarter of his age. Police inquiries established that the boy had suffered a succession of cruel beatings.

In February 1993, Daniel's stepfather, Paul Leslie Aiton, 32, went on trial in the Victorian Supreme Court for the boy's murder. There was plenty of evidence against him. Aiton admitted slapping and "punching Daniel several times in the stomach" to stop him crying. Workmates told of how he had boasted of kicking Daniel between the legs, hitting him on the penis with a wooden spoon, and rubbing his face in his own faeces.

Aiton was sentenced to 22 years in gaol for murder. The judge, Justice Cummins, set a minimum non-parole period of 18 years. He said Aiton had been guilty of "a very aggravated crime with a high level of moral turpitude".

The judge said: "He was small, sick and dependent and you were large, powerful and aggressive. A little over six months after you met Ms Butcher, the body of Daniel Valerio was lying at the coroner's office in South Melbourne".

One restraint on those contemplating attacks on children is universal abhorrence—which continues even in prison. If that did not happen in Bradley's case, it was the exception rather than the rule. But it is unlikely that a person capable of such horrendous acts would be stopped by the intrusion of such a rational thought. It is now mandatory for casualty sections of hospitals to notify government authorities when there are indications of possible assaults on babies and children. Sometimes reactions are hysterical. The public hatred directed at Stephen Bradley was well deserved.

Whether justified or not, universal scorn is but one control. As with the Beaumont children and the Ratcliffe and Gordon girls, the monsters are not only ruthless but extremely cunning and deceptive. The Australian wilderness that was so daunting to the pioneers has to a large extent been tamed. The jungle remains.

ERIC COOKE, RANDOM KILLER

DEATH ON THE STREETS OF PERTH BY NIGHT

I t's quite correct to say that in 1963 the people of Perth regarded their home town as nothing more than that—a friendly town of some 600,000 residents, stretched along an Indian Ocean coastline, where nobody bothered to lock their house or car, where people greeted each other in the street, where parents had no reason to doubt a child's personal safety outside (or inside) the home.

It wasn't that Perth folk were careless or self-satisfied about safety or security. It was just that, despite a "wild west" heritage of pioneers and gold rushes, they liked to trust one another.

Even so, when one in their midst did grossly offend against society, the juries of the west were quite prepared to mete out the ultimate punishment. Since 1901, Western Australia had hanged more people than any other Australian state. In the ten years to 1963, four murderers had been publicly hanged in the grounds of Fremantle's imposing sandstone prison. New South Wales and Queensland had, by contrast, abolished the noose. Victoria had not seen a hanging since 1951.

Western Australia was soon to see another execution. It was to be of a serial killer who during a nine-month rampage terrorised Perth and changed forever the unquestioning friendliness of the nation's most isolated capital.

In the early hours of Sunday, 27 January 1963, poultry dealer Nicholas August was enjoying the company of Rowena Reeves, a barmaid at the Ocean Beach Hotel, Cottesloe. Though married, he was in no hurry to go home. He took Reeves to a late night restaurant and afterwards for a drive along the beachfront. At about 2 am, the two parked in Napier Street, facing the ocean.

They drank some beer and chatted. They were still there at 2.30, August in the front seat, behind the wheel, Reeves in the back.

Suddenly, Reeves saw a man in the middle of the road, staring at them. August saw him too, threw an empty beer bottle at him and told him to "bugger off". Reeves saw the man aiming a rifle, lunged forward and pushed August's head below the seat. She was not quick enough. The bullet smashed through her wrist and hit August. August felt a "hot stinging", as he described it, in the neck and saw blood begin to gush. Reeves screamed: "Start the car and run him down!". August turned on the ignition and opted to speed off, travelling south towards Fremantle. Another bullet whined past the vehicle. August looked back at Reeves. She was lying on the back seat, in a pool of the blood spurting from her wrist.

They escaped and sought treatment. Others would not be nearly as lucky.

At 3.50 that morning, three kilometres inland from Cottesloe, in Louise Street, Nedlands, Sandra Walmsley was sleeping in a front room when she was jolted awake by the doorbell ringing. From inside the house she heard her mother tell her father, retired grocer George Walmsley, 54, to answer the door. He did so. A shot rang out. Mother and daughter rushed from their rooms. George Walmsley was on the floor, fatally shot through the forehead.

At 4 am, in Vincent Street, also in Nedlands, Scott McWilliam, a university arts student, was sleeping at "Mrs Allen's", a crowded boarding house popular with generations of students. He was woken by the proprietor's niece. She said: "There's something wrong with John!". The girl was referring to John Sturkey, a 19-year-old agricultural science student who had been sleeping on the back veranda. She said she had heard gurgling sounds coming from his throat. McWilliam went to Sturkey. Thinking he was choking, he lifted his head from the pillow. As Sturkey's hair fell back, McWilliam saw a bullet wound in his forehead. Sturkey died. Police were called.

The boarders, the local community, and later the whole of Perth, were traumatised. It appeared the killer had come to Mrs Allen's looking for a victim at random. He had found Sturkey. On the balmy summer nights, students had taken turns to sleep in the open-air bed. Anybody could have been sleeping there.

But that was not quite the end of it. After daybreak, another victim, apparently of the same killer, was discovered.

Brian Weir, an accountant, had retired to bed early on the Saturday night at his home in Napier Street, Cottesloe. He wanted to rise early to train at the Cottesloe Surf Life Saving Club. When he did not show up, one of his surf club friends went to his home. The friend found him lying critically injured on a blood-spattered bed, shot through the head. Weir was rushed to Royal Perth Hospital where he underwent an emergency six-hour operation. He had massive brain damage. His hopes of living seemed slim, but he was fit and clung to life. Police had little to go on. August and Reeves had glimpsed their assailant but it had not been a good view. Rowena Reeves had said the gunman was "thin" and "young"—which hardly produced a short-list. Police found spent shells from a .22 calibre rifle. They had a report, at the time of the Walmsley shooting, of a light-coloured Holden vehicle at the corner of Louise Street and Princess Road, about 20 metres from the house. A boot print was found between the houses where Walmsley and Sturkey had been shot. But it was discounted when found to have been left by a delivery man.

Police searched the 400-hectare Kings Park, an expanse into which the killer could have escaped. The afternoon paper, the *Daily News*, screamed: "Park combed for maniac slayer". But the search, though very thorough, was fruitless. A week into their investigation, detectives had interviewed more than 40 suspects and tracked many items of information phoned in by the public. They also began to check the registration of every .22 calibre rifle in Western Australia.

A week after the spate of murders, two men working in the wheat-belt town of Merredin, 500 kilometres east of Perth, reported being shot at. Police set up road blocks around the area. They even dismantled an 80-tonne stack of firewood in search of cartridges. There was mystery over the motives for the shooting. Was there a connection with the Perth shootings?

Newspapers offered rewards of £500 to £1,000 for information leading to the arrest of the gunman. There was no result.

Two weeks after the Merredin shootings, West Perth mother Joy Noble was up at 7 am preparing a family picnic basket when she glanced out the window into her backyard. What she saw froze her blood. It was the naked body of a young woman, spreadeagled on the lawn, her blue nightdress crumpled beside her. She appeared to be nestling an empty whisky bottle. Thinking the woman might be drunk or asleep, Mrs Noble called out to her three times. Then she dialled the police. The body was that of Constance Lucy Madrill, 24, a social worker who shared a house with another woman across the rear laneway from the Nobles' home. Madrill had been raped and strangled.

Madrill had had the habit of leaving the back door propped open with a broom at night so the Siamese cat could enter and leave as it wanted. Police believed that was how the killer had gained entry. Madrill's housemate, Jennifer Hurst, told police that she had said "Goodnight" to Madrill at 11.30 pm. At 1.30, Hurst had got up briefly and glanced into Madrill's bedroom. Nothing had seemed amiss and she had gone back to bed. She was woken next morning by the police.

Police found a length of flex in the house. There were few signs of a struggle in Madrill's bedroom. The hall carpet was bunched, consistent with the killer having dragged his victim out through the back door. He had hauled her feet first about 23 metres from the house, across a laneway and concrete path, into the Nobles' yard. The empty whisky bottle turned out to be one which Joy Noble's husband, Max, had thrown into his yard the night before.

Police Commissioner Les O'Brien did not see why there should be a connection between Constance Lucy Madrill's death and the Nedlands–Cottesloe killings. Six months later, on Saturday, 10 August 1963, he changed his mind.

In Dalkeith, another well-to-do Perth suburb less than three kilometres from the scene of the Nedlands murders, Carl and Wendy Dowd decided to go to a party and arranged for Shirley Martha McLeod, 18, a university science student, to babysit their eight-month-old son, Mitchell.

McLeod, who wanted to be a social worker, told them she'd spend the night studying. They left the neat brick and weatherboard home at the corner of Minora and Wavells Roads with nothing amiss, apart from the weather which was wet and windy. When they returned home, at 2 am, it was a different picture. McLeod was slumped on the sitting room sofa, pen still in her hand, an unfinished sentence in her notebook. The record player was still turning. The electric fire was keeping the room cosy. McLeod looked as though she was asleep, with a peaceful expression on her face. But there was a bullet hole between her eyes. She was dead.

The public went into uproar. There were clear indications that a serial killer was at work. Nobody was safe. Police worked hard to pin down their man. They managed to isolate a fingerprint in the Dowd residence which could not be matched with any known person. Within a week, police had interviewed and fingerprinted 8,000 Dalkeith residents. They fingerprinted 8,000 more the next week, along with 2,800 students from the University of Western Australia.

The press suggested somewhat sarcastically that the police were determined to fingerprint every male over 12 years of age in the state. Civil libertarians started complaining. There were parliamentary calls for outside police help in the investigation. The local force kept up its dragnet.

The breakthrough came on 17 August 1963 when an elderly couple, Mr and Mrs Keehner, were strolling beside the Swan River in tree-lined Rookwood Street, Mount Pleasant. Mrs Keehner spied a Geraldton wax native bush near the riverbank. She went to get a sprig from it. "A glint from the sun made me look down and I saw a rifle", she said later. It was a Winchester .22.

The couple reported the discovery to the police. Police believed it might have been the weapon used by the killer. They staked out the site for two weeks. On 1 September, a man drove up. He was wearing women's gloves and carrying a torch. He went down to the rifle. When he reached it police grabbed him. When they searched him, they found a pair of womens' panties in his pocket. Police took him to CIB headquarters in Beaufort Street for questioning. The man's name: Eric Edgar Cooke, a stockily built, harelipped truck driver.

When police did ballistics tests on the rifle, they confirmed it had been the rifle that had killed Shirley McLeod.

Cooke denied he was the killer. He claimed that on the night McLeod died, on 10 August, he had returned to his home in the Perth suburb of Riverdale at 8.30 pm. His wife, he said, would confirm it. But the next day Sally Cooke swore in a statement that her husband had been out that night until after midnight.

Cooke asked her why she had said that. "Because it's the truth, Eric", she said.

Cooke asked: "What do you think I should do now?".

She replied: "That's for you to consider and make up your own mind about".

Cooke gave police an account of his movements on the night of 10 August. He told Detective Sergeant John Neilsen he had been bowling with a friend that night until 7.30 pm. Then he had driven off alone, roaming the western beach suburbs looking for houses to burgle. In Pearse Street, Cottesloe, he had entered a house by the rear door and had seen a man and woman sitting in the lounge. He had slipped quietly into the main bedroom. He had found no money, but had found a rifle and cartridges.

Cooke said he had gone back to his car with the rifle and had driven off. He recalled walking from his car in heavy rain in the Dalkeith area and opening a door in a house. "I was shocked to find the rifle in my hand", he said. The next thing he remembered was getting back into his car, finding a spent cartridge in the rifle, and ejecting it. He had returned to Riverdale, hiding the weapon in Rookwood Street along the way.

"I can't remember firing the shot, as God is my witness", he said.

On the afternoon of 2 September, police charged Cooke with the McLeod murder. On 3 September, police took him to the scene of the murder of Constance Lucy Madrill. This time, Cooke admitted to the killing.

He said he had gone into the house at night while Madrill and Hurst slept and searched a dressing table for money. He had knocked over a framed photograph. The noise had woken Madrill. "I swung my fist and hit her on the neck and temple—fairly hard [because] it hurt my knuckles", he said. When Madrill had opened her mouth to scream, Cooke had grabbed her round the throat with both hands and squeezed hard, rendering her unconscious. He had dragged Madrill into the spare bedroom, thrown her to a mattress on the floor, strangled her with the lamp flex and raped her.

Cooke had decided to hide the body. He had dragged it into the Noble's backyard, intending to steal a car and take it away. He could not find a vehicle. He had left the body in the yard, stolen a pushbike and ridden away.

Police started to piece together his past to try to understand the man who had become such a monster. He had come to police attention before, in 1955, for stealing a car. A father of seven, he had been by all accounts a loving husband. Sally Cooke was to tell reporters: "I'd like everyone to know that we've been very happy together".

Cooke, an inveterate petty thief and "Saturday night voyeur", had apparently lived a double life. He had been stealing for some 18 years. He revealed to police that up until the time of his arrest for murder, he might have entered 250 Perth residences. On his peeping Tom expeditions he had used the nightsoil-cart laneways which ran past the back fences of countless Perth suburban homes.

He had had a fairly wretched life. Born with a harelip and cleft palate, he had suffered cruel jibes as a child. Early operations had improved his mouth to some extent, but his speech remained indistinct. He started school at the age of six and his impediment went against him. He became a problem pupil and was expelled after eight months.

Cooke was a neglected child, and was also beaten repeatedly by his father. He often had to endure bad headaches and blackouts. He was accident-prone, falling off a bicycle and on another occasion injuring himself diving into a shallow creek. It was thought the accidents might have caused brain damage but this was not borne out by x-rays.

Cooke attended four other Perth schools up to the age of 14 but was never happy. "[Other boys] would make fun of me and the way I talked", Cooke told police.

Leaving school, he had taken up various manual jobs but was directionless. In 1946, at the age of 16, Cooke was admitted to Royal Perth Hospital for three weeks with head injuries. He had intervened during a domestic row to protect his mother and his father had beaten him.

During the Korean War, Cooke had done National Service. He told police he had been "taught to use all types of firearms and was quite proficient in their use".

Cooke had married in 1953. Sally was 18 at the time. They had settled down to married life. Cooke had been getting out at night to steal and do other mischief. Sally Cooke had been aware of his absences. She had referred to them as his "wanderings". When Cooke was charged in 1955 with car theft, his mother-in-law put her home up as bail surety.

The couple had four boys and three girls. There were some problems among them. The first child, a boy, was intellectually handicapped. A daughter was born without a right forearm. Cooke appeared to have fulfilled his fatherly obligations. "He's always been very good to his children and our neighbours admired him for it, too", Mrs Cooke said. "He said the only love he'd ever known was mine and the children's. He wanted to forget about the rest of his life."

It seemed quite a reasonable belief to authorities that Cooke was mentally ill. But they also had to satisfy the strong community demand for justice.

Cooke was committed to trial for murder. His barrister, a prominent local QC, Mr K.W. Hatfield, whom he had obtained on legal aid, sought to show that Cooke was schizophrenic. Hatfield called on the services of psychiatrist Dr Ian James, who had examined Cooke several times through the years at Heathcote Reception Hospital. James on those occasions had tested for possible brain abnormalities, either congenital or caused by his accidents and paternal maltreatment.

Hatfield sought to have Dr James examine Cooke again before the trial. This was refused by the prosecution. Instead, Cooke was questioned by Dr J. Ellis, WA Director of Mental Health Services. Ellis asked Cooke what his motive had been for the shootings in Cottesloe–Nedlands. Cooke replied that he had not known his victims. He had shot them simply because he "wanted to hurt somebody".

Ellis dismissed any notions of schizophrenia or another mental disease. He declared Cooke had a character abnormality which caused him to seek inordinate amounts of attention. "His self-esteem needs bolstering and he will go to any lengths to do this", Ellis said. He added that Cooke had a grudge against society.

After his arrest, Cooke admitted to a total of 41 offences. During his time in custody, Cooke had admitted to several killings. One was of a Perth socialite, Jillian Brewer, 22, on Saturday, 19 December 1959. A hatchet and a pair of scissors had been used in the killing. Cooke withdrew the confession two days later. On 25 October, Cooke said he had killed Patricia Berkman. This crime had never been solved. The attractive 33-year-old had been found lying naked in her South Perth flat, after having been stabbed several times in the face and chest. Her body was found by her lover, a well-known Perth radio star, Fotis Hountas. News of the confession provided a field day for the press. The prosecution sought to try him only for the murder of John Sturkey.

Cooke's trial began on 25 November 1963, before a packed and hostile gallery. The prosecution was a relatively simple matter. The Crown case was completed in a day. Cooke in his evidence claimed he had some mysterious power which made him kill. "It was like a mantle", he said. "I had full possession of my faculties, like hearing and seeing, but this power surge, it was as though I was God—with power over life and death". He said that on the night of 26 January he had stolen a light-coloured Holden from a house in Karoo Street, South Perth, which had the keys in the ignition. He had shot Sturkey and the others during the following hours and then returned the Holden to its garage. [The car's owner, Henry Threfall, did not notice the extra mileage and had no idea, till police turned up on his doorstep, that the vehicle had ever been involved.]

The entire trial lasted three days. The trial judge, Justice Virtue, instructed the jury that they could find Cooke either guilty of wilful murder or not guilty on the grounds of insanity. The jury took just 65 minutes to return their verdict: Cooke was guilty. Justice Virtue sentenced him to death.

Cooke's admissions to other killings had the effect of delaying his execution. Four months after the Brewer murder, a 20-year-old deaf mute named Darryl Beamish had been arrested and had confessed. Despite the fact that Cooke had withdrawn his confession, Beamish's lawyers appealed to the Western Australian Supreme Court against Beamish's conviction on the basis that there had been an admission of guilt by someone else. The appeal failed.

Cooke claimed he had run down and killed a 17-year-old girl named Rosemary Anderson on 10 February 1963, in the Shenton Park area of Perth. Anderson's boyfriend, John Button, a brickie's labourer, had been convicted and sentenced to ten years' gaol for her manslaughter. Button's lawyers appealed on the basis of Cooke's confession and were similarly unsuccessful.

Legal teams for both Beamish and Button applied to the High Court for leave to appeal against the Western Australian decisions. Cooke, in the meantime, was being held in Fremantle Prison, and was being visited each Saturday by his wife.

The High Court refused to grant lawyers for Beamish and Button the right to appeal. One judge described Cooke as "an inveterate liar". The failure of the appeals meant there was no reason to delay the execution. Cooke's father said: "It will be a good thing when the whole episode is over—perhaps then we'll be able to settle down to something like a normal life". Cooke was hanged at Fremantle prison on 26 October 1964.

Brian Weir, the man who had aspired to nothing more on the night he was shot than to get up in the morning and train with his surf club, clung to life for three years. He managed to regain partial control of his legs. His right side remained paralysed, he was blind in his left eye and he could barely speak. He died on 19 December 1965, aged 31, the last sad echo of the career of Eric Edgar Cooke, a man who had never fitted into society and who ultimately hadn't cared.

ABE SAFFRON

THE MANY SIDES OF THE MAN AND HIS MONEY

O ne story, probably apocryphal, about Abraham Gilbert Saffron, the Jewish boy who went to Fort Street Boys High and made a career out of sleaze, involves an appeal by a Queensland nightclub owner. She had a business on the Gold Coast and was being threatened by extortionists demanding protection money. Could Abe help? As the story goes, two men came to the lady's premises in advance of the extortionists and told her to retire to the rear when her tormentors came in. That night, so it is said, the two alleged protection racketeers were admitted to Southport Hospital and the lady in question was never troubled again.

Abe Saffron is surrounded by legend.

But Saffron, despite all the adverse things that have been said about him, including claims that he is a major organised crime figure, has never fitted the gangster image. A slightly built, dapper man, he has been driven since childhood by one motive—to make lots of money.

The easiest way, at least for Saffron, was investment in hotels and nightclubs and in their various ancillary activities. His empire has extended from Sydney to Adelaide, Perth and Brisbane. He has always shunned publicity and has continually indicated he just wants to get on with his life. He has "gone public" a few times when he felt the adverse comment on him had got out of hand. In the early 80s, he contacted this writer at the *Sydney Morning Herald*, saying he wanted to publicly state that he had never been involved with drugs.

Saffron has always had concern about image. In the late 1940s he organised a Christmas party for crippled children. He has been a noted helper of police boys clubs, arranging a "colossal" finance system to help the East Sydney Police Boys Club. He helped raise money for the Miss Australia Quest and contributed to the Lord Mayor's Flood Relief Fund through membership of the Kings

Cross Chamber of Commerce. He has also been appointed a life governor of the Benevolent Society of New South Wales, the oldest charity in the state, to which he had contributed more than $100,000. It has been a good counterweight to the bad publicity, which has been dumped onto him by the truckload.

In the South Australian Parliament in 1978, the then Attorney-General, Peter Duncan, described Saffron as "one of the principal characters in organised crime in Australia". In Federal Parliament in 1982, Senator Don Chipp described him as "one of the most notorious, despicable human beings—if one can use that term loosely—living in this country". In the Victorian Parliament in 1984, Saffron was described as "Gomorrah himself"—a reference to a person code-named "Gomorrah" suspected by the Costigan Royal Commission as being linked with drugs. Saffron said publicly that the suggestion was "an appalling lie".

Saffron attracted enormous police attention at state, national and international level. He was investigated by the National Crime Authority, searched by customs officers, and for years photographed, taped, bugged and followed.

Saffron had—until late in life—an extremely modest criminal record. Two minor convictions remained on the books: one for a betting offence in 1938 which brought a £5 fine; another in 1940 for receiving stolen property, which brought him a bond.

Abe Saffron was born on 6 October 1919, youngest child of a draper. He grew up with two brothers and two sisters in a unit above his father's shop on busy Parramatta Road, Annandale, an inner suburb of Sydney. As a 10-year-old he bought cigarettes at cut-price and sold them, at full cost, to his father's friends at card games. Possessed of good intelligence, he was selected to go to Fort Street and there demonstrated again his business acumen by acquiring used textbooks from boys moving on, sprucing the books up and selling them to the incoming boys. Despite his mother's wishes that he become a doctor, Saffron left school at 15, opting for a career in business.

He started with his father in drapery. The following year he was managing a new shop, with more staff, in Pitt Street, Sydney. A larger establishment in George Street followed. When World War 2 broke out, Saffron enlisted in the Army, but in 1943 switched to the Merchant Navy. He travelled twice to New Guinea. Saffron was afterwards to wear his RSL badge.

At war's end, Saffron could have returned to drapery. Instead, he turned to the hotel business, gaining quick success at Kurri Kurri, in the Hunter Valley of New South Wales, and at Newcastle. In Sydney, he acquired the West End Hotel in Balmain and the Gladstone Hotel in East Sydney. He was married in 1947 to Doreen, a hairdresser, and bought the Roosevelt Nightclub in Orwell Street, Kings Cross.

Saffron had arrived.

He was well placed to take advantage of a revolution in night-clubs which, deep in torpor when he started in the industry, saw the development of elaborate floorshows, bold advertising and late openings.

But from early in his nightclub career there was talk of a darker side to Saffron. In a 1951 article on him in *People* magazine, Saffron acknowledged that he had acquired infamy. "My name seems to have been linked with everything notorious round this town. You'd be staggered at the things I'm supposed to have been mixed up with", he was quoted as saying. A photograph accompanying the article could have been one of a young Frank Sinatra in a Hollywood movie poster. Saffron was sitting with his head resting lightly on his hand at the Roosevelt, with a long fishnet-stocking'd leg framing him. In the same article Doreen, then mother of a son, Alan, and keeper of the Saffrons' austere flat in Poate Road, Centennial Park, told of her initial hatred of the Roosevelt. She complained of how the nightclub scene "seemed to have changed [Abe's] whole personality".

"I hated the long, lonely hours that it kept Abie away from me and I hated his air of preoccupation when he was with me", she admitted in the interview.

Former Sydney haute couturiere, Beril Jents, rented a shop across the road from the Roosevelt. In her 1993 book, *Little Ol' Beryl from Bondi*, she described young Abe as "a good-looking young man, new on the scene ... the younger brother of my friend Ruth's husband Phil [Saffron]". She added: "In those days I remember him as a real playboy—if Abe asked you to come up to his office, you knew not to go".

A complaint like that was trivial compared with what was to come. In 1954, a royal commission into liquor laws, conducted by Mr Justice Victor Maxwell Snr, found that Saffron had employed people to get liquor licences on his behalf and that he had concealed his interest from the Licensing Court. Some of those licences applied to hotels which supplied blackmarket beer to the Roosevelt, which the royal commissioner described as "possibly the most notorious and disreputable nightclub in the city".

Two damages cases from former employees in the early 1950s kept Saffron's name in the papers and cost him a total of £5,622.

In late 1956, Saffron was among a group of men charged with scandalous conduct, following an alleged series of events at a house in Palm Beach. Comments by the police prosecutor on Saffron's morality were less than flattering. But the charge against Saffron was dropped for lack of evidence. Another morals charge was dismissed. Saffron was convicted and fined £10 on two charges of having occupied premises in which obscene publications were found, but the penalties were quashed on appeal. It was all a bit too much for Doreen, however, who took off with Alan for Switzerland where she stayed for six months.

Saffron, not particularly fazed by his brushes with the law, extended his range and his influence. In the early 1960s he made important contacts. One was James McCartney Anderson.

In 1961, despite his continuing marriage to Doreen, Saffron struck up a de facto relationship with one Biruta Aina Hagenfelds. Their bond was an oral promise—the NSW Supreme Court was told much later—for Saffron to provide for her accommodation and lifestyle at a "high material level" for the rest of her life. In return she was to act as a hostess, escort and partner to help entertain business associates. Their union was to produce a daughter.

Saffron was charged with three counts of receiving stolen property. In 1964 he was acquitted on all charges and the NSW Attorney-General decided not to proceed with another five. But the various law enforcement agencies believed Saffron should be closely watched. By the 1970s, he was being repeatedly closely searched by customs officers. His address book, containing 105 names including those of a judge and several police, was copied when he left it behind following a search at Perth Airport in 1973.

The Moffitt Royal Commission into Allegations of Infiltration of Organised Crime into NSW Licensed Clubs, which sat in 1974, was probably Saffron's major setback. A witness described him as "Mr Sin"—a sensational tag. Although evidence was given by a consorting squad detective that the tag belonged not to Saffron but to "another gentleman", it stuck. In the South Australian

Parliament in 1976, it was asked whether Saffron might be the businessman mentioned in a newspaper article as being "almost totally in control of drug-pushing into Adelaide".

Saffron gave his first press interview in 25 years to say that most nefarious activities with which he had been linked were not only untrue but "totally absurd". Quoted in the *Sydney Morning Herald* on 19 October 1976, he said: "On this occasion the accusation that I am involved in drugs is so vile to me that I am compelled to deny it as vigorously as I can through the press. I regard drugs as totally evil ... My business interests are all perfectly legitimate".

The Australian Federal Police, through its intelligence division, explored those business interests. It collected data on Saffron and his purported links prior to 1975 with at least 40, and possibly up to 100, companies nationwide. The data was analysed and compiled in a report produced in 1982. According to a newspaper article in 1985, the information related to Saffron's alleged association with hotels, nightclubs, restaurants, amusement casinos, a sexshop, adult movie clubs and development, investment and finance companies.

"In many cases Saffron's name doesn't appear on company documents although it is strongly suspected that Saffron [exerts] an influence through the use of "front men" and "dummies" or through concealed interests in other shareholder companies", the report said. "The complexity of Saffron's business interests is indeed one of his primary defences, as well as being one of his strengths. That it would take several years to unravel would be no exaggeration".

On 7 March 1978, Saffron copped another rocket. South Australian Attorney-General Duncan described Saffron as a "principal character in organised crime". Saffron "completely" denied the allegations. But they deeply disturbed Doreen Saffron, and marked what Saffron later described as a turning point in his fortunes.

Surveillance continued. Saffron was taped, clandestinely by police in a telephone intercept operation which had not been officially sanctioned, allegedly discussing illegal casino deals and SP bookmaking. Though illegal, the tapes were later officially authenticated.

In 1978 the NSW Premier, Neville Wran, told the State Parliament that Saffron was "not a person of good repute".

Saffron was not prepared to take all of this lying down. When the *Melbourne Age* repeated the "Mr Sin" allegation without attributing it to what was said in privileged proceedings, Saffron sued. In a term of settlement procedure in the defamation action in 1978, Saffron entered the witness box and denied being a criminal or being "Mr Sin". None of his operations was connected with vice or gambling, he swore. He had considered investing money in certain Australian-made films, but it was not the proceeds of vice, gambling, running drugs or any other crime. Saffron won the case.

The 1980s brought new troubles. Several of Saffron's business premises in the eastern suburbs of Sydney were hit by arson attacks. Saffron was also attracting the attention of licensing police at his nightclubs. In 1981, he made seven personal visits to the then Assistant Police Commissioner, William Alan Ruthven Allen, at NSW Police Headquarters. The visits earned Allen an inquiry by the NSW Police Tribunal, which found no evidence that Saffron had paid any money to Allen during these visits.

Allen was not in the clear, however. He was accused of being an associate of both Saffron and Jack Rooklyn. More ominously, he was accused of attempting to bribe the then chief of the Special Licensing Squad at Kings Cross, Sergeant Warren Molloy. In 1982, the NSW Police Tribunal found that Allen had acted in a way which brought discredit on the NSW Police Force. Allen, though disgraced, was allowed to retire on a pension.

Saffron came under the public spotlight again in 1983 with the coroner's inquest into the 1975 disappearance of Mark Foy's heiress Juanita Nielsen who had been editor of a radical Kings Cross newspaper. Nielsen, who had lived in leafy Victoria Street, Kings Cross, had operated on Saffron's turf. She had been a thorn in the side of a redevelopment project at Kings Cross, to which Saffron, according to planning documents, was allegedly linked. Nielsen was last seen on 4 July 1975 at the Carousel Club, one of Saffron's establishments. Saffron, called to give evidence, denied he was linked to the development project which was at the centre of the inquiry into Nielsen's disappearance.

James Anderson, also called to give evidence, proved to be Saffron's undoing. A large, thickset Scot and a former Kings Cross standover man, Anderson had a reputedly ferocious temper and a tendency to be long-winded—to journalists, confidential parliamentary committees and inquests. He did not have a criminal record but lived dangerously. He had survived attempts on his life. Giving evidence at the coroner's inquest, he was startled by an unexpected noise and his hand went straight to his inner coat pocket—as though reaching for a pistol. Whether that was play-acting or not is anyone's guess.

Anderson had had a falling out with Saffron, apparently over money. He told the inquest he had been Saffron's manager and business partner in several Kings Cross nightspots throughout the 70s. They had orally agreed on a formula to split the profits. This arrangement had lasted till 1981, when they came into dispute. Then he put the boot in. He alleged Saffron had been paying police officers regularly for years, including senior NSW licensing police and other officers including an assistant commissioner. He said Saffron had provided "champagne, cognac and a few girls" for police at his Crown Street liquor store, in East Sydney, on Friday afternoons. Police named by Anderson denied they had received bribes. They claimed Anderson hated Saffron. Saffron denied the allegations.

The crunch came when Anderson claimed that Saffron had kept at least two sets of books in relation to his business premises. One, Anderson said, was for taxation purposes. The other was to record what he was really taking. Saffron's reply was: "That is untrue". But he was at a great disadvantage here—in that there were documentary records which might be uncovered which could prove, or disprove, the accusations.

From his answers to intense cross-examination, Saffron appeared to have a somewhat "detached" approach to business, leaving responsibility to managers. According to his evidence, he did not inspect all his accounts and was not sure how many people were on his payroll or how much they were paid.

Whether or not that was true (and it would have provided at least a partial defence), attacks on him kept coming, some from the *National Times* newspaper which, in September 1983, raised allegations over a lease held by Saffron-owned companies on a Public Transport Authority property. The paper had revealed the fact that in July 1978 the NSW government had found that a building in Darlinghurst owned by the Public Transport Authority had been illegally sub-let by businessman Sir Paul Strasser and another developer to two companies owned by Saffron.

TERROR IN VAN DIEMEN'S LAND

Top left: Matthew Brady, "Prince of the Bushrangers", was transported for theft in 1820 and hanged for murder in 1826.

Top right: Martin Cash was transported at the age of 18 for attempted murder but reformed after a career as a bushranger and died peacefully in retirement on an apple orchard at 67 years of age.

Bottom: Reverend Robert Knopwood was accused by bushranger Michael Howe of being involved with the outlaws.

THE BANK OF AUSTRALIA ROBBERY

Top: George Street, Sydney, as it looked in 1826, two years before Australia's first bank robbery.

Bottom left: Justice James Dowling of the NSW Supreme Court ruled that English law could not be applied in a colony that was, to all intents and purposes, an extensive gaol.

Bottom right: Francis Forbes, Chief Justice of New South Wales.

THE RAINBIRD AND OTHER MURDERS

Above: Elizabeth Woolcock, pictured with one of her stepsons and the husband whose cruelty drove her to murder.

THE RAINBIRD AND OTHER MURDERS

Above: Adelaide Gaol gallows. Those guilty of capital crimes in South Australia faced the death penalty and a legal system not afraid to use it.

THE LIFE AND TIMES OF THUNDERBOLT

Top left: Fred Ward, alias "Thunderbolt" or "Captain Thunderbolt".

Top right: Constable Alexander Walker was a little quicker and more skilful than the others who had pursued Ward.

Bottom: Thunderbolt Rock on the New England Highway, south of Uralla, was the scene of a famous confrontation between Ward and police.

THE LIFE AND TIMES OF THUNDERBOLT

Above: The infamous bushranger in death.

SQUIZZY TAYLOR, GANGSTER

Above: This studio shot was just the kind of vain fancy that appealed to Squizzy Taylor, pictured with another racketeer.

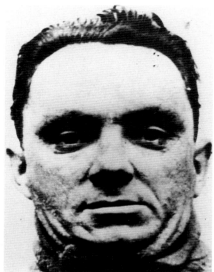

SQUIZZY TAYLOR, GANGSTER

Top left: Squizzy Taylor—the little larrikin who became a colossus of crime.

Top right: A mugshot of Taylor. The gangster's knack of fixing juries and intimidating witnesses meant that he was rarely convicted of any of his many crimes.

Bottom: Darcy Dugan almost achieved the same cult status as Taylor but but didn't have the same good luck when it came to avoiding punishment. He spent a total of 42 years behind bars.

THE PLIGHT OF THE DEFENCELESS

Above: Stephen Leslie Bradley was sentenced to life for Australia's only child kidnap and murder for ransom in the case of Graeme Thorne.

Left: Bradley claimed he made a bogus confession to protect his wife, Magda.

THE PLIGHT OF THE DEFENCELESS

Right: Lottery winners Bazil and Freda Thorne whose luck changed terribly overnight. Since the Thorne abduction the public reporting of a lottery winner's name has been made a personal option on entry.

Below: Graeme Thorne, 8, was lured into a car by his kidnapper, gagged and later murdered ... for the sake of £25,000.

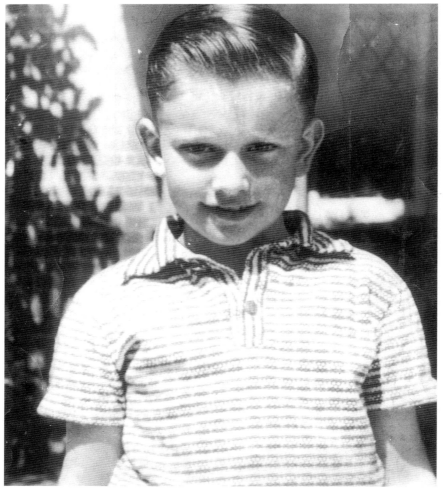

BODY FOUND UNDER LEDGE

THE PLIGHT OF THE DEFENCELESS

Top: Graeme Thorne's badly decomposed body was found wrapped in a rug in a small cave.

Bottom: Police comb the area around Seaforth after the discovery of Thorne's body.

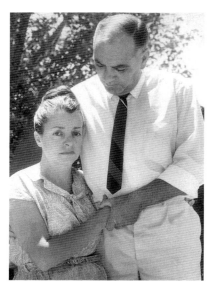

THE PLIGHT OF THE DEFENCELESS

Right: Jim and Nancy Beaumont. While he held on to hope, she tried to accept that her children were gone.

Below: The mysterious disappearance of the Beaumont children still haunts Australia's memory. Pictured left to right: Arna, 7; Grant, 4; and Jane, 9.

THE PLIGHT OF THE DEFENCELESS

Left: Replicas of the Beaumont children were exhibited in every capital city as part of the intensive investigation.

Bottom left: An artist's sketch of the man police were seeking to interview about the Beaumont case.

Bottom right: The extensive search for the Beaumont children went as far as attracting European psychics. Here, police cadets search for evidence in a rubbish dump.

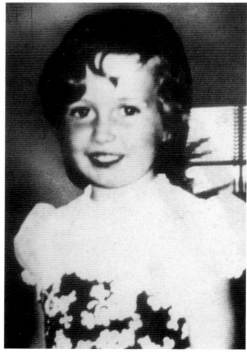

THE PLIGHT OF THE DEFENCELESS

Joanne Ratcliffe, 11, (above) accompanied Kirsty Gordon, 4, (left) to the toilet block at an Adelaide football match. They were never seen again.

ERIC COOKE, RANDOM KILLER

Above right: Eventually admitting to a total of 41 offences, Eric Edgar Cooke was hung on 26 October 1964. A plea of insanity was ignored by the jury.

Above left: Rowena Reeves was one of the lucky ones. She escaped from her confrontation with Cooke badly injured but alive.

Left: Constance Lucy Madrill, 24, was raped and strangled by Cooke and her body dragged into a neighbour's yard.

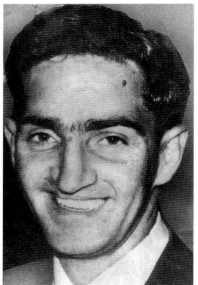

ERIC COOKE, RANDOM KILLER

Top left: Another mystery appeared solved when Cooke confessed to the stabbing murder of Patricia Berkman.

Top right: A family snapshot of a man that Sally Cooke described as a loving father to their seven children.

Bottom: Cooke was led hooded into the Perth Supreme Court to hide him from the angry crowds.

ERIC COOKE, RANDOM KILLER

Above: The scissors used to kill Jillian Brewer. Cooke confessed to her murder and then recanted.

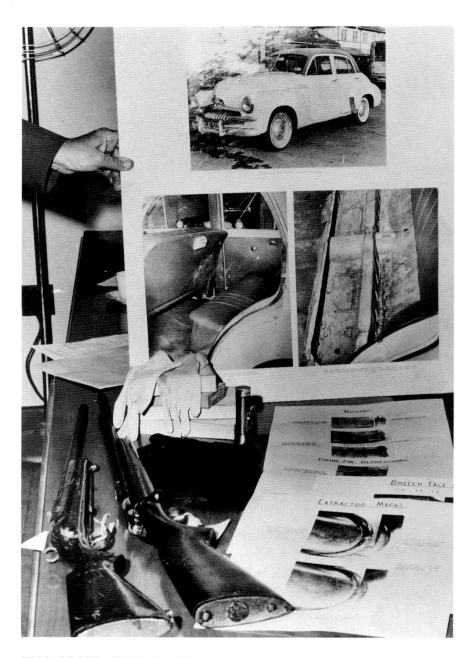

ERIC COOKE, RANDOM KILLER

Above: A collection of evidence—the car used on the night of the killing spree, gloves worn by Cooke when he was apprehended, the murder weapons and blow-ups of the bullet markings.

ABE SAFFRON

Above: Saffron looking very much like a young Frank Sinatra at his Roosevelt Nightclub in Kings Cross. This photograph accompanied the People *article where Saffron acknowledged: "My name seems to be linked with everything notorious round this town".*

ABE SAFFRON

Above: Doreen Saffron pictured with her husband Abe. The woman Saffron married in 1947 when he was just starting in the hotel business has stuck by him through it all.

DOMENICO ITALIANO, THE AUSTRALIAN "GODFATHER"

Top: Domenico Demarte became head of the Society after Domenico Italiano. He did not, however, enjoy a peaceful death like his predecessor.

Bottom: Vincenzo Angilletta had big dreams for the Society's future but he rebelled against their power ... and paid the price.

DOMENICO ITALIANO, AUSTRALIAN "GODFATHER"

Top: Police check the Hampton murder scene where Vincenzo Muratore was gunned down.

Bottom: St Mary's Star of the Sea Church, West Melbourne, was the site of yet another grand scale community funeral with the murder of Vincenzo Muratore.

THE HUNT FOR LARRY BOY

Top left: Peter McCracken, the manager of Elsey station where the attacks by Larry Boy Janba occurred.

Top right: Jessie Garalnganjag worked with Marjorie Biyang in the Elsey homestead kitchen the night that Marjorie died.

Bottom left: Police Constable Roy "Bluey" Harvey spoke admiringly of Larry Boy as a kind of "black Ned Kelly".

Bottom right: Marjorie Biyang's brother Joe McDonald was the member of the search party who finally brought Larry Boy into police hands.

THE PRESSLER CASE

Top: The family at the centre of the intrigue: Clifford and Marjorie Golchert who were killed in their bed.

Bottom: The site of the double murder.

THE PRESSLER CASE

Above and left: Police officers investigate the scene of the crime. The idea of domestic violence in the semi-tropical heat of the canefields captured the attention of a nation.

THE PRESSLER CASE

Top: During his trial, Neville Pressler was found in his cell with razor slashes to his body. In this picture, his wounded left hand is tucked in his pocket as police accompany him to court.

Bottom: Enid Pressler being escorted to trial from prison. The evidence against her was circumstantial but intriguing. Why would a literate man ask Enid to write out his confession? Was the signature on the document a forgery?

THE PRESSLER CASE

Top left: Alan Pressler discovered Henry's body on returning from the cinema.

Top right: Enid Pressler was the only member in the house at the time of Henry's alleged confession and his death.

Bottom: Was Enid Pressler a cold and calculating murderer? The public and participants waited only hours for the jury to decide.

THE DARK SIDE OF ADELAIDE

Left: Dr George Duncan, the victim of a "poofter" bashing that went very wrong.

Below: The body of Dr Duncan was pulled out of the River Torrens by police divers. The other man attacked that night escaped serious injury. It would only become apparent later just how lucky he was.

THE DARK SIDE OF ADELAIDE

Top left: Former Vice Squad officer Mike O'Shea revealed police involvement in Duncan's drowning.

Three Vice Squad detectives were charged over Duncan's drowning: Brian Hudson (top right) Michael Clayton (bottom left) and Francis Cawley (bottom right).

THE DARK SIDE OF ADELAIDE

Above (clockwise from left): The victims: of the "Family" murders—Alan Barnes, 17; Neil Muir, 25; Peter Stogneff, 14; and Mark Langley, 18. Von Einem was never successfully tried for these murders; he was only convicted for the murder of Richard Kelvin.

THE DARK SIDE OF ADELAIDE

Left: Richard Kelvin, 15, who may have been drugged and kept alive for five weeks before he died.

Below: Police surround the area where Kelvin's body was found. The white shapes in the picture are Kelvin's body and a forensic officer.

THE DARK SIDE OF ADELAIDE

Above: Bevan von Einem—the good samaritan who turned out to be a man of unparalleled evil.

Senator Don Chipp told parliament in September 1983 that the building housed a gambling club, a brothel and a sex shop.

"The Government chose to buy out that lease—this is almost incomprehensible—at a cost to the public purse of $2.6 million. There is no record of any action against the gambling club or the brothel. This all reads like an extract from a novel like *The Godfather* or a novel on mobster rule in Chicago or New York," Senator Chipp said.

Saffron kept up his stream of denials. Many allegations against Saffron remained just that: allegations. But Anderson, given immunity from prosecution, had potentially cogent evidence. Two women bookkeepers, also given immunity from prosecution, gave information that they had managed several sets of wages and expenses books for Saffron throughout the 70s. Anderson backed up what they had to say. Anderson's credibility was vulnerable. It was to be disclosed that at that time his tax bill topped $900,000. He was also to be described in the witness box by Ian Barker, QC, as an accomplished witness who told lies, half-truths and evasions in order to get at Saffron. But he was still regarded as a good witness.

The National Crime Authority decided to arrest Saffron and charge him with tax fraud. But the arrest had to be carefully planned. There was talk that Saffron was prepared to flee to Israel, where he had relatives and money.

Saffron was charged on one count of conspiring with Anderson to defraud the Commonwealth of tax between 1 January 1969 and 30 June 1981. He was committed for trial. Anderson was to be a key witness.

The details of the Crown case were complicated and technically difficult. But the evidence from the two bookkeepers was clear. This was that Saffron and Anderson had skimmed off cash profits from Kings Cross establishments and had not declared the total earnings to the Taxation Office. The Crown produced two sets of cash and wages books and tax returns which corroborated the bookkeepers' evidence.

Saffron was said to have been paid $202,000 from Venus Room takings between 1976 and 1980. The defence said Anderson had been paid more than $668,000 in undeclared takings from all the businesses. From June 1979, after a "misunderstanding" about money that should have been paid, a bookkeeper kept a separate book headed "AS" to record cash payments to Saffron. This alone recorded $128,000 up to March 1981. Saffron denied receiving any money recorded in any books.

Saffron made an unsworn statement saying he was innocent. The jury didn't believe him. On the night of 23 October 1987, while the rain poured onto the corrugated iron roof of the old No 16 Supreme Court in Sydney, it returned a guilty verdict. Doreen sobbed. The judge struggled to be heard. Saffron was sentenced to three years imprisonment.

Among his many misfortunes, Saffron was stripped of all his New South Wales liquor licences. At the age of 67, he found himself for the first time in his life a common prisoner. He earned $20 a week in the prison workshop at the Emu Plains prison farm on the outskirts of Sydney suburbia.

The NCA—dubbed later by Doreen Saffron as the "National Crime Assholes", according to one report—sought to continue prosecutions of Saffron. It had on its books allegations that Saffron had paid former Assistant Police Commissioner Bill Allen a total of $2,500 for the purpose of bribing Warren Molloy. Saffron was charged with conspiring with Allen to obstruct the course of justice. He was also charged with conspiring to bribe Molloy, between 1 January and 30 October 1981, to act in a manner contrary to his duty.

The prosecution failed. A Crown witness recanted a statement incriminating Saffron, and James Anderson was found to be a witness whose credibility had been "totally" destroyed. The magistrate dismissed the charges.

Saffron was released on parole on 11 March 1990. He had served 17 months. Doreen drove him home to a spaghetti feast at Vaucluse.

Saffron's battles in the courts were not quite over. Government authorities were interested in the undeclared income which had featured in his trial. In December 1992, after another expensive court battle, a Federal Court judge ordered Saffron to pay a tax bill which, after penalties and interest were added, was likely to top $2 million.

By then Saffron, 73, sometimes spotted joining friends for coffee at the fashionable, Yiddish-style East Sydney restaurant Dov, had joined the Temple Emmanuel, a liberal Jewish synagogue in the eastern suburbs.

Doreen Saffron, who had stayed and stayed with her straying husband, did not often say how she felt about things. But, waiting for the jury's verdict in the tax evasion trial, she did make a response when asked what it was like being married to Abe for 40 years.

"Very interesting", she said slowly. "It's been very interesting".

DOMENICO ITALIANO, AUSTRALIAN "GODFATHER"

THE WORKINGS OF THE MAFIA IN VICTORIA

The impressive funeral at St Mary's Star of the Sea Church, West Melbourne, in December 1962, was well attended. That, as events were to show, was most significant.

One Domenico Italiano had died peacefully in his old age at his West Melbourne home. The funeral was like something arranged for a head of state. Thousands attended the church and its grounds as the pallbearers, including Italiano's son-in-law, Michele Scriva, carried the body to what would be its permanent resting place under an elaborate headstone at the Melbourne cemetery. And it eventually became clear to outsiders why there was so much fuss.

Italiano, whose profile in death was far higher than it had ever been in life, had been regarded as the "Godfather of Victoria", and had been referred to as "The Pope" or "Il Papa". He had been head of the Honoured Society—"L'Onorata Societa" or "N'Dranghita" in Italian—otherwise referred to as "The Black Hand".

From the time the presence of the mafia (using the term in a generic sense to refer to a criminal organisation whose ethnic and cultural roots were Italian) became apparent in north Queensland in the 1920s, there had been vague talk of mafia in Australia. The Calabrian brand went by the names referred to above. From the 1930s, the Honoured Society (we'll call it "the Society" for short) had exerted a small but growing influence on organised crime in Australia. In Queensland, its activities had been concentrated on extortion in the canefields.

In Victoria, the Society moved heavily into the production and distribution of fruit and vegetables. The Society had the huge Queen Victoria Market, known as the "Melbourne Market", sown up. Outsiders had very little chance of getting in while those of

Calabrian and, more generally, Italian extraction were given help getting started, provided they obeyed the Society's rules. It must be pointed out that the majority of fruit and vegetable merchants were honest and hardworking. But like so many migrants, arriving in a foreign country, perhaps not speaking the language and more trusting of their own community than alien institutions, they were also vulnerable to extortion by criminals within that same community.

Because the community kept its internal affairs to itself, little was known about the criminal extortion. It does not appear to have caught the attention of the police in any particular way. That all changed in the events following Italiano's death.

A few months after the funeral, Italiano's right-hand man, Antonio Barbara, known as "The Toad", also died. The death was no particular loss to Australian society in general. Barbara, a violent strong-arm man, had served five years for manslaughter after he killed a woman near Melbourne's Queen Victoria Market in 1936. But to the Society in particular, Barbara's death was far more serious. Combined with that of Italiano, it left a dangerous void at the top.

The places were filled by Domenico Demarte, as the head, and Vincenzo Muratore, who was a prosperous merchant and the Society's trusted financial advisor. But in this world, successions to power were by no means smooth or universally accepted.

Vincenzo Angilletta, 37, was an extortionist and gunman in his native Calabria before he migrated to Australia in 1951 and set up as a producer of fruit and vegetables. He had become part of the system, selling his produce to Society wholesalers. But he had bigger ideas. In the wake of the deaths of Italiano and Barbara, Angilletta decided to make a grab for power. He believed the Society could be a bigger operation, that it could be modelled on the United States Mafia and become a national organisation spreading its tentacles far beyond the Italian community. He wanted to extort shopkeepers of every nationality. Demarte and Muratore rejected the ideas.

Angilletta, enraged by the rejection, was not prepared to back down. He refused to sell his fruit and vegetables to the Society wholesalers. Instead, he sold direct to the general public. Society representatives told him repeatedly that he had broken the rules. He was stabbed, but he refused to take even that as a warning.

The Society leadership decided to step up the pressure. A group picked Angilletta up and took him to Woodend, a country town northwest of Melbourne, where they painted him with human excrement in a ritualistic punishment called il tartaro. It was to be a final warning. But Angilletta chose not to heed it.

Angilletta sold his small market garden in Kew to a Greek family, rather than a Society member, then set up his own group called la Bastarda—"the Bastard Society", decidedly the opposite of the "Honoured Society"—and it attracted support, growing to be 300-strong. Anyone familiar with the mafiosi would know that Angilletta was asking for it. They would not have been far wrong. Demarte, Muratore and a third man met and agreed that Angilletta had to die. Angilletta, anticipating that he was a marked man, started carrying around a small automatic pistol for his protection. It did not do him much good. In the early hours of 4 April 1963, outside his house in the Melbourne suburb of Northcote, Angilletta was hit by two shotgun blasts fired from behind. Forensic tests showed that he was killed with lupara shot—the same type of shotgun pellets used by wolf hunters in Calabria.

Angilletta's associates were not going to take that. They blamed Demarte and Muratore and decided to hit back. On 26 November 1963, Demarte, leaving his North Melbourne home at 3.30 am to go to the Melbourne Market, was hit and seriously wounded by a shotgun blast. Muratore, leaving his home in the bayside suburb of Hampton at 2.30 am on 16 January 1964 to go to the market, was also shot from behind, and was dead before he hit the ground.

The shootings, which became known as the "Market Murders", and the exchange of shootings the "Market Wars", took the Australian community by surprise. The news went nationwide. It was the first time the public at large became aware, and the Victorian police were forced to admit, that organised crime and ethnic-related secret societies were not things that existed only overseas. It also became apparent to police that they were thoroughly unprepared to handle these developments. The police asked the Victorian Government for assistance. The government brought to Australia one of the world's most respected mafia investigators, United States lawman John T. Cusack.

Cusack had been investigating organised crime since he joined the US Federal Narcotics Bureau in 1947. In 1957 he managed to document a key mafia meeting in New York. As a result of his efforts, 60 major organised crime figures were arrested. This was the first major breakthrough by US law enforcement authorities against the Mafia. In Melbourne, Cusack investigated events to see where there was a mafia-style organisation at work. He completed a 17-page report which, never officially released by the government, left no doubt that a mafia-style network was well entrenched.

"It is already engaged in extortion, prostitution, counterfeiting, sly grog, breaking and entering, illegal gambling, and smuggling aliens and small arms", he said. "Its infiltration and effort to control the fruit and vegetable produce business has been exposed. Within the next 25 years if unchecked, the Society is capable of diversification into all facets of organised crime and legitimate business".

Cusack wrote that the Society had five main rules. Aid was to be extended to all members of the Society in any case whatsoever. There was to be absolute obedience to the officers of the Society. Any offence against a member of the Society was to be taken as an offence against the Society as a whole and had to be avenged, regardless of the cost. No Society member was ever to turn to a government agency for justice. Finally, the rule of omerta— silence—was to be observed. No member was ever to reveal the names of other members of the Society or any of its secrets. He wrote that getting anyone within the Society to cooperate was a daunting task. "They realise in silence there is security while testimony against a Society member can bring death", he said.

Victorian police investigating the Market Murders were unable to break the wall of silence. They flew out an expert on the mafia from Italy. He told them that unless the police could make some of the Italian workers at the market more frightened of them than they were of the so-called mafia, any investigation was doomed to fail. As it turned out, nobody was ever to be convicted of the Market Murders. In the meantime, the Society wanted peace. It wanted the publicity to go away and normal business to resume.

The Society was able to bring this about through the agency of a small, smiling man named Liboria Benvenuto, who was related by marriage to the late Vincenzo Muratore. Benvenuto became the Society's head. Born on 15 December 1927 in Reggio, Calabria, he was the illegitimate son of a Capo (Boss) of the Society's counterpart in Calabria, who had controlled seven Italian villages. Migrating to Australia, Benvenuto went into the fruit and vegetable industry and became a well-known identity in the Melbourne Market. Seeing that with the Market Murders full-scale civil war was likely to break out within the market community, he had worked hard as a peacemaker, at one point going to the New South Wales–Victorian border town of Mildura to bring about peace.

Benvenuto's right-hand man was Michele Scriva, who was married to the daughter of the late Domenico Italiano and related through marriage to Benvenuto. Like all characters in this saga, Scriva had an interesting history. Born in Reggio, Calabria, on 19 June 1919, he arrived in Australia in the mid-30s as a 17-year-old, was naturalised and worked as a labourer before getting a stall at the Queen Victoria Market. In 1945 he was accused of involvement in a killing—considered to have been one of the first mafia "hits" in Australia—of Giuseppe "Fat Joe" Verscace. Verscace died after being stabbed 91 times in the inner Melbourne suburb of Fitzroy. Scriva was charged with murder and stood trial along with two other men, Domenico Demarte (later to be one of the victims in the Market Murders), and Domenico Pezzimenti. They were all acquitted, but Scriva was not destined to fade from the scene. In North Melbourne in 1950, one Frederick John Duffy, 36, attempted to intervene in a fight and was stabbed to death. Scriva was charged with his murder, convicted and sentenced to death. The sentence was commuted to life imprisonment and Scriva was released after ten years.

The combination of Benvenuto, seen as the conciliator, and Scriva, whose record suggested something else, seemed to have the right effect. Things settled down and for the next 20 years the Society went about its business making money through legitimate enterprise, extortion and drug dealing. Its lower profile meant the risk of public exposure could be minimised. Members of the Victorian Bureau of Criminal Intelligence tried to monitor the Society's activities, but even when there were indications that the law was being broken, little was done to arrest the ringleaders. Collecting evidence was frustrated by the rule of omerta.

This cosy state of affairs was blown somewhat by developments elsewhere—specifically the murder of anti-drug crusader Don Mackay in Griffith, in the Riverina area of New South Wales, on 15 July 1977. The information that flowed from that, through police inquiries and royal commissions, focused attention closely on mafia activities in Victoria.

Police at one stage investigated allegations that Benvenuto was involved in moving marijuana from Griffith to Melbourne. A truck would be driven from Griffith with fruit and vegetables concealing marijuana. The truck would be parked in Carlton and the key left above the front tyre. A second driver would drive the truck to a secret spot, remove the marijuana and then return the vehicle. The original driver would then take it to the market.

On 10 May 1983, violence sparked again. Benvenuto, who at the time was working with his son-in-law, Alfonso Muratore, found his four-wheel-drive vehicle blown up in the car park of the Melbourne wholesale fruit and vegetable market. Gelignite had been strapped beneath it. Nobody was hurt. Police found a shotgun in the car. Questioned, Benvenuto said he could not think of any motive for the bombing, declaring: "I have no enemies, only friends at the market. I don't know why anybody would do this. I have never done anybody harm".

A year later, two associates of Benvenuto were found murdered in the Murrumbidgee River in the Riverina area of New South Wales. Rocco Medici and his brother-in-law, Giuseppe Furina, both from the Melbourne suburb of East Keilor, were tortured and their bodies dumped on 5 May 1984. One of them had had his ears sliced off, a supposed mafia warning to others that the victim had "heard too much". Benvenuto was godfather to one of the Medici family and was a close friend of Furina. The murders, believed to have been connected to the Society drug dealings, were never to be solved. Victorian police asked Benvenuto to go to its Homicide Squad offices to be interviewed about the murders. Benvenuto walked in wearing a pork-pie hat and said: "I'm so sorry I can't help but I don't know anything about it".

In 1988, Benvenuto was a sick old man. He called a small-time insurance broker, Giuseppe Arena, to his bedside in Beaumaris. Some people believed the Godfather wanted Arena to take a senior position among the Society elders. Arena was no stranger to violence. He had served two years for manslaughter after he killed his wife's lover in 1976. Ironically, a defence witness had told the court that Arena was so well liked that he was known as "The Friendly Godfather". Arena was more than he seemed. He was a close friend of a violent member of the Australian underworld. In 1982 Arena put his family home up as surety for the man who was charged over a $2 million heroin deal. Arena later went to the engagement party of the criminal's daughter.

On 10 June 1988 Benvenuto died of natural causes. A huge crowd gathered at St Patrick's Church in Mentone for the funeral. Within days, Arena seemed to grow in status with certain members of the Italian community. Others resented his apparent new authority. Within three weeks, Arena had sold his business and "retired" at the age of 50, even though he appeared to have been in no financial position to do so. On 1 August 1988, six weeks after Benvenuto's death, Arena was taking out the rubbish bins in the back yard of his suburban home at Bayswater when he was shot dead from behind. Arena left an estate of $216,768.57. A check of his affairs showed that he was involved in money laundering for some alleged mafia heavyweights. He also had at least one corrupt contact within the Tax Department.

In May 1989, Michele Scriva died a respected elderly Italian gentleman. He was described by relatives as "truly a great man among men". So, just as when "The Pope" and "The Toad" died, the deaths of Benvenuto and Scriva, and that of Arena, left another power vacuum. Three men were given the job of running the Society in Victoria. They were a retailer, who ran a successful inner suburban business, a fruiterer, who was also a property developer, and the son of a man connected with the 1963–64 Market Wars. But the wheel of violence had not stopped turning.

The main stronghold of the Society in Victoria retained its grip on the fruit and vegetable industry, demanding payment from some retailers and wholesalers in return for smooth operation of the industry. But it depended on a continuing grip of steel, and ruthless retribution to anybody who opposed the system. There was always resentment of extortion, and revolt was never far below the surface. After the death of Benvenuto some merchants decided they had had enough of paying. Some even began to employ Australian gangsters as a show of strength. One well-known identity at the market, Alfonso Muratore, son-in-law of Liborio Benvenuto, who had worked closely with Benvenuto at the market, decided he wanted a change of scene.

Only weeks after Benvenuto died, Muratore, father of three, left his wife—Benvenuto's daughter—for another woman. He also left the markets and tried to make a fresh start. He opened a coffee shop. His abandonment of his wife and desertion from the scene entirely was taken by Society elders as a great insult. What was even worse, in their eyes, was that in 1992, no doubt longing for the industry that was in his blood, he returned to the wholesale fruit and vegetable market. And that was not the end of it. Muratore had a few more goodies in store for them before he was to get his comeuppance.

Some of the major victims of the huge extortion rackets were a group of national supermarket chains which bought fruit and vegetables at the market. The huge Coles–Myer group was a prime target. In 1990, at least one senior Coles–Myer executive started to realise that there might be a problem in the buying of fruit and vegetables. He put a young man, John Vasilopolous, in charge of the area to try and sort out the buying procedure.

A few months after, on 19 December 1990, John Vasilopolous was in bed in his Ivanhoe home reading a book. It was 10.30 pm. He heard a knock at the door. He called out and asked who it was. A man speaking with an Australian accent said: "Open the door, John". Vasilopolous opened the door just wide enough to see a man, armed with a shotgun, crouching in the porch. He turned to run and was hit with one of two blasts. He called out to his wife and two daughters to stay inside as he lay bleeding on the ground. Medical reports show that he was hit in the left thigh, right leg, left side of the stomach and chest, right upper arm, left forearm and elbow. Police formed the view that he was shot on the instructions of the Society elders, as a warning not to interfere with the activities of the market.

Coles–Myer did try to change the system. They brought in a major produce merchant, T. Costa Pty Ltd, to buy its fruit and vegetables in a bid to beat the mafia "tax". But the extortionists simply switched their attention to T. Costa Pty Ltd. The merchant's representative received instructions that when they bought from producers, they had to provide receipts, which would enable the Society to impose a tax of 50 cents per case of fruit and vegetables bought by Coles–Myer. As an incentive to cooperate, a Costa purchasing officer was bashed with an iron bar in the suburb of Sunshine. A senior Costa official was warned that if receipts were not handed over to the Society, he would be shot.

Coles–Myer told the police the company had been paying an estimated $3 million a year to organised crime interests. For its own information, Coles–Myer wanted to find out more on what it was up against. A private security agent organised a secret meeting between Coles-Myer representatives and a man they hoped could shed light on the Society's activities. The man the security agent contacted was Alfonso Muratore.

Coles–Myer representatives met Muratore on 19 July 1992. He explained to them some details of what had been happening. Muratore was no fool, he knew the risks. He remembered the shotgun killing of his father in 1964. If he had any notion of becoming complacent, soon after his meeting with the Coles–Myer representatives he had acid poured over his car and he was assaulted at the market, leaving him with a blackened eye. He began carrying a small pistol for protection. He did not go to the police for help. Even though he had left the Society, the mafia code had been instilled into him that going to the police was not the thing to do.

On 4 August 1992, two weeks after his meeting with Coles–Myer representatives, Muratore was shot dead—murdered in almost the same circumstances as his father. He had been about to get into his car outside his Storey Street home at 1.30 am to drive to the market. A hooded gunman fired at close range, hitting him twice in the head. A companion of Muratore was hit in the leg. Muratore was fatally wounded less than a kilometre from where his father had been slain. From the point of view of those in the Society who allegedly ordered his murder, there was a great difference between father and son. Vincenzo Muratore had been trying to protect the Society. Alfonso had been betraying it.

At least three other major fruit and vegetable merchants immediately employed armed security guards after the murder of Muratore because they were told their names were on a death list. A relative of Muratore received death threats and eventually moved after his house was vandalised.

In 1992, still active in law enforcement, John Cusack, the man who first exposed the Honoured Society in Victoria, said he was saddened but not surprised, to see the violence continuing. He said that even 30 years earlier the fruit and vegetable market was the centre of the Society activities. "They were entrenched in the markets", he said. "There were honest Italian merchants there who had to pay extortion. The organisation was able to keep newcomers out. They were able to create a monopoly".

THE HUNT FOR LARRY BOY

At Elsey Station in late 1968, a particularly savage "build-up" was beginning—that time of the year in the Northern Territory when temperatures and humidity soar and the race is on to muster the last cattle of the season before the weather becomes deadly to man and beast. The Aboriginal "housegirls", Amy Dirngayg, Jessie Garalnganjag and Marjorie Biyang were running late the evening of 20 September. The first bell from the homestead had rung, bringing them up from the blacks' camp to prepare meals for the manager, Peter McCracken, his wife Mary, and the other munanga (European) station hands. The second bell meant meals were to be served.

Amy Dirngayg, nicknamed "Cookie" and boss of the homestead kitchen, noticed that 18-year-old Marjorie appeared worried, and had to remind her to set the table. "We thought she was upset about something, and knew that she had an argument with her husband", Amy recalls.

After tea the "girls" washed up, hanging up pannikins and utensils on crude wire racks strung across the kitchen, and cleaned the benches. After that, Marjorie refused to go back to the camp with Amy and Jessie. It was puzzling behaviour. "She said to us, "I can't go down to the camp. I'm going to camp right here in the kitchen. I'm going to sleep here in the kitchen"", said Amy. "We said "What? No, you can't stop here, you've got to come with us, with your family in the camp. You'll have to look after yourself here, you can't stay here". But she wouldn't listen, so we went back to the camp, leaving her behind".

It was the last time Jessie and Amy would see Marjorie alive.

At about 8.30 pm, Marjorie went to bed with a 21-year-old

white stockman, David Jackson, with whom she had apparently been having a relationship for some months. On two occasions during the night he heard sounds outside his quarters, and he saw a torch flashing. He thought he could see someone in the shadows and reached out. A person was there but fled. At about 3 am, somebody violently attacked the two with a tomahawk. Biyang was struck repeatedly on the head, throat and body. Jackson was hit on the head and chest.

Peter McCracken, hearing screams, raced to the scene. He found Jackson propped against a wall, his face and chest covered with blood. He was barely conscious, and had no idea who had attacked him. McCracken followed a trail of fresh blood to a nearby saddle shed, where he found Biyang's body. Though it was still three hours before dawn, it became obvious who had carried out the attack. In the blood on the floor of the jackaroo's quarters there were bare footprints: McCracken recognised them as those of "Larry Boy" Janba, Marjorie Biyang's Aboriginal husband.

Elsey Station, 400 kilometres south of Darwin, is one of the most famous cattle runs in the Northern Territory. The first homestead was built on Yangman tribal land at Warloch Points when the station was first settled and stocked between 1877 and 1882. By the time Jeannie Gunn wrote her evocative tales of the "Land of the Never Never" at the turn of the century, poor water supplies had forced a move for the Elsey homestead to its current site on the Roper River, well inside lands traditionally owned by the Mangarryi people.

The conquest of Mangarryi and Yangman lands in the late 1800s was characterised by brutality. From the beginning of settlement white stockmen made a practice of "stealing" Aboriginal women. Nevertheless, the nature of the cattle industry allowed Aboriginal people continued contact with their traditional lands and, during the wet season "lay off", time to maintain a strong ceremonial life on Elsey. As one history of Elsey has put it: "As long as they adapted to the requirements of the pastoral industry, [they] could remain in touch with the country, through work and outside of work".

Up until the 1960s life on Elsey was hard, both for the white cattlemen and women trying to get a living, and for the Aboriginal stockmen and their families in the Aboriginal camp. In this, Elsey was little different from many of the other cattle stations: a white manager and a handful of white station hands, with an Aboriginal camp—away from the homestead—of about 80 to 100 men, women and children. At the height of the mustering season up to 30 Aborigines would be employed at Elsey, though during the September of 1968 there were only two small "stock camps" of Aboriginal workers, plus the three housegirls at the homestead.

Police Constable Roy "Bluey" Harvey, 32, 188 centimetres tall, red-haired, fair-skinned, was stationed at Mataranka, 30 kilometres west of Elsey homestead. His "beat" covered 7,800 square kilometres. He had worked in the bush most of his life, including 11 years at remote police stations in the Northern Territory, and had participated in manhunts before, including trailing after a murderer through the desert west of Papunya in the Centre. He had a good relationship with local Aborigines, and probably expected few problems when called out that night to find Larry Boy. Fifteen years later, he was to tell a journalist: "Larry Boy had his day planned before I was even awake that morning".

Larry Boy Janba had worked as a ringer on Elsey for about seven years, before being dismissed by McCracken in 1965. From then, he lived at nearby Mataranka Station with his mother. After his marriage to Marjorie, he had lived in and around the bush near Elsey homestead. Jessie Garalnganjag describes him as being a loner in those days. "He never came up and talked to us much, Larry Boy, he never came up", she said. "He was just on his own. He would just go out hunting every day. When he got plenty of tucker he would pass it back wrapped in paperbark to everyone. Share it out to people like his brother-in-law, blackfella way. He would bring tucker to his wife and the others, to get tobacco back. That night [the night of the killing], we knew he'd had an argument with Marjorie, he didn't come around at all, not even for cards".

After the attack Larry Boy took to the bush north of Elsey, retreating to familiar territory—the cabbage palms and pandanus of the melaleuca channel country and wetlands known locally as "the Jungle". To outsiders this piece of real estate was, to say the least, unprepossessing. A 100-square kilometre stretch of mosquito, snake, crocodile and wild pig infested swamp 11 kilometres to the east and north of Elsey homestead, it was going to be a nightmare for the searchers. But Larry Boy had no such problems. It might be said his spirit lay in that country. He was the grandson of "Goggle-Eye", a principal figure in Gunn's book,

We of the Never Never, and son of Yiworrorndo, who had an unsurpassed knowledge of the area.

Marjorie Biyang's brother, Joe McDonald, who was part of the party that went to search for Larry Boy, said long afterwards: "He was a pretty tough young fella, hard to catch, you know? Of course he knew that place, his father used to live in that place— Jungle Dick [the name given to Yiworrorndo by Europeans in the 1940s] ... And he knew that place like the palm of his hand. He knew every channel. He grew up there".

In the first days of the hunt, Harvey was joined by Darwin-based Detective Bob Jackson and a forensic expert Sergeant Pat Slater, police from Larrimah, Katherine and Maranboy, and five Aboriginal trackers. Three weeks later, the search involved five police and 22 civilians, five four-wheel-drive vehicles, a motor cycle, 40 horses, a police boat, and a helicopter with fuel supplied by a DC3 aircraft. As the search progressed, police enlisted the help of Aborigines with special knowledge of the country such as Clancy Roberts, eldest brother of Jessie Garalnganjag.

It had been obvious early in the search that it was going to be difficult to find Larry Boy, who was believed to be armed with a .22 calibre rifle and other weapons. No tracks were found. There was talk that Larry Boy would travel up to 60 kilometres a day. There had been a sighting, unconfirmed, that he was seen near Katherine to the north. Four search parties went out, some patrolling bush up to 200 kilometres from the Elsey homestead. On the tenth day, after Larry Boy's tracks were finally seen and the remains of fish and wallabies that he had left behind at temporary camps were discovered, Larry Boy's whereabouts were narrowed down to the Jungle.

The searchers went in, but got nowhere, despite searching 12 hours a day. Fatigue and illness set in. Boots were falling apart in the harsh conditions. McCracken was hit by influenza and seven Aborigines from Elsey succumbed to viral infections. Two journalists sent there were forced back sick after a few days. Bluey Harvey, who ultimately came down with pneumonia, wrote afterwards: "Sickness was to be expected, meals when you could get them, there was rarely a lunch break and often it was one meal a day in the evening. There were times when you'd be sweating like hell, the next minute soaking wet [from rain], the tropical weather was taking its toll ... I hoped the mozzies were treating

Larry Boy the way they were treating us, as we were certainly very popular with them".

Harvey and an Aboriginal tracker Bennett had led the frustrating search from the beginning, as they circled and re-circled the swamps. On a number of occasions, they followed tracks that appeared to lead them west towards Mataranka, where Larry Boy's mother and sisters were camped. On each occasion they realised they had been tricked. Larry Boy had laid deliberate false trails walking backwards to fool his pursuers. It was three weeks into the search before they realised that Larry Boy had wrapped his feet in wallaby hide to cover his tracks. Station tracks were graded each evening so that any tracks left by Larry Boy crossing at night could be quickly discovered. Each day the police patrolled all the crossings in the hope of finding a trace of their suspect. Apart from fragmentary finds of food scraps of wallaby, flying fox and cut cabbage palms, there was no sighting of the fugitive.

Harvey's search teams were being additionally frustrated by bureaucratic obstruction. On 10 October, 19 days into the search, police headquarters in Darwin announced that it was withholding all police searchers with the exception of Harvey, and that helicopters would no longer be supplied. So Harvey found himself regularly arguing with his superiors in Darwin over the hire of horses and supplies. Protests to Canberra and the Minister for the Interior, Peter Nixon, achieved little more than assurances that protection would still be given to the Elsey homestead. Darwin's *Northern Territory News* protested, and supported local station owners' vows to keep up with the search, now into its fourth week. One extra police searcher, Barry Frew, was sent to Elsey. Harvey wryly commented: "He is an experienced man and dressed for the job ahead of him, and not wearing a nicely pressed uniform and Julius Marlow dress shoes". On the 23rd day of the search, in frustration McCracken decided to hire a helicopter for two days at his own expense.

There could be no peace in the local community which was concerned that Larry Boy would raid the homestead for food. Jessie Garalnganjag remembers the homestead girls being individually escorted by police each night to their camp. As fear grew, they moved into the homestead. There was little doubt that Larry Boy was not too far away. At times it became obvious that it was he who was following the searchers, easily eluding them as they attempted time and again to trap him. He was constantly a jump ahead. Joe McDonald recalls that they nearly caught him on a number of occasions, and that at times he was watching them from only a few metres away: "There was one time he was watching us from under a dead palm tree ... we pulled up having dinner once ... just all having a yarn about him and we took off again, another search you know? We walked away from the dinner camp and he came up behind, picking up all the bumpers [cigarette butts] from the ground!".

At one point Harvey found a cache of tobacco and cigarette papers placed by the edge of a path in the Jungle, and tracks of Larry Boy, only 20 minutes old, covering those of the search party. Harvey became convinced that one of the local Aborigines was supporting Larry Boy. He relegated the suspect from horseback to foot patrol. On the 30th day of the search, a party found a food wrapper at the junction of Salt Creek and the Roper River. It was only five kilometres from the camp of Larry Boy's mother, and the wrappers matched food bought by his mother two days before. Aboriginal people have since denied that any such assistance was given to Larry Boy. They have pointed out that he was able to live off the bush, and that there were numerous times when he raided stock camps to steal food. Jimmy Conway recalls one such occasion, when he was with a stock camp east of the station. The camp cook discovered a large amount of food missing one morning, as well as Larry Boy's tracks leading from the camp. "He used to just sneak in and take it at night, when no one was looking", Conway said. Joe McDonald recalls: "Well, they found out that he used to go into the stock camp kitchen, steal damper and food. No, I don't know of anyone who helped him. His mother lived in Mataranka and they were keeping an eye out there. He used to get his own tucker, I never heard of anyone helping him out".

Whether locals were assisting Larry Boy or not, by the fifth week the searchers appeared no closer to finding him. Senior police came down from Darwin to instruct Harvey to "keep up the pressure and to attempt to make contact with Janba and tell him that no harm would come to him if he gives himself up". The same message was given to the Darwin media. An exhausted Harvey commented later: "The thing that amused me was the "try and make contact" bit. What did they think we had been doing for the last 33 days? Someone jokingly suggested we drop him a mob of leaflets to this effect and that McCracken pay for the plane!". Harvey's cynicism had not lessened six days later on 30 October when he was informed by Darwin that, after 39 days, he was to be relieved. He was told he was to go back to the homestead for the "hand over gear". "What gear?, I asked … [that night] I gave what gear we had, some used water bottles and a couple of old .303 rifles. I then went home to Mataranka".

At 5.30 the next morning, McCracken woke Harvey at the Mataranka police station to report that Larry Boy had raided Elsey Station the night before and stolen bread, meat and sandshoes, and that horses were ready to go if Harvey wanted to join in. Harvey's replacement had already organised patrols around the homestead. Harvey and Bennett followed the sparse tracks that appeared to lead from the Elsey schoolhouse towards Mataranka. Bennett spotted leaves on the ground that grew only on trees in the Jungle, indicating that Larry Boy was brushing out his tracks as he retreated from the homestead. The Elsey schoolteacher drove up and reported that a bucket had been stolen from the school. Harvey's ears pricked up. This, he thought, might have been Larry Boy's first serious mistake! If Larry Boy needed a bucket, he could not be heading to well-watered Mataranka or the Jungle channel country. Instead he could only be heading for a water-scarce area: the limestone cave country north of the Jungle, where fruitless searches had been carried out from time to time over the previous 40 days.

After a hard ride to the area, right in the centre of a recently graded road Bennett spotted a toe mark, clearly identifiable as Larry Boy's. On the other side of the road was a small branch of a tree from the Jungle area. Larry Boy had crossed, doubled back, and was headed north. He had left no tracks, but plenty of leaves. Harvey and Bennett followed them to the entrance of a cave. The cave had previously been inspected. But Bennett looked at the entrance closely, and realised that the cobwebs covering it had been slit down one side. Bennett said: "We got him, Bluey!".

Harvey realised that he had left his revolver on the yard fence before riding out that morning. He borrowed Bennett's .22 rifle and crawled into the cave. The cave forked, and outside one of the forks was the bucket. Harvey got into difficulties, finding himself unable to breathe because of the foul air. He got out and sent

Bennett off to fetch the other searchers. Within an hour or so a crowd of men stood at the entrance to the cave. They had been waiting weeks and weeks to catch Larry Boy.

It was finally left to Joe McDonald to capture the fugitive. McDonald said later: "All the ringers and everyone was there. You couldn't see him down there, but he could see you in the sun. Everyone was there trying to smoke him, smoke-bomb him, you know? I said to myself, "I'll give 'im a go, and try and get in this hole". I tried at first but it was no good, it was too dark for me, so one of the coppers, Bluey Harvey, give me a torch. Well, I crawled in on hands and knees and I put a torch on him and he put a torch back to me and I ducked my head. He said, "You Wampu Kelly?" and I said, "Yeah, me Wampu Kelly". He [Wampu Kelly] was another bloke, coloured bloke, big fella, but he wouldn't fit in that hole, it was too small for him.

"I said, "Come on, we're going outside, family wants to see you. Don't be frightened, nobody going to get you". So he followed me out. He started mucking round with the gun, trying to shoot me first in the cave there. He just couldn't turn around … If he had a chance I reckon he would have shot me inside the cave there. Anyway he followed me out and I held him by the hand and he came up backwards. As soon as he got out in the daylight he seen all that mob and he asked the policeman if he could go back in and pick up his gear back in the cave. I said, "Don't let him back there, you mob'll never get him again". So I sent young Roger Gibbs and Wilson McDonald. They was only small then, little fellas, and they crawled into the cave and pulled all the gear out".

The boys recovered the .22 rifle, 39 rounds of ammunition, a tomahawk, tobacco, cigarettes and food. Larry Boy had no clothes and had been using his naga (loin cloth) as a dilly bag. Harvey took Larry Boy back to the Elsey homestead and unsuccessfully tried to find Larry Boy's bloodstained clothes. Then he took him to Mataranka where he charged him with murder. It had taken 40 days from the time of the killing.

At the Supreme Court trial in February 1969, the jury found Larry Boy Janba not guilty of murder but guilty of the manslaughter of Marjorie Biyang and guilty of the unlawful wounding of Jackson. The jury agreed that Larry Boy had been provoked "to the stage where he lost all self-control". He received concurrent sentences of eight years on the manslaughter charge, and five years for the wounding, and was sent to Darwin's Fannie Bay Gaol. He was never to see his country again.

On 11 June 1972, two months before he was due to be paroled, Larry Boy died in gaol, after an illness lasting several months. A coroner the following year found that he had died of melioidosis, commonly known as Nightcliff Gardeners' Disease. At the time it was assumed that the disease, caused by soil organisms, had been contracted by Larry Boy during his time on the run in the bush. Today's medical knowledge suggests that this is unlikely, and it is probable that the illness was contracted in gaol.

The manhunt for Larry Boy Janba occurred at a time when the "frontier" in the Northern Territory was giving way to modern transport, but many elements of the harsh old days were still alive and well. In hospital recovering from his injuries, the white stockman Jackson was quoted as saying: "I don't know what the fuss was all about: it was all right, it happens all the time". When Northern Territory journalist Jim Bowditch went to Elsey, he noted that the white ringers participating in the search deeply resented Larry Boy's reaction to a white stockman sleeping with his Aboriginal wife. Bowditch said that comments were directed at him by one searcher: "Here's the boong lover now, we'll show you how to fix the black bastard when we catch him!".

Not so Bluey Harvey. During the hunt he often told his trackers, with some admiration, that Larry Boy was "like a black Ned Kelly" in his skills, being on the run for so long. He said that when he questioned Larry Boy after the arrest, Harvey discovered that at times during the search Larry Boy had been close enough to his pursuers to touch them as they went past. Over the years, he also expressed admiration for the enormous skills of the black trackers he had worked with in the 20 years he was on the force. On his retirement, reminiscing on the manhunt, Harvey said: "I nearly gave up that last day!". It was at that moment of truth that the skill of Bennett and the courage of McDonald had come to the fore and saved the day.

THE PRESSLER CASE

DOUBLE MURDER AND DOUBLE-DEALING

reater love hath no man than this, that a man lay down his life for his friend.

In Central Queensland in 1960 that noble sentiment was to take on a new meaning. A mother, police said, had shot her brother-in-law in a callous attempt to shift the blame from a son convicted and sentenced for a cowardly double murder.

Sounds complicated? It certainly was. The case came to intrigue not just the wealthy canegrowing district of Bundaberg, 300 kilometres north of Brisbane, but ultimately the whole nation. It was a story of convoluted relationships, deep brooding feelings, motherly love; of a dark Freudian landscape opening up against a backdrop of rugged provincial independence.

There were three particular people who could not be intrigued. They included Clifford and Marjorie Golchert, who owned a farm at Kalkie, near Bundaberg, and who were battered and shot to death in their bed on the night of 14 May 1959.

What added to the air of mystery was the "exotic" location. It was murder in the canefields, violence in the semi-tropics, death in a sea of prosperity, dishonour in a community committed to the work ethic. Bundaberg, a typical provincial rural town, was (and is) prosperous, populated by hardworking people generally of British and European heritage, who owed their existence to sugar. The town had its own sugar mill. Like all sugar belt towns, for most of the year it was surrounded by a sea of green.

Kalkie is today as it was in the 1950s—comprising a school, a couple of houses belonging to cane farmers and their workers and the waving sea of green and gold shutting off the horizon for anyone standing on the ground.

The Pressler family at Kalkie were well known and wealthy. They had a sugar cane farm. The matriarch was Enid, a widow of several years. Aged just over 50, she was tough and resolute. She had gone to live in the Bundaberg township, in Clifford Street. But she still called the tune at Kalkie. Her 29-year-old son, Neville, a giant, heavily muscled bull of a man, ran the property. He had a wife, Mary, and two young daughters. Also on the property was Enid's brother-in-law, Henry Edward Pressler, a shy retiring bachelor of 67 years, nicknamed "Heini", whose only occupations were pottering about the farm, fishing and reading.

The Golcherts were the Pressler's neighbours. Marjorie Golchert was very attractive. The couple had been married for seven years but had no children. They were quiet, respectable, unpretentious, financially secure, by all accounts happy and devoted.

On 14 May, Neville Pressler left the farm with his family and drove to his mother's home. The family remained at his mother's place while he went off on his own to a store to buy clothes. After that, he visited the Queen's Hotel in Bundaberg where he met up with some people he knew. Present in the company was Clifford Golchert. The group were talking about going on a fishing trip. Golchert said he would like to go but he would first have to go home and milk the cows. He got up and left.

Soon after, Pressler left, went to his mother's place, picked up his family and returned to Kalkie, arriving at 5.30 pm. He tried on his new clothes and, as was his habit, drank some overproof rum.

That night, Clifford and Marjorie Golchert were battered and shot to death.

The next day, Neville Pressler and his family left on a holiday. The Golcherts' bodies lay undiscovered for several days. They were found by members of their family who had become worried when they had not heard from them.

After news of the killings spread round the district, a relative of Neville Pressler sent him a telegram telling him there had been a tragedy and asking him to come home.

A post-mortem examination confirmed the manner in which the Golcherts met their deaths. The funeral was held. Neville Pressler was a pallbearer.

Police interviewed Neville. Because he lived in the vicinity, he was on the suspect list. They also interviewed Henry Pressler. If they had any suspicions, Henry would have been a far less likely culprit than Neville.

What police claimed to have obtained from Neville Pressler was damning to him. It was, they said, a confession. They said Pressler had given it to the arresting officer, Inspector Bill Cronau. In the alleged confession, Pressler said he had done it.

According to the confession, Pressler said he got up through the night and put some clothes on. The next thing he remembered was being at the Golchert's place hitting Clifford and Marjorie over the head with an iron bar.

"Cliffie and Marj were then lying together in this bed in the sleepout. Marj started to cry and I hit her over the head and I saw that her finger was half cut-off", he allegedly said.

"They were both howling so I shot them to put them out of their misery. I got the gun from the dining room where it was usually kept and I found some bullets on the top of the shelf in the kitchen cupboard.

"When I shot Cliffie in the head, the blood spurted out. The dining room light was on. I must have switched it on when I came in. I think I put the gun back where it was kept and ran out of the house. I locked the back door and took the key with me.

"I ran out of the yard, down the yard towards where the new people were living. When I got to the paddock, I fell over some soil on the side of the road and I noticed I had the key and piece of pipe in my hand.

"The pipe was wet and sticky. I threw them away in the cow paddock. I went home and had a big nip of rum. When I got up next morning I saw my clothes had blood on them so I put on some clean clothes and hid the dirty clothes in the bathroom.

"On Sunday morning when my wife burnt a lot of rubbish in the copper I took my shorts and shirt and burnt them with the rubbish. My wife did not know I did this. I don't know why I went down there that night. We had always been the best of mates".

The police charged Neville Pressler with two counts of murder. The scenario they drew up was that he had been to the Golcherts' home when Clifford Golchert was away fishing. He had propositioned Marjorie Golchert and she had refused, scoffed at him and told him she would tell her husband.

Pressler had become worried about this, and had decided to take action to stop it getting out. He had waited for Clifford Golchert to return home. When the couple were in bed he had attacked them with an iron bar and a .22 calibre rifle.

Enid Pressler, hearing Neville had been charged, reacted with outrage. She loudly protested his innocence and said he would have the best lawyers available. She managed to get the services of Dan Casey, an up-and-coming lawyer destined to become one of the finest defence barristers Queensland has ever seen.

Casey had a degree of personal commitment to the case. He certainly knew the area. He had grown up in Bundaberg, where his father was the police sergeant. Sergeant Casey had in fact bought a horse from the Pressler family so that young Dan Casey could learn to ride.

But mere personal commitment on the part of counsel could not counter what Pressler had stacked against him, though Pressler denied he had made the confession. He was committed for trial.

Pressler maintained from the outset of the trial that the police had fabricated the statements attributed to him. On 4 November 1959, the trial's third day, he was found in a police cell with razor slashes to his left arm, wrist, hand and both ankles. Police discovered him, used handkerchiefs to stem the flow of blood, then rushed him to hospital where the wounds were stitched. A razor was found in the cell. There was no reason to suppose he had not inflicted the wounds on himself. But if it was a desperate plea for sympathy, it was ill-conceived. The trial was resumed a week later.

Casey based Pressler's defence on his denial that he made the confession. In his own evidence, Pressler said he had been friends of both the Golcherts. He denied killing them. He said that when interviewed by the police, he had been in "a state of nervous exhaustion". He said Inspector Cronau had tried to induce him to lower his guard.

What value Pressler thought he would get from his evidence was countered by evidence from his own brother, Geoffrey. Geoffrey Pressler said he was in an adjoining room while Pressler was being interviewed at the police station. He said he had heard "nothing untoward". He added that, after the interview, Pressler had met him and told him privately that he had committed the crime.

Trial judge Justice Joe Sheehy said in his summing-up to the jury: "There is no medical evidence. The prisoner himself has not suggested he was drunk on the night of the murders. The only ground is that it is a horrible murder, committed on people he was friendly with, and there was no motive.

"The main defence is that he did not do it and that the only thing against him is the writing of that confession claimed to have been made and signed by him at a time when his mind was influenced. It has been put to you that his mind was so overborne that he became a jelly.

"It has been claimed that Inspector Cronau put his arm around his shoulders. It has been suggested that it was false comfort and crocodile sympathy".

Justice Sheehy said that against this was the definite sworn evidence of Inspector Cronau and Detectives Buchanan, Sullivan and Murdoch as to oral statements made to them. There was the pipe with human blood on it and hairs which corresponded with the hair of the dead woman; and there was the door key missing from the back door and which the prisoner had discovered in his own cow paddock.

"These things were found by the police after the confession and might not have been found without the prisoner telling where they were. The prisoner said he found them the morning after the murder on the road and threw them into the paddock then".

In the end, the jury had little to decide on. They found Neville Pressler guilty of murder. Justice Sheehy sentenced him to life imprisonment.

Casey, interviewed years later, in 1987, said to his biographer, Kerry Smith: "I did my best, tried every trick. Pressler had made a full confession to Bill Conau and this couldn't be overcome. Joe Sheehy, the judge, an old Crown Prosecutor, gave a savage summing-up against Pressler".

Then the real drama.

On 7 June 1960—just over a year after the Golchert murders—inoffensive Henry Pressler was staying with Enid and other members of the Pressler family, including Alan Pressler, in Bundaberg. Enid encouraged the family—except Henry—to go to the picture show. She and Henry stayed home.

At 11 pm that night, Alan Pressler returned home. Enid asked him to "go into Uncle's room and see if he is all right". Alan Pressler walked into Henry's room and found him dead, with a bullet wound through the head.

Enid Pressler was interviewed by Constable James Mahoney. She said: "Henry gave me a statement today about lunchtime and said he had done what Neville was in gaol for and that he could not live with himself any longer.

"Henry went to bed about six o'clock and he got up and had a cup of tea—he often does things like that.

"Uncle dictated the statement today at about 11 o'clock. I wrote it out and asked him to sign it and said we would go and see [solicitor] Mr Boreham this afternoon but I don't want to have to go to town twice, but he wouldn't sign it.

"He gave the daughter a pound to go to the pictures this afternoon. They left about twenty past seven and he signed the statement about half past seven. I got frightened and locked myself in my bedroom and I tried to read for most of the night. At about half past ten I heard a noise on the sleepout side of the house like a window shutting loudly, but I did not get up as I was too frightened.

"I waited until Alan ... came home about 11 o'clock and I asked Alan to go into Uncle's room and see if he was all right.

"Alan came back almost immediately and said, "I will ring the police". I said to Alan, "Did he shoot himself?". Alan rang the police and also Dr Schmidt".

The alleged written confession of Henry Pressler read as follows: "Marjorie Golchert came round to see Mary one afternoon and there was no one home but me. We talked for a while then I asked her how it was that she did not have any children. She said she had almost given up hope. She was in a joking mood. I asked her if I came over some night when Cliff was away fishing would she be nice to me and she answered as she walked to her car, "You never know, I might".

"I was unsettled from then as I thought from how she had spoken that she would be quite agreeable to me going to see her. That Friday I knew Cliff was going fishing so I went over to see Marj. She turned me down straightaway and called me an old fool and laughed at me. She told how Cliff would laugh when she told him and I was very angry and went home and went to bed.

"I worried what would happen when she told Cliff. I must have gone to sleep later when Cliff seemed to be at my door. I don't know if he was really there or if I had a nightmare. Cliff was taunting me and sneering at me and trying to get at my throat. I jumped out of bed and ran after him. I went over to Neville's house to get his gun. I could not find it so I grabbed what was on the kitchen table and got a piece of piping from the woodheap and raced over towards Golchert's looking for him.

"I thought I could see him just ahead of me so I threw the clothes after him to try to stop him. When I got to his house I couldn't see him about but there was a light on in the sleepout. I went in and they were both in bed. Cliff was leaning over and he was either getting in or out of bed. I remember I hit them both a lot of times with the piece of piping. As I was hitting Cliff I remember thinking it was either him or me.

"Then I got his gun there and I was looking for bullets in a drawer. I found them on a shelf and shot them both. I wiped the gun on my flannel and also the light switch and drawer and the tin the bullets were in. I locked the door as I went out and took the key and piece of piping with me. I threw them in the grass on the side of the road. I walked around the paddock a lot before I went to bed ... there was blood on my clothes so before daylight I went up to the irrigation shed and burnt them.

"I scattered the ashes of the pyjamas in the cane but the flannel was hard to burn and the ashes went into a lump so I buried them near the shed ... I never thought Neville would be blamed for it or he could be found guilty of something that he could not do.

"I am sorry and this dreadful mistake must be cleared up. I can't stand it any longer".

On 8 June, Enid Pressler made a public statement that Henry had confessed to the murders of the Golcherts. She said he had dictated his confession to her, that she had written it out in an exercise book, and that he had signed it. It was now open to the government, she said, to pardon and release Neville.

Police suspected Enid Pressler's story. She had admitted writing the statement. But why couldn't the literate Henry Pressler have written it himself?

Eric Pressler, Henry Pressler's brother, told police he could not understand why Henry Pressler would have chosen to dictate rather than write the confession.

"My brother had a good education and was quite well-read", Eric Pressler said. "He spent a lot of time reading good literature".

Police wanted the original document so they could get an expert to examine the real and purported signatures. Enid Pressler said she had given it to Mr Boreham. Mr Boreham initially declined to hand it over, hampering police inquiries.

In the meantime, police reviewed the old file records of their investigation into the Golchert murders. Henry Pressler had been interviewed several times. The records indicated that at the time of their inquiries, police were satisfied Henry was not involved in the Golchert killings.

When police got the original confession document, they gave it to two forensic handwriting experts, one from Sydney and one from Brisbane. The experts concluded not just that the purported signature of Henry Pressler had been forged but that the forgery had been done by Enid Pressler.

On 20 June 1960, police charged Enid Pressler with Henry's murder. Their scenario was that she had written the statement, then taken a firearm, put it to Henry's head, forced him to sign the statement, and pulled the trigger. In the police view, everything else had been play-acting.

News of the charge rocked Bundaberg. Enid Pressler was committed for trial. The trial attracted national attention. As with all such cases there was plenty of pre-trial comment, plenty of theories. One was that the police had taken an absurdly simplistic line: he is supposed to have made the confession, he has been shot dead, so charge his sister-in-law. It was a line of logic, some critics said, that could have appealed to a schoolboy.

Dressed in floral frocks and looking very soft and matronly, Enid Pressler engendered enormous public support. For some reason she appealed particularly to women. She probably believed that her greatest chance lay in a tacit appeal to an arena far broader than the court where she was due to be tried. But leaving that aside, she had a strong defence. All the evidence against her was circumstantial. What material evidence existed to link her to the shooting? She was represented by Dan Casey. The big hurdle was going to be the handwriting evidence.

In the meantime, Neville Pressler petitioned the government to accept Henry Pressler's purported confession as genuine and release him from gaol.

The Crown produced the handwriting experts. That was to prove that Enid had written the confession. The Crown produced evidence that the angle and location of the wound were inconsistent with Henry having put the weapon to his own head.

If such evidence had the potential to be persuasive, it was reckoning without Dan Casey. On 3 November 1960, when he addressed the jury, he was at his brilliant best. He said: "The Crown claimed that they had made a case of overwhelming circumstantial evidence that Mrs Pressler went in and shot Henry Pressler in his room.

"But where was the evidence that Henry Pressler did not commit suicide? Where was the evidence as to the state of his room, whether the blinds were up or down and whether the lights were on or not?

"The Crown has set up Mrs Pressler as a cunning, clever, designing, callous woman who, to free her son, had determined to destroy the uncle and forged a confession by him, making it appear that the uncle suicided. On the other hand they tried to show she was almost an idiot.

"The Crown has left many holes in its case and left it to you, the jury, to fill them in as though you are a pack of jackals hunting down a prey, instead of a jury. They left a complete blank for you to fill in—as if you were ghouls enough to do".

At 10.30 that night, after several hours deliberation, the jury returned a verdict: "Not guilty".

Neville Pressler hoped that this would lead to his exoneration. That hope was to be dashed. The Court of Criminal Appeal, headed by the Chief Justice Sir Alan Mansfield, unanimously dismissed his petition. The court ruled that, on legal precedent, Henry Pressler's "confession" was not admissible. And that was where the matter stopped.

Neville Pressler, who was divorced by his wife Mary after he was sentenced, served 16 years, doing most of that time on a prison farm. He was released in 1975 and remarried. When interviewed in 1992, he was a successful smallcrops farmer at Emerald in central Queensland and had several children. He maintained his innocence.

Just over a year after her trial, Enid Pressler paid £22,500 for Neville Pressler's farm. She lived on in Bundaberg, sticking undeviatingly to the story that Henry Pressler had made his confession to her and suicided. Bill Conau remained unconvinced of her story. In 1986, interviewed by Kerry Smith, he said he believed there had been a miscarriage of justice—that a guilty person had been acquitted. He said: "I believe it was a mother trying to protect her son".

Whatever the truth, there was nothing that could be done about it. Enid Pressler went to the grave in 1988 taking whatever secrets she might have had with her.

As an ironic footnote, it is interesting to see what happened to Henry Pressler's impressive estate of £4,000 in savings. On 22 January 1962, probate was awarded on his estate at the execution of his last will and testament. The sole beneficiary was named. It was Enid Pressler.

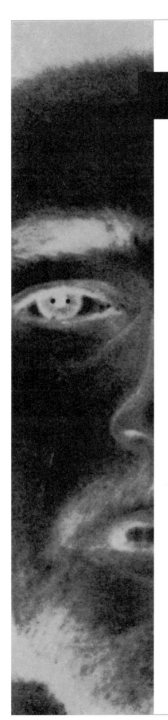

MADNESS, MURDER AND INTIMIDATION

International terrorism had been seen by Australians from afar for decades. The world stopped when Palestinian terrorists invaded the Israeli Olympic quarters at Munich in 1972. Would such fearful terrorist activity eventually come here? It did, courtesy of some radical Croatian activists who brought their feuds with them, set up military-style training camps, returned home for insurgency operations and often ended up dead. Australia was not entirely innocent. The turmoil of the Vietnam war saw to that. But the bombings that rocked our capital cities in the 60s and 70s were a shock for which we were not really prepared.

As the various intelligence organisations and politicians continued to squabble over terrorism, the problems of the outside world came to trouble us, ready or not. The Hilton Hotel bombing in Sydney in 1978 was allegedly associated with an extremist religious group and the visit to Australia of the Indian Prime Minister. It opened up a law enforcement and judicial nightmare that continued for many years and its practical aftermath was that security was tightened everywhere. In the mid-1970s, it was easy to walk unchallenged into Parliament House in Canberra. After the Hilton blast, in came the metal detectors and x-ray scanning of baggage. At that point, Australia lost much of its innocence.

We have reviewed the Croation bombings in this book but we could have chosen to look at the murder of the Turkish consul and his bodyguard in Sydney by so-called Justice Commandos for the Armenian genocide or any of too many other incidents; there is, unfortunately, no shortage of terrorist activity in this country. Whatever has blown up on the international front — the Gulf War of 1991, the long-standing Lebanese conflict or the tragedy of Bosnia — it is no longer possible for governments in an increasingly multicultural Australia to sit back and pretend that we are still isolated.

On the strictly domestic front, there was little cause for joy in the 70s. The nation had to come to grips with several horrors—the rampage of the Morse murderers in northern New South Wales, for example, and Adelaide's homosexual murders. The first of the latter, the killing of Dr George Duncan, did not have death as its aim. It was a manifestation of traditional violence towards actual or suspected homosexuals. The killings that followed were not accidents. The sexual mutilation and murder of seven boys and young men over an 11-year period, and the further saga of horror where seven young women were murdered in the late 70s, raised profound questions, some of them about Adelaide, others about the structure of a society where such atrocities could be committed in our very midst.

In Brisbane, violence, like the corruption exposed in the celebrated Fitzgerald Inquiry, has always been up-front. There was nothing subtle about the message extortionists delivered to the Whiskey au Go Go nightclub in 1973. Always, with licensed premises and late-night openings, there is scope for extortion, corruption of licensing police and general skulduggery. The lesson that must be learnt from that massacre is that if not strictly checked, the underworld activity that always surrounds late-night financial honeypots can produce a holocaust, with the innocent caught in the flames.

The Great Bookie Robbery in Melbourne was, unlike the Whiskey au Go Go caper, a military operation that went right ... at least in its execution phase. The subsequent history shows that criminals, used to the underworld with its own internal checks and balances—informers, rivals, predators—are not well equipped to handle the massive wealth that occasionally tumbles into their hands from a security system that has been totally breached. Not that there were convictions over the robbery, and there is evidence much of the money was invested one way or another, but the underworld by and large retained its own and exacted its toll. Although Norman Lee was acquitted over involvement in the Great Bookie Robbery, he tried another caper in 1992 and paid with his life.

The painters and dockers murders, part of a battle for control of the union, was simply gangster activity with a trade union touch. Many former prisoners went to the docks for work. The justification was that it gave them a chance to go straight. The Melbourne docks were unlike the Sydney docks where the socialist Left held sway. The Costigan Royal Commission was meant to get to the bottom of what was happening on the waterfront. Instead, it went to the bottom of the harbour.

The Costigan lid-lifting operation uncovered the extent of tax avoidance schemes in which the painters and dockers were minor players and the real operators were in the Establishment. This book, focusing as it does on physical violence, makes little mention of fraud and other white collar crime. The question might be asked as to who the real villains are: those who risk life and limb to obtain their loot or those who live behind a facade of respectability.

THE CROATION BOMBINGS

I N T E R N A T I O N A L   T E R R O R I S M   I N   A U S T R A L I A

On the night of 4 July 1963, nine expatriate Croatian terrorists crossed the Yugoslav border from Italy, near the city of Trieste. Their purpose was to kill foreign tourists, blow up railway lines and commit similar acts of sabotage. Despite being heavily armed, their mission was a failure. They were all captured a few weeks later and put on trial.

Thus began the story of a string of unsolved terrorist bombings and incidents which plagued Australia from the mid-1960s to the 1970s. The nine Croatian terrorists—or freedom fighters, as they would term it—had lived in Australia immediately before the incursion and were members of a shadowy group of young men called the Croatian Revolutionary Brotherhood (HRB).

Shortly after the Yugoslav court sentenced the nine terrorists in 1964, there was a sensation in Australia. While walking down a street in the Sydney suburb of Petersham, a Croatian migrant, Tom Lesic, was almost blown apart by a bomb. He lost both legs, part of his abdomen and most of his eyesight. Later Lesic claimed that he had been handed the bomb by "a communist". Documents tabled in the Senate in March 1973 show that ASIO, however, were sceptical of this explanation. They believed he had been ferrying the bomb himself.

The documents also set out the oath taken by members of the HRB. Standing before a table draped in black on which was placed a rifle and dagger in crossed position, a crucifix and two candles, a prospective swore silence and loyalty to the Brotherhood. The punishment for offences against the Brotherhood's principles, said the oath, was death.

The events of 1963–64 were modern Australia's introduction to terrorism, the use of indiscriminate violence for political ends. Ultimately this campaign of terrorism led to a violent upheaval in the Australian Security Intelligence Organisation (ASIO). That was in March 1973 when the newly elected Labor Attorney-General,

Lionel Murphy, staged a raid on ASIO headquarters. Murphy believed ASIO was hiding information on Croatian terrorism from the new government and was determined to teach the security service who was boss. Just why he believed this stemmed from the inability of ASIO (and the state and Federal police) to find those responsible for the ten-year campaign of political terrorism is unclear. It was perhaps the longest string of unsolved crimes in Australia's history.

Terrorism is a political crime and the 1963 incursion and the Lesic bombing saw the stirring of a potent political brew. Croats fought Serbs, fascists fought communists, and behind the scenes the Commonwealth Police and ASIO watched the fray and tried to plot the terrorists' next move.

The events of 1963–64 began a period of ten years during which Croatian emigres launched two guerilla incursions into Yugoslavia from Australia. Inside Australia itself, in the same period, there were at least 12 bombings, numerous wild demonstrations and countless individual threats of physical violence to individual Yugoslavs. Yet no one was ever charged with bombings and the few who were charged were only convicted on minor matters.

The postwar Croatian community in Australia was both highly nationalistic and parts of it were deeply influenced by fascist ideology because in 1941 the invading Nazis had set up a puppet state headed by Dr Ante Pavelic. His bloody rule saw the deaths of countless Serbs, Gypsies and Jews. Following the war, Pavelic and many of his supporters escaped on the Vatican-assisted "ratlines" to Latin America and elsewhere. From there they reorganised a worldwide emigre movement dedicated to re-establishing Croatia and smashing communist Yugoslavia.

It was from the jungle of Croatian emigre organisations and factions in Australia that the Croatian Revolutionary Brotherhood emerged.

On 27 August 1964, Prime Minister Menzies issued a ministerial statement on "Yugoslav immigrant organisations", criticising the violence but blaming all sides for the tension. For the next two years, things were apparently quiet. But behind the scenes Commonwealth Police and ASIO were active in building a picture of the mysterious and violent world of Croatian emigre politics.

In 1966, Commonwealth police barged into the Geelong home of another member of the Brotherhood, Adolf Andric, and proceeded to cart away letters, documents and personal possessions. The booty from the raid showed that the local Croatian Revolutionary Brotherhood was still active, was involved in bomb making and was part of a secret, Europe-based terrorist group. Indeed Andric, who was an industrial chemist, was turning his scientific knowledge to the manufacture of poisons, bombs and detonators. As well, the documents revealed that military-style training camps were held, the latest being at Tumbi Umbi near Gosford on the New South Wales central coast over Christmas 1965.

Andric was not charged by police and many believed that this was because the government was in sympathy with the anti-communist aims (but not the methods) of the Brotherhood. Andric himself was to be killed in 1972, on another Brotherhood incursion into Yugoslavia organised from Australia.

Apart from the police raid, the period of calm following the 1963 incursion ended on 17 November 1966 when a mail bomb exploded prematurely in the Melbourne Mail Exchange. The bomb, inside a hollowed-out book, was designed to explode when the book was opened. The book was addressed to Marjan Jurjevic, a Croatian who publicly attacked the extremists in his community and who was a leader of the rival Yugoslav Settlers' Association, which was despised by the Croatian nationalists. Though it was clear that the bomb was made by a political enemy of Jurjevic's, there was no evidence for police or ASIO and no arrests were made.

Six weeks later, on New Years Day 1967, another bomb made from several kilograms of gelignite exploded on the patio of the Yugoslav Consulate in Sydney, at 3.30 am, shattering windows and damaging walls of the building. Again the perpetrators could not be found.

That year was to be a significant one for the Commonwealth operations against the Brotherhood. A few days after the consulate bombing, Commonwealth police interviewed a Brotherhood leader, Josip Senic, who had been deported from Sweden. Two years earlier, Senic had stowed away on a ship to Europe, after the Commonwealth Police vetoed the issue of a passport to him. Senic's purpose was to reach Europe and take over the Brotherhood's operations against Yugoslavia—which he in fact did, in the process possibly killing an Australia-based rival, Geza Pasti. Senic's movements showed that Australia-based Croatians were clearly a key part of a worldwide terrorist network.

ASIO tended to accept that the Brotherhood were "hotheads" and that the mainstream Croatian independence organisation in Australia, called the Croatian Liberation Movement (HOP), was not terrorist. ASIO itself used right-wing Croat individuals in its operations and surveillance of left-wing Yugoslavs. Yet secret ASIO documents released in 1973 showed that even this group was training for military operations.

One document said:

The HOP has held several camps since 1962, at which members were issued with Army-type uniforms and Ustasha badges, and were instructed in the aims of HOP ... the HOP in Australia claims that they have played no part in the organising, recruiting or sending of terrorists from Australia to Yugoslavia, and that the HOP was opposed to the almost certain death of young Croats attempting the impossible. The HOP requires its members to remain steady, physically and mentally alert, so as to join the armies of the free world should the opportunity develop to fight communism on an international scale.

ASIO could fairly be said to have been working on an anti-Communist brief.

Its approach to Croatian affairs appears to have been directly affected by this. By contrast, the Commonwealth Police did not have any such brief and treated the matter as one of classic "crime intelligence". The result was that in the period 1967–68, police-gathered intelligence was superior to that of ASIO, the official "intelligence" organisation.

In March 1967 the police raided the homes of a number of suspected Brotherhood leaders, including the home of HRB leader, Jure Maric, and took away large numbers of documents, some of which were tabled in the Senate in March 1973.

These revealed quite open plans for further guerilla incursions, discussions of logistical problems such as storage of weapons, communication codes, letters which revealed the links between the Brotherhood and Croatian terrorist groups in Europe, bomb-making formulas and instructions on the most effective way to sabotage train tracks and derail trains.

Interviewed in 1968, Jure Maric told his Commonwealth Police interrogators that the Brotherhood was "dying" and had only five members. This was not entirely false. Both the Commonwealth Police and ASIO and accepted that the raids and the surveillance of the Brotherhood (as well as internal fights) had knocked it off balance.

ASIO claimed for years that no organised threat of Croatian extremism existed in Australia and that the bombs were the work of unorganised individuals. This advice was politically reassuring to the Liberal government but very shortsighted, and after a certain point, wilfully so. Ultimately it was to form part of the explosive mixture of events that led to a major crisis in the early days of the Whitlam Government.

The analysis of the Commonwealth Police was more guarded. After acknowledging that the Brotherhood now appeared to be "dormant", they concluded their March 1968 analysis with the prophetic words: "No doubt a few dedicated ones ... will revive their activities, possibly under different circumstances. With their past experiences, they are possibly now better equipped and more able to conceal their revolutionary activities".

The threats continued, but it became increasingly difficult for the Commonwealth Police and ASIO to identify the source. In May 1969, Canberra's David Jones store carried a display of goods from more than 40 countries, including Yugoslavia. All were decorated with flags and symbols of the trading country. After a number of telephoned bomb threats the store management withdrew the flags and other emblems, causing a protest from the Yugoslav Government. Protests in Parliament brought a sarcastic reply from a government senator, emphasising the anonymous nature of the threats and stating falsely that the matter was in the hands of the Canberra police.

A few weeks later at 12.45 am the roar of yet another bomb rent the night air as it exploded against the door of the Yugoslav Consulate in Sydney, causing extensive damage. At a police lineup, an eye-witness identified Brotherhood member Josip Senic as being near the consulate shortly before. But he had a "watertight alibi". Then, on 29 November, someone threw two sticks of gelignite at the rear of the Yugoslav Embassy in Canberra, where it bounced off a wife fence and exploded relatively harmlessly. Still nobody was charged.

This was too much for some government ministers. The External Affairs Minister, Mr (later Sir William) McMahon, referred to the lack of arrests and suggested that many Croatian extremists were concluding that they could act with impunity. He pointed out that the only court action to that time, against a demonstrator who burnt a flag, resulted in a derisory $5 fine. He added: "I find it hard to believe that it is not possible to penetrate these groups by one means or another".

The Commonwealth Police and ASIO both responded defensively. But their conclusions differed significantly. The response from the Commonwealth Police was:

> Australian Croats are involved in an international conspiracy directed against the Tito government of Yugoslavia and it seems that members of the Croatian Revolutionary Brotherhood will persist in their attempts to attack the people and premises of the Yugoslav Government in Australia.

ASIO's new Director General, Peter Barbour, put an entirely different point of view. He said:

> It should be understood that, so far, evidence is lacking that any of the bomb attacks on Yugoslav establishments have been planned by specific organisations, rather than individual extremists. The detection of individuals, or small isolated groups, is obviously a more difficult matter than the penetration of established organisations.

All through this period, any real action against terrorism was unfortunately hindered by rivalry and suspicion between the Commonwealth Police and ASIO.

A classic example, related in secret documents tabled in Parliament, occurred when Inspector Kerry Milte arrived unannounced at the business premises of a well-known Croatian nationalist leader, Srecko Rover, and began to question him. Rover, not surprisingly, did not want to discuss matters with Milte. Milte made it clear that the interview was serious by giving the official warning that he could choose not to answer questions. According to those documents tabled in the Senate in 1973, Rover said: "Why don't you phone ASIO first before you talk to me ... I would really like you to phone ASIO because they know all about me!".

From 1970 to the end of 1972, all hell broke loose as a series of bombs exploded in Sydney and Melbourne. It began in October 1970 with the bombing of the Yugoslav Consulate in Melbourne. Police examining the ruined building next day found a second bomb, attached to an oil storage tank.

In July 1971, St George's Free Serbian Orthodox Church in St Albans was extensively damaged by a bomb. Four months later, in the early hours of the morning, a bomb exploded outside the Adriatic Trade and Travel Centre in George Street, Sydney. The next month it was the turn of the Hub Theatre in the Sydney suburb of Newtown. Its crime had been to screen a film praising the role of partisans in the war against Nazism.

All through this period, drama began to be played out on the stage of Federal Parliament as Labor MPs accused Liberals of being soft on right-wing terrorism but tough on anti-Vietnam war protestors, whose only crime was to demonstrate in the streets.

In Labor's eyes the Attorney-General, Victorian Liberal Ivor Greenwood, refused to believe there was a real threat of Croatian terrorism. A review of documents which were secret at the time indicates that he turned ASIO's negative and tentative statement that "evidence is lacking" into a positive assertion that organised Croatian terrorism in Australia no longer existed, and that anyone who claimed it existed was politically motivated. According to his critics, Greenwood ignored the Commonwealth Police's careful warning of the "possible existence of a submerged group similar to the [Brotherhood] being responsible for the direction of these disturbances".

The year 1972 opened with the explosion of a bomb set against the statue of the Serbian Chetnik leader, General Mikhailovich, in Canberra. On the night of 6 April there were two simultaneous bombings. One bomb exploded on the balcony outside the flat of Marjan Jurjevic (the same man who was the target of the book bomb in 1966). The other bomb exploded outside the premises of the ANZ Bank in Melbourne.

In June 1972, there was another raid on Yugoslavia. Nineteen men crossed the border and this time a minor war broke out as the Yugoslav army encircled and shot and killed most of them. Of the 19, six were Australian citizens and three others had previously lived in Australia. Among them were the Andric brothers, who were both seen as leaders of the Croatian Revolutionary Brotherhood by ASIO and the Commonwealth Police.

This raid proved that the Brotherhood had never died, in spite of ASIO's advice to Greenwood. But then, in September, there was another bombing. This time it was in broad daylight, shattering the George Street windows of the Adriatic Travel Centre and sending shards of glass spiralling down into a crowd of shoppers. Sixteen people were injured. Miraculously, nobody was killed.

Incredibly, among the injured inside the Travel Centre was Tom Lesic, the Croat whom ASIO believed had blown himself up in

1964. Just as he had in 1964, Lesic tried to blame "communists" for the bomb, claiming that he himself, and not the travel centre, had been the target of the attack.

The September bombing came amid a worldwide spate of aircraft hijackings and bombings associated with another nationalist cause, that of the Palestinians. In its own small way, the bombing put Australia on the map. Unlike other terrorist incidents, not once did any political group take the "credit" for the bomb or use the occasion to reinforce demands.

Greenwood was to maintain that Croatian terrorism was not a problem to the bitter end, which came in December 1972, when his party was defeated.

Getting to the bottom of the string of unsolved bombings became a top priority for the new Attorney-General, Lionel Murphy. But a more practical event also began to exercise his mind. The Yugoslav Prime Minister, Mr Bejedic, was due to visit in March 1973, and would be an obvious target for the bombers and would-be assassins.

Both the Commonwealth Police and ASIO mobilised their forces in preparation for the visit. But Murphy was suspicious of ASIO's commitment to the cause of defending the Yugoslav dignitary. On the grapevine he heard that top bureaucrats from ASIO and other government departments had held a meeting which, he thought, was planning to restrict information to the new Labor Government about Croatian terrorism. On the night that he got wind of this, Murphy rang the Canberra regional chief of ASIO and demanded to see his files at eleven the same night. He hoped to find out how ASIO was conniving at a conspiracy to deny him the truth about Croatian terrorism.

The Canberra files told Murphy little. The Canberra chief explained that the original files were held in ASIO's Melbourne headquarters. The long-held rivalry between the Commonwealth Police and ASIO then came into play. Fearing that ASIO might destroy vital documents when tipped off that he intended to visit, Murphy agreed that Commonwealth Police should precede him to the ASIO building in St Kilda Road.

When he arrived at around 9 am he found the press waiting, an angry and frightened ASIO staff herded into their auditorium, and all the safes sealed by the Commonwealth Police. Murphy searched the files, found what he wanted—which did not reveal a conspiracy—and tried to calm things down. He gave a speech in Parliament which attracted the attention of the nation. Greenwood gave a spirited speech in reply.

But the damage, in the eyes of overseas intelligence agencies such as the US Central Intelligence Agency, was done. How could any overseas intelligence organisation trust the national intelligence group with information which could not be totally secured? ASIO would never be the same again. The first Hope Royal Commission, established in 1974, investigated ASIO and recommended a number of changes to its interpretation of its brief.

The Murphy raid began a series of events in which the string of unsolved bombings got lost in the rush. Shortly after, the Yugoslav Prime Minister Bejedic arrived amid the tightest security ever seen in Australia. During and after the visit, which stirred angry protests, state and Commonwealth police staged a series of dawn raids on the homes of dozens of Croatian nationalists. This in turn provoked Liberal, Country Party and Democratic Labor Party senators to call a Senate inquiry into the events. The matter dragged on and it became clear that whatever problems existed with ASIO and the Croats, they were largely due to incompetence rather than conspiracy.

The dramatic Murphy raid set the tone for a government keen to reform but with little experience of power. Perhaps the lasting damage from the bombings was not to the bricks and mortar blown apart but to the reputation of Australia abroad, to the security and police forces who never found the bombers, and to Australia's first Labor Government in 23 years.

THE DARK SIDE OF ADELAIDE

SEX, FEAR, PERVERSION AND A SERIAL KILLER

When author Salman Rushdie visited Adelaide in the early 1980s, he was horrified. Destined within a few years to inflame the entire Islamic world with his writings, Rushdie could hardly be described as a shrinking violet. But what he saw in Adelaide, the "City of Churches", home of a national cultural festival, sent him into a spin. Returning to London, he wrote: "Adelaide is a perfect setting for a Stephen King novel or a horror film. You know why those films and books are always set in sleepy conservative towns? Because sleepy conservative towns are where those things happen".

What Rushdie was referring to was a string of murders of males—beginning with the drowning of Dr George Ian Ogilvy Duncan in 1972 and including in the next 11 years several boys and young men who were not only killed but sexually mutilated. What had impressed itself on Rushdie's mind were the horror details that had come out in one of the associated court cases.

Adelaide, the city without a convict past, set on the meandering River Torrens, planned by a military engineer to be forever surrounded by gardens, had revealed its darker side. The beauty of the original concept continued but the Gothic underbelly had become apparent.

On the night of 10 May 1972, a group of men descended on the banks of the Torrens. They were looking for homosexuals who were known to frequent meeting spots along the river's banks. They found two of them, near the University of Adelaide foot-bridge, and threw them into the water. One, whose name was Roger Wesley James, suffered a broken ankle. The other, Dr Duncan, came off far worse. His body was recovered the next morning. A post-mortem examination revealed that Duncan, a man of slight build, who had only one lung as a result of tuberculosis when he was a child, had drowned. Severe bruising under both arms indicated he had been thrown by a number of people.

The drowning was deemed to be murder. The South Australian Police Homicide Squad investigated. What their initial inquiries revealed was very serious indeed. There was a possibility that the men who had gone down to the Torrens looking for homosexuals were police. The inquiry was taken over by two commissioned police officers, Chief Superintendent Col Lehmann and Superintendent Paul Turner. After nine days they had discovered the identities of three police possibly involved. The three, Vice Squad detectives Michael Clayton, Francis Cawley and Brian Hudson, were interviewed but refused to answer questions. Coroner Mr R.E. Cleland conducted an inquest several weeks later, the three policemen appeared and again refused to answer questions. The next day they were suspended from duty and charged with a breach of police regulations and subsequently resigned without ever answering the questions. Cleland found Duncan had died owing to violence. He ruled there was insufficient evidence to identify those responsible.

The South Australian Police Commissioner, Harold Salisbury, ordered investigations to continue. On 27 July 1972 he took the unprecedented step of calling in two senior officers from Scotland Yard's Homicide Squad to conduct an independent investigation into Duncan's death. The public saw this at the time as a move on the part of the police to alleviate misgivings that there might have been a cover-up. Chief Superintendent Bob McGowan and Sergeant Charlie O'Hanlon, from Scotland Yard, concluded their investigation on 25 October. They failed to find sufficient evidence to recommend a prosecution. Their report was never released, neither by the police nor the State Government, giving rise to continuing suspicion.

There were sporadic bursts of publicity during the years that followed. The case had a nasty smell. Duncan, a quiet, inoffensive man who was undoubtedly homosexual, did not deserve to die. But what more could be said? That question was answered on 30 July 1985 when a former Vice Squad officer, Mick O'Shea, made a number of revelations about the case. These appeared in a series of articles in Adelaide's morning newspaper, *The Advertiser*. O'Shea said police had "closed ranks" to protect their own, that some police had been suspects, but because of their intransigent attitude the coroner's inquest had never been likely to identify those responsible. O'Shea claimed vital aspects of the case either were not given enough attention by investigators or were not investigated at all.

O'Shea said that among the issues that had not been pursued was scientific evidence which would have implicated certain police. He claimed that as well as the three Vice Squad officers, a fourth man had been named as having been present on the occasion. But the investigating officers had never interviewed him. Nor had he been sought for interview by the investigators from Scotland Yard.

The Advertiser's revelations were dramatic. O'Shea said that on the night Duncan drowned, members of the Vice Squad had been at a city hotel farewelling one of their members. They had talked about going down to the Torrens to "flick poofters in". After Duncan had drowned, senior police had given "clear directions" that the facts on what police got up to, particularly what the Vice Squad did in policing homosexual activity, were not to be told. O'Shea said there had been a "general level of disharmony" in the Vice Squad at the time, which he said had caused mistrust and open malevolence between senior officers and junior ranks, and between individual members. He claimed that in this atmosphere there had been a conspiracy of silence to protect police thought to have been involved in Dr Duncan's death.

The articles had an immediate and significant impact. Senior officers announced the establishment of a new task force to investigate Duncan's death and O'Shea's allegations. The matter was also raised in State Parliament. A reward was posted offering $25,000 and a guarantee of immunity for any witness who offered information. Following this, an eye-witness gave a fresh statement in which he claimed he could identify those responsible for Duncan's death. The Duncan task force completed its interim report on 10 January 1986. It was forwarded to the then Crown Prosecutor, Paul Rice, for consideration as to whether there was now enough information for the laying of charges. Three weeks later, on 5 February 1986, members of the task force arrested officers Clayton, Cawley and Hudson, and charged them with the manslaughter of Duncan.

The three appeared before Chief Magistrate Nick Manos in the Adelaide Magistrate's Court in September 1986, to face committal proceedings. Roger James, then aged 41, who had been thrown into the Torrens with Duncan, gave a graphic description of events. He said he had given evidence at the coroner's inquest but that he had been untruthful. He said he had also lied to the two Scotland Yard officers.

James said that at the relevant time he had been a practising homosexual. He told the court he had been walking home along the banks of the Torrens about 11 pm watching ducks when he heard a voice saying: "Do you give it or take it?". James said he had immediately been put on guard and had said: "Neither". He said: "It was not a normal approach for a homosexual to make. It was a fairly overt approach". When asked by Rice how this approach had been different, James said: "I don't think I would like to go into those details. It would be pornographic".

James said the person repeated the question. Then a group of four had walked along the path towards him. "When they were almost level with me, one of them sort of projected out of the group, feet first into the river", he said. "He just suddenly emerged out of the group … then the person who had spoken to me started pushing me towards the river. Somehow I collided with the group that had thrown the other man. I grabbed hold of a coat pocket so that I ended up with my back to the river. I remember thinking I had better hang on to the coat pocket and I remember being hit in the head, just with a fist, and somehow I lost my grip".

James told Rice he had been hit more than once and was pushed backwards, his foot slipping between planks. "I felt and heard something snap and then I went into the river. I remember calling out, "Don't panic". But I was the one doing the panicking. I think I was calling out to the person who was thrown into the river just before me. I turned around to see just where he was, but there was just the top of his head and two of his hands above the water. He was just opening and closing his hands. I remember being amazed because I always assumed someone drowning would splash, yell and panic, but he just slipped away and it was like he was never there".

He said he had called out to those on the bank that a man was drowning. He had scrambled back up the bank. The group had returned and one of them had pushed him back in, saying: "Go save your mate!". James finally got out of the water. The man who had initially approached him stripped to his underpants and dived in, swimming to the place where Duncan had disappeared. But Duncan was gone. Then he got back onto the bank and with the others fled along the bank. James said he panicked. "I thought, "My God they have seen me and I have seen them kill this guy and they have run off ... and will come back and do me in!""

James said he crawled along a path towards Victoria Drive, which ran alongside the river. He had hidden in bush and tried to flag down a car. Another driver saw him and stopped to assist. The good samaritan's name was Bevan Spencer von Einem—a name which had no significance at the time, and indeed it appears von Einem was there quite innocently, but 14 years later that name would convey the most sinister menace.

On 29 October 1986, Manos dismissed the manslaughter charge against Brian Hudson. He said that while there was some incriminating evidence, a reasonable jury properly directed would not and could not convict him. Clayton and Cawley did not have it as easy. On 12 November 1986 Manos found there was sufficient evidence for the pair to face a Supreme Court trial for the man-slaughter of Duncan. The two were tried in the South Australian Supreme Court in September 1987. After a three-week trial, the jury retired to consider the evidence. Nineteen hours later, it returned verdicts of not guilty.

But that was hardly the end of it. Between 1979 and 1983, Adelaide had seen five more ghastly killings. They were of males and, although the victims themselves might not have been homo-sexual, the perpetrator—or perpetrators, whatever the case was—clearly had unusual hangups in that direction. The killings, dubbed the "Family" murders by the headline-hungry media, involved abduction, drugging, sexual assault and, finally, mutilation.

Alan Barnes, 17, disappeared in June 1979. His mutilated body was found seven days later on the banks of the South Para reservoir northeast of Adelaide. Scientific evidence suggested he died the day before his body was found, as a result of blood loss caused by a horrific injury to his anus. Two months later, the remains of Neil Muir, 25, were found on the banks of the Port River at Port Adelaide. Muir's body had been cut into numerous pieces and placed in garbage bags which had been thrown into the water, possibly from a nearby bridge. Peter Stogneff, 14, left home in August 1981 with the intention of wagging school. He failed to return. Ten months later, in June 1982, his skeleton was found at Port Gawler beach, north of Adelaide. The skeleton had been cut into three parts with a saw.

Mark Langley, 18, was last seen by friends in February 1982 near the River Torrens. His mutilated body was found nine days later, in bushes in the Adelaide Hills. A sharp instrument had apparently been used to inflict a wound stretching from near his navel to the area of his pubic hair. The body hair immediately around the wound had been shaved. Several segments of his small bowel were missing. A post-mortem concluded that his death had been due to loss of blood from an injury inside his anus.

By now, the South Australian Police Major Crime Squad had set up a special team of detectives. Police worked on the quite obvious theory that the murders were linked. The team, headed by Detective Sergeant Trevor Kipling, concentrated on known homosexuals and had questioned a number of suspects. One was Bevan Spencer von Einem, the man who had picked up the injured James the night Duncan died. Von Einem was well known to them. They questioned him several times over the Barnes and Langley murders.

Then a fifth victim turned up. He was Richard Kelvin, 15, abducted in June 1983 just 50 metres from his North Adelaide home. Seven weeks later his mutilated body was found in bushes in the Adelaide Hills. Post-mortem examinations revealed similar anal wounds to those of the other victims. Police believe Kelvin was drugged and kept alive for up to five weeks before he died. Investigations revealed that Kelvin's body contained traces of four drugs. Von Einem was questioned once more and this time he did not deflect the questions. Three of the drugs found in Kelvin's body were found in von Einem's possession. Hairs from von Einem were found in Kelvin's jeans. In December 1983, he was charged with Kelvin's murder and committed for trial.

Giving evidence in his own defence at the SA Supreme Court, von Einem denied ever meeting Kelvin. When confronted with the evidence that he had indeed done so, von Einem made the fatal mistake of changing his evidence in front of the jury. He said he had given Kelvin a lift and that he had let Kelvin off near his home. On 6 November 1984, the jury returned a guilty verdict and von Einem was sentenced to life imprisonment. A record non-parole period of 36 years was imposed.

Four years passed while police quietly worked on the other four murders, always having in mind that von Einem was the prime suspect. New witnesses were located and interviewed, some repeatedly. Fresh developments were reported by the ever-hungry media. On the afternoon of 18 September 1989, in a move that surprised nobody, detectives swooped on Adelaide's Yatala Prison, where von Einem was held in a protective wing, and charged him with the murder of Alan Barnes. Several weeks later they charged him with the murder of Mark Langley.

The committal hearing provided an extraordinary insight into happenings at which few people could have guessed. The evidence that unfolded before magistrate David Gurry shocked even hardened reporters assigned to cover it. The hearing was held before a packed court, with many people queuing for admission at the start of each day's proceedings. Von Einem, a tall thin person with neatly cut grey hair, sat impassively, shuffling only occasionally, maintaining a level gaze in the direction of prosecution and defence counsel.

Crown Prosecutor Brian Martin, QC, presented the "similar fact" evidence which he alleged was incriminating to von Einem. This included the causes of death, anal injuries and use of drugs. He put to Gurry that the circumstances surrounding the deaths of Kelvin, Barnes and Langley were so "strikingly similar" as to indicate that the same person was responsible for all three. Martin said von Einem regularly picked up young male hitchhikers, drugged them and sexually abused them. He called 22 witnesses, including former hitchhikers and associates of von Einem.

The testimony of the first prosecution witness, whose identity was suppressed from publication, stunned the court. The witness was known as "Mr B". He was a self-confessed homosexual and a former associate of von Einem. His evidence was sensational. He not only linked von Einem with the five victims of the Family killings but also implicated him in two other long-standing mysteries—the disappearance of the three Beaumont children and of Joanne Ratcliffe and Kirsty Gordon. A suppression order prevented South Australians reading or hearing broadcasts of the evidence for nearly two weeks. But once reported it put the case in the national spotlight.

During four days of testimony Mr B described how he and von Einem picked up and drugged hitchhikers before sexually abusing them. He said that on the night Alan Barnes died, in June 1987, he had met von Einem at the site known as "Number One" beat, an area frequented by homosexuals on the banks of the Torrens. He and von Einem had gone for a drive looking for hitchhikers. They had seen a youth in the city's northern parklands.

"We picked him up and asked him where he was going", Mr B said. The youth—later identified as Alan Barnes—had said he wanted a lift to Salisbury and had got into the back of the car. Barnes had been given some drinks containing alcohol and tablets of a drug called Rohypnol, which when taken with alcohol could induce unconsciousness. The three went to a cafe in North Adelaide for something to eat. Barnes was becoming affected by the drugs.

Mr B said von Einem went to make a telephone call and had come back saying he had rung a man and arranged to meet him at the Number One beat. When von Einem and Mr B arrived at that location the man, identified only as Mr R, had approached the car, acknowledged von Einem and suggested they go for a walk. They returned five or ten minutes later. Mr R left. "Bevan got back in the car and said, "Do you want to come with us and do some surgery on this guy?"," Mr B told the hushed court. Von Einem had said they were to going to "make a video about what happened" and were going to kill Barnes, then dump the body off a bridge. "I asked if Mr R was coming, he said "Yes", and I decided to leave", Mr B said. A few days later he had seen von Einem who said the youth had died and Mr R was concerned that he (Mr B) had seen the youth. Mr B said von Einem had threatened him and warned that, if anything was said, he would be implicated.

Jane, Arnna and Grant Beaumont had disappeared from Glenelg Beach on 26 January 1966. Joanne Ratcliffe and Kirsty Gordon disappeared from Adelaide Oval on 25 August 1973. All were presumed dead, and no trace of them had been found. Had von Einem accounted for them as well? Mr B's evidence about the fate of the children left onlookers gasping.

Mr B said von Einem had told him he had picked up all those children. Von Einem had told him he had gone to Glenelg beach, where he regularly used to go in summer to "perve" on people in the showers, had picked up the three children and done some "brilliant surgery" on them. He had "connected them together". One of the Beaumont children had died and von Einem had dumped the body. Von Einem had given no explanation of what happened to the other two. Mr B said in cross-examination that von Einem had not mentioned the names of the two girls he claimed to have picked up at Adelaide Oval, but he had formed the belief that von Einem was talking about Joanne Ratcliffe and Kirsty Gordon.

Von Einem denied involvement in any of the offences. There was nothing more substantial to connect him with the child abductions. But on 11 May 1990, after two months of hearings and more than 2,000 pages of evidence, Gurry committed von Einem for trial in the Supreme Court on charges of having murdered Barnes and Langley. Von Einem's lawyers launched an abuse of process action in the Supreme Court in a bid to have a permanent stay of proceedings. They said that because of the prejudicial publicity, their client would never get a fair trial. This action commenced in the Supreme Court before Justice Duggan several months later. It failed but Duggan, who was appointed in December 1990 to conduct von Einem's trial, apparently took heed of the arguments raised on von Einem's behalf.

After a pre-trial hearing, Duggan ruled "similar fact evidence" inadmissible. Crown Prosecutor Martin then said there would be two separate trials on the charges of murdering Barnes and Langley. But two days later the Crown withdrew the Langley murder charge. Then Duggan ruled that even if the Barnes murder trial went ahead, evidence from von Einem's trial for Richard Kelvin could not be produced as evidence. Duggan also ruled out evidence concerning von Einem's involvement with hitchhikers and his alleged associates. On 1 February 1991 the Crown withdrew the second charge of murder. Essentially, the Crown had the majority of its evidence ruled inadmissible and therefore had little hope of a successful case against von Einem.

Throughout all this, von Einem broke his silence and spoke to the media just once, and that was to deny any involvement in any of the Family murders or, despite his conviction, that he had murdered Richard Kelvin. He told the journalist who interviewed him inside Yatala Prison that he "could not believe it" the day Sergeant Kipling jumped over his back fence to arrest him for the murder of Kelvin. "You know, I didn't have the means to keep someone for seven weeks somewhere", he said. "It's not the case, there's no one out there who can say that von Einem kept Kelvin at my place or whatever, because it didn't happen, not with me. It did with somebody else, who I don't know".

Three years after Dr Duncan met his death at the hands of his assailants, South Australia became the first state in Australia to decriminalise homosexuality. That act of enlightenment undoubtedly made life easier for that minority and directed the attention of at least some of their persecutors elsewhere. But the sexual mania that accounted for the killings that followed knew no laws, and was unresponsive to enlightenment.

THE WHISKEY AU GO GO OUTRAGE

FIFTEEN DIE IN A NIGHTCLUB INFERNO

Late in 1992, the Queensland Government received a rather strange request. James Richard Finch, the notorious mass murderer, asked that the top joint of his left hand little finger, kept in a bottle of liquid on a shelf in the gaol museum, be returned to him in England.

Finch, English by origin, was a strange one. A petty criminal and standover man, semi-literate, he lived a life of lie. He was an obsessive, submissive homosexual who pretended to be tough but was merely an unintelligent bully-boy. He also had a violent, unpredictable side to his personality. He had served a 14-year sentence for shooting and wounding a Sydney hitman, Stewart John Regan. After serving his time, he had been deported to his home country.

Finch claimed, after his conviction over the Whiskey au Go Go firebombing in Brisbane in 1973, to have bitten his finger joint off to gain publicity for his claim that he had been framed. It was proved a companion had sliced it off with a razor.

But worst of all he lied to family, friends and supporters about that fateful night in March 1973 ...

The Whiskey au Go Go nightclub, at the corner of Amelia Street and St Paul's Terrace in the inner-city suburb of Fortitude Valley, had operated through the Vietnam years. The typical crowd during that time had included the youth of the era. People had gone there to see off family members going to the war, welcome them home, or have a function to celebrate—or commiserate—in the event of someone getting his call-up notice.

On Army pay nights the Whiskey management, like other nightclubs such as Tomcats and The Lands Office, had asked football clubs to supply burly forwards to keep the sometimes rowdy soldiers in order. A Brisbane journalist was one of those hired. He was a member of Brisbane's Western Suburbs Rugby League Club at the time and was in the Whiskey au Go Go a week before it was bombed.

The journalist believes there was a lack of professionalism in the way in which the club was managed. The very decision to use footballers instead of trained staff, he said, demonstrated that. Some months prior to the bombing the Whiskey au Go Go fire management, in response to complaints from residents about noise from the nightclub, had sealed the windows and installed air conditioners.

The nightclub, in common with others in Brisbane and the Gold Coast at that time, was under pressure from the underworld. On 24 February 1973, the Torino nightclub, a few hundred metres from the Whiskey au Go Go, had been firebombed. It was closed and empty at the time. On 4 March 1973, Brisbane's *Sunday Sun* told of a proposed underworld racket to extort money by threatening to use bombs. The newspaper said Sydney criminals planned to hold about 40 nightclub and restaurant operators in Brisbane and the Gold Coast to ransom for a total return of between $10,000 and $15,000 a week. If they did not pay up, the report said, a nightclub in full swing and not easily escape-proof would be firebombed.

John Andrew Stuart, 32 at the time, was a hardened, professional criminal, originally from Sydney. He had intellect and charisma. He had good looks—something women did not overlook when he became well known. But he was hardly the sort of chap you'd invite home to dinner. According to later prison records, he had spent two one-year periods in mental institutions and had eight major and minor convictions, including breaking and entering. His convictions included attempting to kill and escaping from lawful custody. He was to be diagnosed as having a psychopathic personality and possibly a schizophrenic illness, a form of psychosis.

Stuart was part of the extortion gang. He needed some help. He knew Finch and was friendly with him. He knew Finch was in England. Stuart's brother, Dan, said later: "John kept telling me he needed money to bring Finch out from England".

Finch, 28 at the time, was not as smart as Stuart, and was able to be dominated by him. Stuart told Finch he needed him in Brisbane to help with some jobs as he expected "some trouble with the nightclubs". Finch agreed to participate.

Dan Stuart said later: "He [John Stuart] showed me letters from Jim Finch written in his own hand in which Finch had written that they were going to "fix these gentlemen"". According to Dan Stuart, the "gentlemen" referred to were nightclub owners in Fortitude Valley from whom John Stuart, Finch and others hoped to extort $100 a week in protection money.

Stuart had paid Finch's $600 air fare to return from England.

The target was the Whiskey au Go Go nightclub, which had apparently objected to paying the protection money. The idea was to firebomb it. The firebombing was meant to scare, to frighten the nightclub owners in southeast Queensland for ever and ever.

Like arsonists before and since, Stuart had little understanding of the nature of petrol in a confined space. So many times, fire investigation officers will say, people intending to burn down premises, for whatever reason, will think they can pour the petrol and throw a match through the open door before making their escape.

In fact, they are caught out often, by a minute spark from an electrical appliance while they are pouring the petrol. Or, when the match is thrown, by the petrol fumes that have been caught in their clothing, or been breathed into their lungs ...

Let alone who else might suffer, or how far the fire might spread.

This was the trap John Stuart was unwittingly setting. If he had cunning in many other directions, he did not have knowledge in the only thing that really mattered—whether the blaze would amount to more than a scare for proprietors.

In the lead-up, Stuart went through the normal careful, criminal preparations. A getaway car, with driver, was needed. Recruited for the purpose was Ian Hamilton, a former Queensland state boxing champion.

Finch claimed later he had argued strongly with Stuart against the venture. "Stuart told his contacts who were paying him that he would supply a third man to bomb the Whiskey", he said. "He told me if I didn't do it he would be in grave danger from them. John said I owed it to him after all we had been through—being bashed by prison officers in Grafton and in other gaol escapades".

Stuart had said: "Haven't you got the heart? Are you a coward, Jim?". Finch said he had responded to the taunt and decided to go along with it.

Stuart was well known to police. Prior to the firebombing, he was preparing the ground carefully for his exclusion as a suspect. He had decided to go up-front, to make a big public noise about his concerns, and to raise a warning about the very enterprise he was secretly planning. He contacted Brisbane journalist Brian Bolton.

"I have known Stuart for 10 years and he has kept numerous appointments over the past five weeks to tell me of Brisbane's nightclub bombing threat", Bolton was to write. "He warned me it was "coming shortly"". On the day before the bombing, Stuart met Bolton again and told him he had warned police about the pending firebombing campaign.

Bolton said Stuart had told him: "It will happen in the next three or four weeks. I'll have to go and tell someone in authority. I've been keeping a close lookout for two men from Sydney who I knew intended muscling in on nightclub extortion in Brisbane and the Gold Coast. They arrived in Brisbane on Monday ... I saw them in one of the clubs on Monday night ... but they didn't recognise me.

"But I knew they were here to put on the squeeze and if club operators didn't start paying up it wouldn't be long before the first place went up".

Bolton was to add: "Stuart agreed yesterday to go on television in Brisbane next week to make a public warning about the threatened bombings of big turnover clubs and restaurants from Brisbane to the [New South Wales] border.

"He said that even though he thought it would be three or four weeks before the first torch bomb which would incinerate nightclub patrons in an eruption of flame he wanted to act quickly to warn everyone he could.

"He asked me to accompany him last night on a round of Brisbane nightclubs to warn proprietors".

On that same day, Stuart gave Finch details of the plan. Stuart told him he had been paid $5,000 for the "job" from underworld figures and others. The getaway car was to be a black Holden sedan, obligingly stolen for the purpose by Hamilton.

On the night of 7 March 1973 patrons gathered in the disco-theque of the Whiskey au Go Go to hear the Delltones, whose famous band members included Peewee Herman. The Delltones entertained the crowd of more than 100 with their typical surf numbers, including Hangin' Five and the ever-popular Mr

Baseman. Their support group was a band called Trinity, which was making a debut performance. There was nothing to indicate what disaster was to befall them. The Whiskey au Go Go's manager, Mr Brian Little, was at the opening of a new nightclub, Blinkers.

That night, Finch and Stuart went to Dan Stuart's home in the Brisbane western suburb of Jindalee.

Dan Stuart said later: "At 11 pm John and Finch asked me for a fuel drum. They always carried fuel drums with them. They always milked cars".

Finch and John Stuart left in a car just before midnight. On Finch's later account, Stuart drove up a side road where he saw a black Holden parked at the roadside. Finch got out and Stuart drove on. As confirmed later by Dan Stuart, his plan was to establish an alibi by being seen at several places in Brisbane that night and using journalist Bolton to strengthen it.

At the car, Finch met two men. "When I saw [them], they reminded me of the Black September terrorists at the Munich Olympics", he said later. The two men had donned their black balaclavas so that only their eyes and mouths were visible.

"They said they'd heard of me and that I had a good name among crims. They said they were glad to have me aboard".

Finch spoke to the two men. Then he dressed the same way they did, including putting on a balaclava. The three rehearsed their techniques several times before setting off for the Whiskey au Go Go. In the boot were two nine-litre drums of petrol, standing upright, three-quarters full. On the way to the nightclub, the men stopped to loosen the caps on the drums and to open the boot, leaving it slightly ajar for quick opening.

Finch was to say later that at the time Stuart was talking to Bolton, he and his accomplices were making their move on the Whiskey au Go Go.

"We came up to the Whiskey in one clean swoop, pulling up outside the nightclub in the main street, St Paul's Terrace", Finch said.

It was just after 2 am. Finch and Hamilton leapt out each side of the car from the back seat. Hamilton whipped off the petrol caps while Finch grabbed a drum in each hand.

They sprinted to the entrance to the nightclub. "I raced straight in and dropped the drums on their sides just inside the doorway", Finch said. "As the petrol began to spill, in about a one or two yard circle, the torch [Hamilton] dropped a match and set fire to it. There was a sudden whoosh and it just started to burn".

The blast blew out the electrical connections. The fire sucked up carpet, rubber underlay, paint and old timber, giving off carbon monoxide gas. The fire and the gas swept up the stairwell. It took about 30 seconds to reach the discotheque.

Ray Roberts, a guitarist with Trinity, said: "We were on a break at the time and all of a sudden there was some kind of commotion down at the other end of the club. I thought there was a brawl. There was a red glow and someone shouted, "Fire, get your gear and go!". Lola Roy, who was sitting with friends celebrating the forthcoming marriage of a friend, said: "We smelled the smoke and then the lights went out from the front progressively to the back. We made for the fire escape".

The air conditioning system took in the fumes and spewed them out into the crowd. Those closest to the air conditioning outlet were immediately affected. People started to fall. People could not see where to go or what to do. Two of the exit doors were apparently locked. The windows had been sealed. Oxygen was sucked away. Those inside were breathing carbon monoxide. Some got out a rear fire escape. Others screamed for friends they could not find. Some fell and were clambered over. Windows were smashed and patrons leapt the five metres to the footpath.

Roberts said: "I smashed my way through a side window. No one else used that window but me. I got cut about the left arm and head but got out. People were screaming. It was a nightmare. Horrible".

Janice Maddox, who was waiting outside the club for Roberts, said the heat became intense. "We heard screaming and shouting and then the police and firemen arrived", she said. "A friend I had come to meet was among the dead. I recognised him from his clothing. Soon afterwards two waitresses were brought out dead".

Police and ambulance men who went through the ruins found bodies horribly charred. Others had burns that would not have been enough, on their own, to have killed them. The death toll was ten men and five women. Among the dead were two members of the band. Others were Lesley Gordon Palethorpe and William David Nolan, military policemen. Four of the dead were teenagers.

Sometime in the early hours of that same morning, Stuart went to the *Sunday Sun*. Arriving at work later that day, Bolton found two notes on his desk expressing disappointment that Bolton had not turned up for their trip around the nightclubs. One note said: "I waited from 8.55 till 10.40. Why didn't you appear? I've been to Blinkers [another night spot] and every one looking for you".

Dan Stuart said Stuart also went to Finch's flat. Stuart later told his brother: "You should have seen Finch. He was in the lounge chair eating some grapes, about to put one in his mouth when I told him about the 15 people. He said "Fucking hell!" and ran out the door". Finch ran into the bush and went into hiding.

Stuart got back in touch with Bolton who was to write: "Stuart told me yesterday: "The two men from Sydney I have told the police about are not experienced in crime. No experienced crim would do anything like that. It's unheard of. Apart from killing and maiming innocent people just to get extortion, they're facing certain gaol terms. But these two blokes are hop-heads and they wouldn't give a damn about who gets hurt or how many".

A policeman, of any description, gets experience at one thing, and that is hearing "a story". Just about everyone tries it on, from the little lady getting a parking ticket to the hoodlum caught in the act of cracking a safe. Some of the things people try are ingenious. Police don't often get caught. They were not going to be taken in by Stuart's ploy.

Pat Lloyd, a former policeman turned Brisbane reporter, said on the same day: "The police radio network was alive with calls today ordering special watches to be kept for several well-known criminals who are missing. At least one of the men being sought is classed as a potential killer, he has a history of violence".

On 12 March 1973, police arrested Finch and Stuart. They got Finch in a shopping mall. Hamilton went missing. A criminal named Billy Stokes was later charged, convicted and gaoled for the murder of Hamilton. Hamilton's body was never found.

In custody Stuart refused to speak, be interviewed, or sign anything. But both he and Finch were charged with the murder of one of the club patrons, Jennifer Denise Davie. She was the nominal victim. For reasons of speed and efficiency, Finch and Stuart only needed to be convicted of the one murder, although it was open to the police to lay 15 charges of murder.

The committal hearing began in May 1973. It was one of the

most sensational on record. Both pleaded not guilty. Throughout the hearing, which went into June, Finch and Stuart took to swallowing pieces of wire, usually in the form of wire crosses held together with rubber bands which dissolved in the stomach and released the wire into the intestines. Finch and Stuart attempted unsuccessfully to get separate trials. They protested endlessly that they had been "verballed" by police—that the police had made up incriminating statements and attributed them to them. The two were committed for trial.

Stuart was absent from the courtroom having operations to get the wire crosses removed. The trial proceeded under Justice Lucas. Central to the police case was an unsigned record of interview in which Finch confessed to his and Stuart's role in the firebombing. They claimed they had made no confessions.

Part of the evidence against them was an alleged confession by Finch to a cellmate, an Aboriginal named Robert Arthur Murdock. Murdock was hardly the sort of witness whose credibility would remain unchallenged. He was a psychopathic rapist who was later to spend all his days in prison for repeated degrading offences, including a four-day attack on his female probation officer when he repeatedly assaulted her. Known as "The Black Stallion", he was kept for ten years in a cage in Townsville prison because he could not be trusted among men as he would inevitably try to rape anyone who came near him.

Regardless of what arguments might or might not have been raised about Murdock's evidence, it corroborated much of the other Crown evidence. Stuart did not come to court to hear any of the evidence against him. In an historic legal precedent he was convicted in his absence, along with Finch.

The two failed with numerous appeals. Finch applied to the High Court for leave to appeal against his conviction on the grounds that he had not been given the opportunity to cross-examine potential jurors to see whether or not they had been influenced by "saturation pre-trial publicity". In November 1975 the full bench of the High Court unanimously refused the application.

Stuart fought hard against his imprisonment. He protested, wrote letters and appealed to whoever would listen. In November 1977, he climbed onto the roof of Boggo Road gaol and pulled bricks and guttering from the roof to form the words: "Innocent— victim of police verbal".

He also wrote poetry which was circulated amongst his supporters and increased the regard they held for him.

Brian Bolton quoted what was thought to be the first poem Stuart wrote, called "Symbols":

> *Just as the blooming of a flower*
> *Or the eagle drifting in the blue*
> *Or the rising sun's first golden hour*
> *Or spring time's ever brilliant hue*
> *Or like the wind unchained and free*
> *Or the ripples of a moonlit sea*
> *If the truth of beauty is enough to know ...*

It was poignant enough to be referred to after his death. On New Year's Day 1979, Stuart was found dead in his cell. A post-mortem examination revealed that he had had an acute heart infection. Suicide was ruled out. A coroner's inquest found there was no evidence of extensive violence, although he bore "numerous old scars".

Over the next decade, Finch sought backing for his claim of innocence. He attracted the support of legal experts, journalists and sympathetic women. He sought to have his case reopened so that he could prove his innocence and establish that he had been victim of a police verbal.

He was a prolific letter writer, in many cases writing daily to close friends and those who could help him. In the letters he wrote often of how close he was to God, how he had been wronged and what a good citizen he would be if he was released and was given the chance to prove his innocence. He deceived a remarkable woman, Cheryl Cole, who professed her love for him and led a group seeking his release.

Cole said publicly she was in love with Finch and that they had corresponded for years. In February 1987, she and Finch were married in a special prison service, largely arranged by journalist Dennis Watt, the one other person who took a keen personal interest in Finch and his predicament.

Released from gaol and deported to Britain, with Cheryl Cole still in Australia, Finch contacted Watt and said he had something to tell him. Watt got the nod from his newspaper to travel to Britain to interview Finch. He did not expect what Finch was to say—that he had indeed torched the Whiskey au Go Go, just as had been alleged. News got back to Australia. The Queensland Government was miffed. It was quickly stated that Finch had only been convicted of one murder, and that he was liable to be extradited to Queensland to do more time—a lot more time. Finch quickly withdrew his statements, saying that he had been "confused".

Cheryl Cole went to Britain to join Finch but, as with Watt, her illusions about him were to be rudely shattered. He subjected her to fits of uncontrollable violence. He treated her with animalistic brutality. He told her that throughout his prison life he had had homosexual partners in his cell. After a few months, she returned to Australia.

Finch remained in England, took up residence with his sister, and got a job as a nightwatchman in a factory.

Stuart's brother, Dan, who had been under police protection and in hiding since the firebombing, gave an interview with Don Pederson of the Brisbane *CourierMail*, confirming that Finch and Stuart had carried out the bombing.

It was a suitable final word. Both Finch and Stuart had adapted well to the Hitlerian notion of the big lie. Tell it big enough, and long enough, and repeat it enough, and people will start to believe.

THE CROATION BOMBINGS

Above: The George Street bombing occurred in broad daylight in one of Sydney's busiest thoroughfares. Sixteen people were injured; miraculously no one was killed. All of a sudden the safe and peaceful lives of ordinary Australians were shattered by the threat of terrorist attacks.

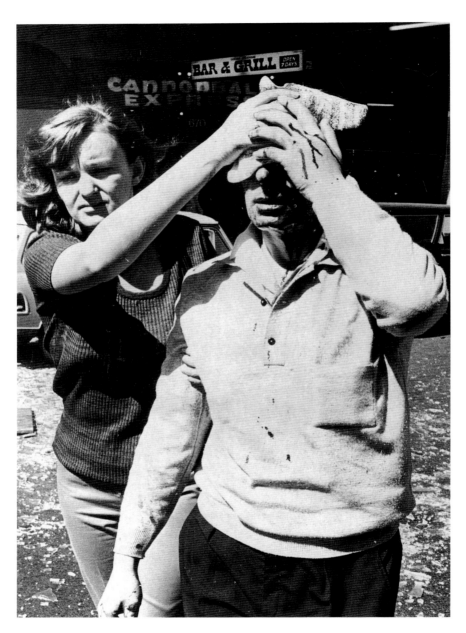

THE CROATION BOMBINGS

Above: Australia suffered a painful and bloody introduction to international terrorism through a series of bombings in the mid-1960s and 1970s.

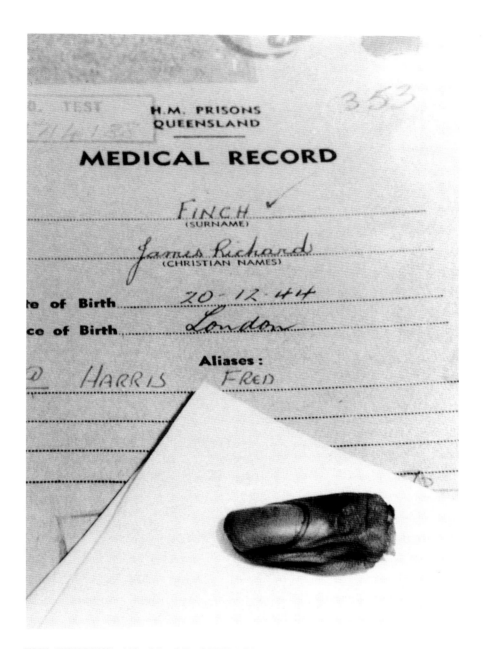

THE WHISKEY AU GO GO OUTRAGE

Above: The fingertip that James Finch lost in a publicity stunt.

THE WHISKEY AU GO GO OUTRAGE

Top: Finch and his trusting bride Cheryl Cole at their wedding in prison. It was only on his release that she became aware of his true brutish nature.

Bottom: Robert Authur Murdock, aka the "Black Stallion", was so violent he was kept in a cage in a Townsville prison for ten years. He allegedly heard Finch's confession.

THE WHISKEY AU GO GO OUTRAGE

Top left: John Andrew Stuart, the hardened, professional criminal whose intellect, charisma, good looks and poetry helped convince supporters of his claims of innocence.

Top right: The testimony of Dan Stuart was amongst the strongest evidence against his brother John and Finch

Bottom: The Whiskey au Go Go Nightclub in the aftermath of the firebombing that killed 15 people.

THE GREAT BOOKIE ROBBERY

Left: Police believe the bandits set up an ingenious peephole system during their Easter "practice run".

Below: The bandits entered the building through the Queen Street door and caught the lift to the club on the second floor.

THE GREAT BOOKIE ROBBERY

Above: Victorian Club Secretary, Frank Murray, with the cash boxes and padlocks that had contained the bookmakers' millions.

BATTLE FOR THE WATERFRONT

Above: The leaders of the warring factions: Patrick Shannon (left) and Billy Longley (right).

BATTLE FOR THE WATERFRONT

Top left: Freddie "The Frog" Harrison was gunned down in front of dozens of his workmates, yet all claim not to have seen a thing.

Top right: Alfred "The Ferret" Nelson disappeared before the election. His body was never found.

Bottom: The blasted body of Desmond St Bernard Costello was found dumped in an excavation ditch.

BATTLE FOR THE WATERFRONT

Top: Doug Sproule (left) and James Bazley (right) were both targets of pre-election violence.

Bottom left: Jack "Putty Nose" Nicholls, secretary of the union: "the rotten system has cut my life short".

Bottom right: The royal commission headed by Frank Costigan started its investigation at the waterfront and ended up in the nation's boardrooms.

THE TRURO MURDERS

Top left: The discovery of Veronica Knight's body was the first step on the trail of a serial killer.

Top right: The skeleton of Julie Mykyta, 16, was only located with the aid of James Miller, accomplice to murder.

Right: The remains of Connie Iordanides, 16, were found a kilometre from where Veronica Knight's body was discovered.

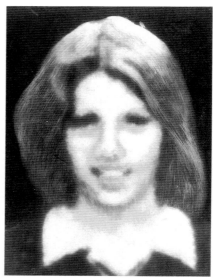
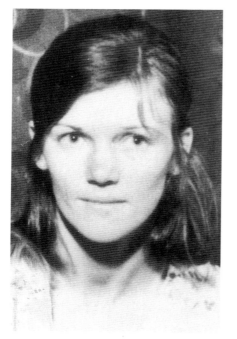

THE TRURO MURDERS

The Truro body count continued with the discovery of the remains of Sylvia Pittman, 16 (top left), Tania Kenny, 15 (top right), and Vicki Howell, 26 (left).

THE TRURO MURDERS

Above: Human remains are carried away in plastic bags from the Truro site by Major Crime Squad Detective Peter Foster.

THE TRURO MURDERS

Above: A police forensic officer carries the wrapped remains of Julie Mykyta from the Truro "dumping ground".

THE TRURO MURDERS

Top: It is difficult for the general public to imagine the face of a serial killer. Christopher Worrell is believed to be the man responsible for the Truro murders.

Bottom: Police examine the remains of Tania Kenny, 15, after Miller guided them to the grave site in May 1979.

THE TRURO MURDERS

Above: Worrell's accomplice James Miller showed police the location of the Truro victims' bodies.

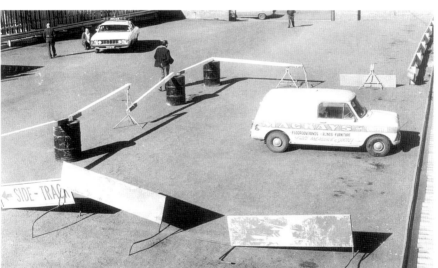

THE MURDER OF DONALD MACKAY

Top left: Donald Bruce Mackay. The mysterious death of the anti-drug campaigner galvanised a nation and shook up the crime world and the legal system.

Top right: A reward was posted by the NSW Government one week after Mackay's disappearance.

Bottom: Bloodstains and three spent cartridges were found with Mackay's car at the back of the Griffith Hotel.

THE MURDER OF DONALD MACKAY

Right: The search for Mackay's body was exhaustive. Two workers from the Water Resources Commission check the local irrigation channel.

Below: The township of Griffith turned out in force to a community service for Mackay who at that time was missing and presumed murdered.

THE MURDER OF
DONALD MACKAY

Top left: There was an attempt to implicate Barbara Mackay and her son in her husband's murder.

Top right: Frederick Joseph Parrington, who reached the position of executive chief superintendent in the NSW Police Department, was departmentally charged over his conduct of the investigation.

Bottom: The Woodward Royal Commission found that Mackay had been murdered by a Griffith-based organisation and that Robert Trimbole was the practical head of the group.

BARLOW AND CHAMBERS

Above: Kevin John Barlow (left) and Brian Geoffrey Chambers (right) pictured after the Malaysian Supreme Court rejected their appeal on 18 December 1985.

BARLOW AND CHAMBERS

Left: Chambers was involved in drug dealing from the 1970s. For him getting caught was only a matter of time.

Right: Kevin Barlow. With a taste for alcohol and marijuana and an aversion to work, he followed the promise of a good time and easy money to the gallows.

BARLOW AND CHAMBERS

Top left: Hired by Musarri as a minder, John Asciak recruited Barlow for the drug run with Chambers.

Top right: Debbie Colyer-Long was Barlow's landlady and Asciak's lover. She was the fatal link between Barlow and Chambers.

Bottom: Mr and Mrs Barlow. Lawyers, governments and members of the public joined family members in attempting to have the death sentences lifted.

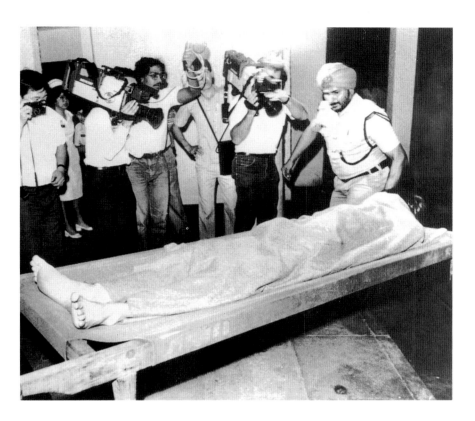

BARLOW AND CHAMBERS

Above: Barlow's body in the mortuary the morning after the hanging. Barlow and Chambers were the first Europeans to be executed under Malaysia's drug laws.

THE WALSH STREET SHOOTINGS

The fatal shooting of Constables Damian Eyre (top left) and Steven Tynan (top right) was believed to be an act of revenge for Graeme Jensen's death.

Bottom: Outside 222 Walsh Street, the bloody aftermath of the murders. The white Holden Commodore served as the bait.

THE WALSH STREET SHOOTINGS

Top: Victor Peirce's Richmond home was demolished in the police search for evidence connected with the Walsh Street case.

Bottom: Anthony Leigh Farrell (in the centre of picture) was one of three men arrested on charges of murdering Constables Tynan and Eyre.

NEDDY SMITH IN THE SPOTLIGHT

Above: Arthur Stanley "Neddy" Smith. The notorious criminal who lifted the lid on crooked cops.

NEDDY SMITH IN THE SPOTLIGHT

Above: Paul Hayward was arrested in Bangkok on drug-related charges. Justice Woodward believed he was involved in a massive heroin importation ring with Smith.

Top right: Detective Sergeant Roger Rogerson. His relationship with Smith was to have far-reaching implications.

Bottom right: Detective Bill Duff. He joined Smith and another criminal, Murray Riley, in a birthday celebration at a Redfern restaurant.

Above: Dangar Place in Chippendale where Lanfranchi was gunned down.

Left: Warren Lanfranchi's meeting with Detective Sergent Roger Rogerson was engineered by Neddy Smith.

THE GRANNY KILLER

Above: Gwendolin Mitchelhill, 84, was in the habit of carrying large amounts of cash. Police at the time believed robbery may have been the motive behind her death.

Left: Robbery did not seem to be behind the murder of Lady Ashton, 84. Her apartment was full of priceless antiques but her murderer attacked before she entered her front door.

THE GRANNY KILLER

The fear continued to build with attacks on Margaret Pahud, 85 (top left) and Olive Cleveland, 81 (top right).

Right: With the murder of Muriel Falconer, 93, police had their strongest clue—a footprint in the blood around the body.

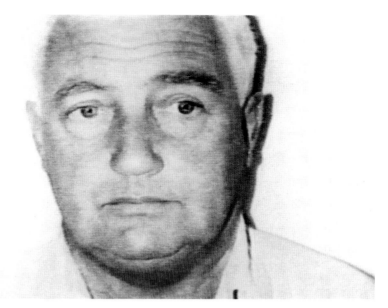

THE GRANNY KILLER

Top: John Wayne Glover was sentenced to life imprisonment for the string of murders that had become known as the "Granny Killings".

Bottom: John Glover and Gai Rolls on their wedding day. She thought Glover had the potential to better himself. His mother-in-law, however, saw him as a fortune seeker.

THE GRANNY KILLER

Above: Frail they may appear but the elderly of Mosman remained fiercely independent even after six women were brutally murdered.

THE GREAT BOOKIE ROBBERY

AUSTRALIA'S ANSWER TO THE GREAT TRAIN ROBBERY

For nearly a century, Melbourne bookmakers had met at the old Victorian Club, at 141 Queen Street, to settle up on the first business day after a major weekend metropolitan race meeting. They were the biggest and richest bookmakers in the state, catering for the punting needs of the biggest races in the country. It was a system which had stood the test of time. Huge sums of money arrived on settling day by armoured car. Once inside the club, there was almost no security. It all worked on trust. For years, members of the Victoria Police Consorting Squad had had an informal arrangement whereby three detectives would drop in to check that all was well. Nothing had ever happened. No one expected anything would.

The millions of dollars in cash present each settling day had attracted the attention of criminals. For any gang which had the resources and the daring to stage a robbery, there was untold wealth to be had. As head of the CIB, Detective Superintendent Graham "Slippery" Davidson, was later to comment, it was simply a matter of plucking an over-ripe plum. Several gangs, including one led by the notorious criminal James Edward "Jockey" Smith, had conducted preliminary checks on the feasibility of committing the robbery but the job had always appeared too daunting.

One man, Raymond Patrick "Chuck" Bennett, had the dash, brains and imagination to consider the whole matter as a serious proposition. Bennett was a natural leader of men, well liked and charismatic. Those who knew him said he was a master strategist with a meticulous eye for detail. He had been a known armed robber for years, and came from the old school which refused to talk to police about anything. According to violent standover man, Mark Brandon Read, Bennett was in a class of his own. "He was a thinker and a top gang war tactician", Read said. "He was also a master planner and one of the Australian underworld's foremost bank robbers".

At the time of his contemplating the supreme "bust" of his career, Bennett was somewhat indisposed. He was rotting away in a prison cell on the Isle of Wight, half a world away. But that was just an inconvenience. Late in 1975, Bennett took advantage of the freedom granted in pre-release leave to jump on a plane and fly to Melbourne to case the Victorian Club. A young policeman spotted him in the suburb of Moonee Ponds. After accomplishing his mission, Bennett slipped quietly back to England to complete his gaol term, content in the knowledge that when he was again a free man he could turn his attention to the job that others just talked about.

When he flew back to Australia, Bennett quickly went about recruiting a gang of nine. According to Paul Delianis, now a retired deputy commissioner of the Victoria Police, and at the time head of the Consorting Squad, the group was probably the best gang of armed robbers ever assembled in Australia. "They had specialised in commando-type raids for years", he said. "They copied the methods of an English group called the Wembley Gang which had used similar commando tactics".

Bennett did not want any novices. Though the entire gang he recruited has never been conclusively identified, it is believed that one of the key members was Ian Revell Carroll, a man with the imagination and patience to carry out big jobs. Another apparent member was a more "downmarket" criminal, Anthony Paul McNamara. Most of Bennett's gang, if caught, would have been known to police. That was one of the pitfalls of collecting such professionals. The one man in the gang who did not fit that pattern—who was unknown in the Melbourne underworld and unknown to detectives—was most useful to Bennett. Described as a "time and motion expert" and living in a northwestern suburb of Melbourne, he had in fact been part of a planning team for major armed robberies in Melbourne, Perth and Sydney.

Bennett took his crack group to a secret training camp in rural Victoria. He behaved more like a football coach than a career criminal, giving an instruction to his men that for three months they were to swear off booze and keep away from women. He was far from a wowser, but bitter experience had taught him that no matter how dedicated the criminal and how good the plan, loose lips could destroy a job before it started. He reasoned that if he picked the right men and they could remain silent, before and after the job, they stood a good chance of getting away with it. He did not want anyone, other than his crew, to know they were planning the biggest armed robbery in Australia's history. The men, it is understood, followed his directions for the most part, though they might have sneaked off for a drink or two when Bennett was not about.

When the time came to attempt the robbery, Bennett felt he and his team were ready. He knew how the system at the Victorian Club worked. He had no doubt that he would be able to get in, get the cash and get out. And as well he wanted to get away with it—to make it a quick, clean heist, with as little trouble and as few clues as possible, although the gang would have to keep watch for the Consorting Squad police coming for a routine check. If it was necessary to shoot, they would have to do it. He knew that once the crime was committed, the police would throw every resource available into solving it. He counselled his men to remain calm, be quiet and, when they got the loot, not to start throwing it around, as Peter Macari had after ripping off $500,000 in the "Mr Brown" Qantas hoax in Sydney a few years before. Bennett organised "laundering" for the loot, and called upon a close friend, Norman Lee, a Melbourne dim sim manufacturer, for help in at least this regard.

The date selected was 21 April 1976. It was just after Easter and it was not selected at random. Bennett knew that the haul would be tripled if the Victorian Club was hit then, because the bookies would be gathering to settle not just for one race meeting but for three—at Caulfield on the Saturday and Monday, and at Moonee Valley on the Tuesday. As part of the preparation, and to further minimise the chance of failure, Bennett organised a virtual dress rehearsal. According to information later given to police, the gang went into the deserted premises of the club over the Easter holiday and practised what they were going to do. His plan was to use a team of six to storm the club, backed by at least three others.

On the big day, 46 bookies were to go to the Victorian Club to settle. Cash from 116 bookmakers was delivered by a Mayne

Nickless armoured car. Just after midday a man arrived at the club, saying he was there to fix the refrigerator in the bar on the second floor. At 12.07 pm that man, with armed accomplices, suddenly burst into the area where the bookmakers were settling. The six wore balaclavas and were heavily armed. They ordered 31 people to lie on the floor. One guard went to grab his .38 revolver, but a gang member saw him and bashed him to the floor with the butt of a submachine gun. The gang ripped out the two phones in the room. They used bolt cutters to open the eight Mayne Nickless metal cash boxes, which contained up to 118 calico bags, all filled with untraceable bank notes. They put the bags into three large mail sacks. As fate would have it, that day the Consorting Squad was preoccupied with other matters and did not make the usual visit. It probably saved some police lives. The gang used the empty cash boxes to jam the service lift, then moved quickly down the back stairs and into the lunchtime traffic of Queen Street.

Just as Bennett had planned, the operation was slick, nobody panicked, and it was over in just 11 minutes. "Without Ray Chuck's thinking, the Great Bookie Robbery would never have been pulled off", Mark Read said. "Ray was a criminal leader whose personal courage gave strength to the men who followed him".

News spread quickly. The nation was aghast. The official statement of the haul said $1.4 million, but it was probably a lot more. Exactly how much was grabbed was to remain known only to the gang members themselves. It could have been as much as $15 million. The bookmakers remained tight-lipped. Many people believed the amount said to have been stolen was grossly understated because the bulk of the cash had not been documented, in order for the bookmakers to avoid turnover tax. News spread overseas. For something as good as this, everybody would want to know about it. Britain had had its Great Train Robbery. So Australia was saying: "Cop that!". The same tactics Bennett had devised were in fact to be used in huge robberies in France and America. International police intelligence indicated the jobs were almost carbon copies of the Great Bookie Robbery.

In Victoria, police responded immediately by setting up a task force. Police in all states were notified. Their inquiries went deep into the underworld throughout the nation. The Victorian police investigation was headed by Alan "Buckets" Anderson. It did not take police long to draw up a shortlist of ringleaders. If Bennett's name was being bandied around in the underworld, it was certain to get back quickly. Police were soon confident that they knew at least some of the perpetrators. Anderson came to believe the gang could not possibly have had the information necessary to carry out the job without a very special form of assistance. "There had to be some inside information", he said.

A group of Sydney-based criminals known as the "Toecutters" also started making inquiries, but for a different reason. The Toecutters were an infamous group which used to torture armed robbers who were known to have done big jobs and to steal their money. Bennett's name started being bandied around, and to the Toecutters he meant trouble. They decided to leave him and his men alone—Bennett would never be stood over and no amount of money was worth what would happen if they tangled with him.

The gang, for its part, did not bother putting its feet up. Within days the members began to put their detailed money-laundering plans into operation. Some of the money was immediately invested in real estate in New South Wales, Queensland and Victoria. The gang had a female expert based in Sydney handle the complex property investments. Police investigations have shown that some of the money went to Manila, via Canada. There was so much money from the robbery that it became an embarrassment. The gang had to find ways of concealing it. Some were quite novel. Bennett's mother collapsed in the waiting room of a Melbourne solicitor. When ambulance officers arrived they cut off her clothes to attempt external heart massage. They found $90,000 in cash concealed in her clothing.

Police turned their attention to Bennett's known associates. One was Norman Lee, Bennett's close friend. "They were like brothers", one policeman said. Police formed a view that Lee had been part of the gang and that he had afterwards been a money launderer. They decided the way to get to the robbers was to try to follow the money trail. It was about the only avenue of inquiry open to them, as there were virtually no clues at the scene. None of the victims could identify the robbers. Bennett had anticipated the police move on Lee. But he was confident, believing Lee would honour his promise to look after the money, and that he would never crack under police questioning. He knew Lee would rather go to gaol than tell the police anything. Lee was, in underworld terms, "staunch".

Police charged Lee, then 28, with the armed robbery of $1,387,540 from the Victorian Club. Police alleged that he once took $60,000 in cash to his solicitor's office inside a plastic garbage bag. He was also charged with receiving $124,000 from the robbery. Police alleged he laundered $110,000 through his solicitor's trust account. Lee had allegedly used the money to buy equipment for his factory and to renovate his home.

Lee did not panic. Even when arrested he stuck to Bennett's plan and did not say a word. He even refused to give his name to police. Detectives got his safe from his office and took it to the quadrangle inside the Russell Street police complex. They were looking for cash or incriminating paperwork. They asked Lee for the keys. He just looked blankly back at them. They were forced to get a safe expert to cut it open for them. It was empty. Purely out of principle, Lee had refused to cooperate with the police and open it, even though there was no evidence inside which could incriminate him.

Lee was acquitted. The magistrate said that while the money might have come from illegal activity, it was impossible to say that it came from the Great Bookie Robbery. Anderson today says he remains convinced that, if they had successfully prosecuted Lee, other arrests would have followed. "I have no doubt that Norman Lee was totally involved in the robbery of the Victorian Club", he said. Lee went off to celebrate his acquittal with a meal in Melbourne's Chinatown. Within days of Lee's acquittal, the police task force on the robbery was disbanded.

It appeared that Bennett and his gang had got away with it, and indeed at the time of writing nobody has been convicted of the robbery of the Victorian Club. But justice sometimes moves in mysterious ways. It would be wrong to suggest that the criminals ended up laughing all the way to the Swiss bank. Nearly every member of the gang was to suffer in one way or another—so much so that their collective fate became known as "The Curse of the Great Bookie Robbery".

While Bennett was quite popular with many in the underworld, he was not without enemies. He was hated by one group which was led by two brothers who were master standover merchants, Les and Brian Kane. The Kane brothers were well known in illegal gambling circles and ran a successful protection racket involving several casinos. The Kanes were also well connected with the notorious Painters and Dockers Union and were a major force in the Victorian underworld. Together with Bennett's gang, the Kanes' gang was regarded as the most professional in Victoria. But the gangs were rivals. Neither side trusted the other and, in a bar at the Richmond Hotel, factions from each became engaged in a vicious brawl, in which Bennett himself nearly lost an ear. The fight sparked virtual all-out war.

Les Kane made some drunken threats against Bennett's family. In the minds of some criminals, those threats marked Kane out for death. Not long after, on 17 October 1978, three men marched into Les Kane's home in the Melbourne suburb of Wantirna and, according to police, pushed him into the bathroom and opened up with machine guns. They allegedly disposed of the body. It has never been found. Some police and criminal figures say the remains were put through Lee's dim sim factory.

Three men, Bennett, Vincent Francis William Mikkelsen and Laurence Joseph Pendergast, were charged with Kane's murder, tried and acquitted. But Bennett was charged with an armed robbery offence (unrelated to the Victorian Club robbery). On 10 November 1979, Bennett was sitting quietly outside Court 10 at the Melbourne Magistrate's Court waiting for the committal proceedings to begin when, in broad daylight, in front of police, public and court staff, a gunman opened fire and killed Bennett in cold blood. As the mortally wounded career criminal grabbed his wounds and staggered a few short steps, shocked police grabbed him, thinking it was an elaborate escape bid. Elaborate it was, but it was no escape bid, it was an audacious murder plot. The gunman had detailed knowledge of the buildings and had organised his escape by bending back tin sheets on a fence at the rear of the property.

There were many rumours about the identity of the gunman. A strong theory was that he was Les Kane's brother, Brian, who had refused to accept the court's verdict that Bennett was not guilty of Les's murder. The theory that Brian Kane had done the payback attracted the attention of Bennett's associates. On 16 July 1981, Mikkelsen's brother-in-law, Norman McLeod, was shot dead as he sat in his car outside his home in the suburb of Coolaroo. The car had been owned by Mikkelsen. Police believe Mikkelsen had been the intended victim. In November 1982, it was payback time again. Brian Kane was sitting next to a girl in the Quarry Hotel in the suburb of Brunswick when a lone gunman came in and shot him dead. The killer was never found, but was believed to be a friend of Bennett's who had been in prison in another state and had escaped. The third man charged with Les Kane's murder, Laurence Pendergast, went missing from his Warrandyte home in August 1985. No sign of him has ever been found. Police believe he is dead.

Without Bennett, "The General", many of his gang went their own way. The huge volume of money was scarcely going to go unnoticed, whatever means were adopted to disguise it. For years, police nationally and internationally believed they came across evidence of where it had gone. Some of it was used to buy into the vice, drug and arms network of Asia. One gang member established a girlie bar in Manila which became a known port-of-call for all Australian criminals overseas. Police investigations showed that Australian drug syndicates were established with cash from the robbery.

Ian Carroll went on to become one of the best planners of armed robberies in the country. He would plan the jobs and then send a "kit" to the location. Each kit would contain handguns and heavy calibre weapons for each crew member. The kits also contained plans, disguises, bandages, sutures, pain killers, antibiotics—in case one of the team was shot—and even magnetic strip signs to disguise the bandits' vehicles. But maybe the particular combination of courage, cunning and ruthlessness that had marked Bennett's career was missing in Carroll. He was shot dead during an argument in the back yard of his Mt Martha safe house in Melbourne in 1983, a killing which has never been solved.

Anthony Paul McNamara took to drugs and like so many other criminals ended up a victim of the needle, dying of a drug overdose in Easey Street, Collingwood in 1990. Some suspect he was deliberately given a drug overdose and in fact murdered. Two brothers suspected of being involved in the Great Bookie Robbery went on to organise their own stick-ups—not so successfully as one was later gaoled for 15 years. The "time and motion man", who could have lived forever without a criminal record, just did not know when to quit. He moved to Sydney and was later convicted over his part in a railway payroll grab. He has served his time and vanished from public view.

A man who organised the cars and helped launder the money

moved to Manila where he became an international vice, drugs and firearms broker. When he returned to Australia he drove a Rolls Royce and wore flashy gold jewellery valued at $322,000. He became a major financial contributor to an Australian Rules football club and a heavy punter with interests in several harness horses. He was the principal figure in eight Costigan Royal Commission references handed to the National Crime Authority (NCA) and he was the subject of three Australian Federal Police secret task forces. He was eventually arrested by the NCA and sentenced to 11 years gaol for drug offences.

The quiet man of the robbery, Norman Lee, faded from public view after his acquittal, eventually selling his business and moving to Singapore. That might have been the last that was ever heard of him. But, in 1992, he was back to his old tricks when he joined in the attempted robbery of an armoured van in Melbourne. Members of the Police Special Operations Group were waiting and Lee was shot dead.

Many original gang members were unable or unwilling to use the money made from the heist to get out of crime altogether. Whether it was greed, whether it was because they knew no other life, or simply because they missed the adrenalin surge from planning and committing violent crime, few of them were able to walk away. Though the crime at the Victorian Club was grand in its conception and brilliant in execution, they remained essentially small men, inhabiting the same jungle as before. According to Delianis, the luck ran out for the gang when they got away with the Great Bookie Robbery. "Perhaps if we had more evidence and they had gone to gaol, they would be alive today", he said. "They were in a dog-eat-dog business and they paid the price. Live by the sword, die by the sword".

BATTLE FOR
THE WATERFRONT

VIOLENCE AND DEATH IN A MELBOURNE UNION

Freddie "The Frog" Harrison was a gunman, standover man and debt-collector for illegal gambling houses and SP bookmakers, one of Melbourne's most feared and violent gangsters. He had, according to police, killed at least two men and wounded many others. With his wide-brimmed hat, expensive overcoat and flash cars, he looked every inch the gangster. In fact he loved the image and could be found at the pictures, watching the latest George Raft or Jimmy Cagney crime movies. Harrison also had close links to an industrial union with tentacles throughout the waterfront, the Federated Ship Painters and Dockers' Union (FSPDU).

For decades "The Dockies", as they were commonly known, had been more than a union. Criminals had joined in 1939 to avoid wartime manpower regulations. From then on, the union had represented an uneasy alliance between men who did a dangerous and physically demanding job and criminals who used The Dockies as a front. Work on the waterfront was on a casual basis. Workers would turn up when they wanted to see what jobs were available; a crook could give the appearance of full-time employment.

The fact that there was a criminal element in the union became obvious enough. Union members became involved in the underworld gang wars that regularly flared in the streets and pubs of Melbourne. Men went missing, others were gunned down in broad daylight as the affairs of the underworld became inextricably mixed with those of the union. There grew up within the union a feeling of self-reliance and contempt for outside authority. An FSPDU secretary, Terry Gordon, was quoted as saying: "We catch and kill our own".

On 1 February 1958, Freddie Harrison went pig-shooting in New South Wales with two FSPDU members, Harold Nugent and John Eric Twist. On the weekend, there was a falling-out in the group and a shot was fired, badly damaging Nugent's hand. Police were to believe forever after that Harrison fired the shot. Nugent was always to claim it was simply an accident. The men returned home and, on 6 February, Harrison was at No 13, South Wharf, returning to a trailer he had borrowed from a friend. At 4.40 pm he was kneeling, about to uncouple the trailer from his 1953 Ford Customline, when a man walked up to him and said: "This is yours, Fred!". The man then blasted Harrison with a shotgun from less than a metre away.

Constable Reginald George Wilkinson noticed a boy scurrying off near the docks with something hidden in his cardigan. He apprehended and searched the teenager, and found he had been carrying a cardboard ammunition carton containing 12-gauge shotgun cartridges. There were 22 of them, and a further two shells in the boy's pocket. The box had originally contained 25 shells. The boy, Charles Joseph Wootton, aged 15, of Punt Road, Windsor, told police he had found the box. The shells contained number four shot, the same type used to kill Harrison 150 metres away. Wootton was Harold Nugent's stepson.

But the police continuing to investigate the killing walked into a virtual brick wall, which was enormously frustrating because there had been plenty of witnesses. At least 30 dockies had been standing nearby when Harrison was gunned down. They had been working on a ship, the *River Murchison*, moored at the wharf. They told police they had seen nothing. Several had to concede that something had happened, because they had been close enough to be spattered with Harrison's blood and brains. But they told police they were unable to remember anything about the gunman. The killing of Harrison was never solved, although police always believed that it was John Eric Twist, later suspected of being involved in drugs, who had pulled the trigger. If he was responsible, Twist was to take the secret with him to the grave when he died of cancer in Queensland in the 1980s.

The tale of Harrison and his kind was to be repeated again and again in the violence that surrounded the FSPDU. Police were to say later that of Victoria's top 100 criminals, at least 70 had links with the union which was at the forefront of new developments in organised crime. They were into illegal gambling, later huge armed robberies, and still later, the smuggling of drugs, illegal aliens and weapons. There was hardly a trick that the Dockies did not exploit. After the death of union secretary Jimmy Donnegan from a liver complaint in 1970, a violent power struggle began which, on the surface, was over control of union affairs. In reality, it was a battle over who would control a large slice of the Melbourne underworld.

There were two camps, one run by the popular union secretary, Pat Shannon, and the other by an FSPDU executive, Billy "The Texan" Longley. The two, and their backers, were not backward in demonstrating what an advantage it would be to vote for them. Shannon wanted to be re-elected as secretary, Longley wanted the union presidency. Among the supporters were some of Melbourne's most violent criminals. The two camps, split into the white ticket (Shannon) and the blue reform card (Longley), lobbied hard. The election was to be on Friday, 10 December 1971.

About three weeks before the election, one of Longley's closest friends and supporters in the union, Robert John Crotty, was attacked and beaten with a housebrick outside a South Melbourne hotel. Crotty suffered multiple fractures of the skull. Witnesses told police: "Crotty fell over and hurt himself". Crotty was incapacitated, and was to spend the last seven years of his life as a virtual vegetable before dying in 1978.

The attack on Crotty marked what was an undeclared war, and there were more victims. Billy Longley lived in a heavily-fortified house in Port Melbourne. A shotgun was fired into the gate to his home. A week before the election, Longley went into hiding, though his wife and child remained in the house.

Three days before the election, Alfred Desmond "The Ferret" Nelson, the union's unofficial welfare officer, good friend of Shannon and a popular figure on the waterfront, went missing. Police investigating got information that he had been abducted from his home in Langridge Street, Collingwood, as he was having his shower. The first suggestion was that he had been "buried" with his two-door, automatic Valiant Charger sedan. Six weeks after the disappearance, police found the car deep in the Yarra slime off No 21, South Wharf. They jemmied open the boot fully expecting to find the body but only found a child's car seat and some hessian bags. "The Ferrett" had always used the seat for his pet dog, a silky-haired terrier. Nelson's body was never found. Five men were supposed to have been involved in his abduction but there were no arrests.

The next to go was Desmond St Bernard "Cossie" Costello, a well-known criminal and former friend of Nelson. Costello was hardly a pushover. Nearly ten years earlier he had been acquitted of the shooting murder of Melbourne criminal, Osmond James "Hoppy" Kelly. Now he was thought to have been involved in the killing of Nelson. The job the killers did on Costello was very efficient. His body, blasted by a .12-gauge and a .410-guage shotgun, was found dumped in an excavation ditch on the site of the new Eastern Freeway at Clifton Hill. An arm was shattered and part of a hand had been blown away. Police heard claims that he had been dragged, bare-footed, from his home in East Preston, that he had asked for a cigarette and been refused, that when the moment came he had tried to protect his face with his arm and the shotgun blast had gone straight through it. Police held two theories. One was that Costello had been killed as a payback for the murder of Nelson. The other was that a gang of criminals wanted the money he was reputed to have gained from a $587,000 armed robbery in Sydney.

On the union's election day, 10 December, there were at least two gunfights. About 7.15 am, 45 minutes before polling was to begin, a carload of men arrived at the Williamstown docks. They forced their votes into the box and then stayed in their car, with a machine-gun trained on other voters. Another group arrived and a gun battle ensued, in which three men were reportedly shot and 50 shots were fired into the car. The car itself was taken away and cut up with oxy-acetylene torches to keep it away from the police. One ballot box was reportedly stolen and votes for the Longley team taken out and replaced with votes for the Shannon team. Then there was another gunfight, at the union offices in South Melbourne.

The next day firefighters found the burnt-out car of a Shannon supporter, union vigilance officer Doug Sproule. When asked about the incident, Sproule said: "It could have been spontaneous combustion". On 30 December, two dockers were hit by a gunshot blast fired from a car in Gertrude Street, Fitzroy. One of them, Lawrence Chamings, 23, was shot in the shoulder. On 24 January 1972, the FSPDU South Melbourne office was firebombed. Union papers, including some of the ballot, were destroyed in the fire.

The following morning a bomb was thrown at the Longley house, which had been vacated by Longley's wife and daughter 15 minutes earlier.

The next day the election results were proclaimed at a meeting of the union. The Shannon ticket was declared the winner. Allegations about ballot-rigging were raised immediately.

In March a young painter and docker, Ronald "Joey" Hamilton, was shot and seriously injured when he opened the door at his sister's City Garden home. A few days later a shotgun blast shattered the window of a house in St Kilda. Police believed the offender got the wrong house and was looking for a neighbour, Charlie Wootton, now a well-known painter and docker who had moved on since the time he was apprehended carrying away the shotgun shells from the scene of the Freddie Harrison murder. Next to become a target was James Frederick Bazley, who stood as vigilance officer on the Longley ticket. In May 1972 he was outside his home in North Carlton when 14 shots were fired at him. He was hit in the thigh and shoulder. In September, while he was sitting in his car at Carlton, he was again shot at and again hit twice, in the head and hand. Though his survival on both occasions was lucky, it was not to dissuade Bazley from a life of crime. And the violence, even by the loose standards of the painters and dockers, was out of control.

Pat Shannon as union secretary wanted to claw back some sort of public respectability for his organisation. In May 1972 he said: "Remember, no stray bullet or bomb has harmed a non-unionist". Even that was to be an empty boast. The head of the Victorian Homicide Squad, Detective Inspector Kevin Carton, was so concerned about the continuing violence that he wrote a secret report to the State Government calling for a judicial inquiry into the union. He got no response.

In April 1973, the inevitable happened—innocent people got caught in the crossfire. In suburban Melbourne, Zlatko Kolvorat left his home with his two sons, Nicholas, 10, and Peter, 12, to get fish and chips for the family's Easter Saturday night dinner. He knew it would take five or ten minutes for the fish to cook and decided to buy his sons a lemonade in the nearby Moonee Valley Hotel while he had a beer. As the family were sitting drinking together, painter and docker Lawrence Richard Chamings walked in. Following Chamings was another man armed with a .32 calibre pistol. He pointed the gun at Chamings and started firing repeatedly. One of the shots hit Kolvorat in the stomach. Kolvorat pushed Peter to the floor and tried to grab Nicholas. Nicholas turned towards the gunman and was hit between the eyes, falling mortally wounded into his father's arms. Another drinker in the hotel was wounded. The gunman chased Chamings across the bar. Armed himself with a pistol, Chamings knew he had no time to draw it and that his only recourse lay in escape. He tried to get through a door into an outside toilet block but did not make it. The gunman shot him down.

Kolvorat, whose innocent trip to buy dinner had resulted in the death of his son, said of the gunman: "He was laughing while he was shooting". Police arrested one Barry "The Bear" Kable and charged him with the shootings. But Kable was acquitted. In Sydney later, Kable was attacked by three men, bashed, and left with a blood clot in the brain.

The war continued. At 9.55 pm on 17 October 1973, Shannon was drinking in a hotel in South Melbourne when a man walked in carrying a .22 calibre rifle. He pumped three shots into Shannon, killing him instantly. Police arrested four men over the murder: Billy Longley, Kevin James Taylor, Gary Leslie Harding and Alfred Leslie Cannott. Harding made a three-page statement to police, telling them his version of events. In court, the Crown alleged that Longley paid Taylor $6,000 for the hit and that Harding pointed Shannon out to Taylor in the hotel. Harding's evidence was that he waited in the car and Taylor ran up, threw the gun into the back seat and said: "I shot him, I got him". Longley, Taylor and Harding were convicted of Shannon's murder. Cannott was convicted of manslaughter. Within 12 months Harding was dead, hacked to death in his Pentridge Gaol cell.

Shannon was replaced as secretary of the union in 1974 by Jack "Putty Nose" Nicholls, who was very defensive of the union's reputation. But the reality belied what Nicholls was saying. The Dockies continued to be a law unto themselves. Many branched out into full-time crime—and many paid with their lives. Victor Frederick Allard left the docks to become a major heroin dealer. In 1977, he was shot in the stomach while drinking in a St Kilda hotel. He later agreed to break the underworld code of silence and became a secret police informer on a major drug ring. The police offered him protection but he told them he felt safer on the street where nobody would suspect he was a double agent. He was wrong. On 9 February 1979, he was shot dead in an execution-style hit in Fitzroy Street, St Kilda.

Many other unionists died violently through underworld feuds and power plays. But Longley, the man some said was at the top of many death lists, continued to survive. There was a price on his head, but he also had strong men on his side. Always maintaining his innocence of the Shannon killing, Longley was desperate for a new trial which he hoped would clear his name. He saw publicity as his only hope. In 1980 he did what was considered, till then, the unthinkable: he told the inside story of the union in a most public way by agreeing to be interviewed for a series of articles in *The Bulletin*. The resulting articles caused a bigger explosion than any bomb thrown by a docker on the outside could have done. Longley told of how the union served as a front for organised crime and that millions of dollars were made through illegal activity and corruption.

"Don't let anyone kid you that there is not corruption on the Australian waterfront", he said. "It is rife. The private sector is open slather to graft and corruption. You can simply name your price. Millions have been made from criminal activities and corruption. The money comes from ghosting, slings robberies etc … I could name 20 or 30 people who have been knocked by painters and dockers. They have either been killed for money or simply their mouths. This is just not in Melbourne, but in Sydney, Brisbane and Perth".

"Ghosting" was a word that pricked up many ears. It had been rumoured for years that shipping agents were prepared to spend big dollars to ensure that ships were not held up in docks. Quick turnaround was important and if money could grease the wheels so that they turned more quickly, then so be it. Ghosting was simple. The Dockies might need 15 men to do the job but bill the agent for 60 men's wages. The men who did not turn up but were paid were known as ghosts.

Longley said ghosting had been occurring. Not only that, he said that one of the organisers of that racket had at one time taken out a contract to murder someone and killed an innocent person instead. Longley said that the man had got away with it. Victorian police launched an investigation into Longley's claims but came back with a report which played down the statements. Prime Minister Malcolm Fraser was, however, far more interested. Longley's claims, particularly relating to ghosting, concerned him greatly. He decided that only a royal commission could settle the question once and for all of what was happening in the union. In that, Fraser was supported by the Victorian Government.

The two governments picked a mild-mannered Queen's Counsel with a love of Italian food and little experience in criminal matters. His name: Francis Xavier Costigan. Costigan opened his hearings in the Williamstown Court, Victoria, on 1 October 1980 with more than 200 union members protesting outside.

One of the Dockies' staunchest and loudest defenders was Putty Nose Nicholls, who said allegations of the union being a front for organised crime were nonsense. "It makes me dirty when our members, good members and citizens, are persecuted for the crimes of a few", he said. Nicholls hated the commission and on 16 June 1981 failed to answer a subpoena to give evidence before Costigan in Melbourne. Two hours later his body was found, slumped over the front seat of his light blue Falcon sedan. He died from a single bullet wound to the head. A letter, deemed to have been his suicide note, said: "To my members and executive, I tried very hard but the rotten Fraser government did not want me to survive. Do not think I have taken the easy way out but the rotten system has cut my life short. I had big ideas for advancement but these were chopped short. Farewell Comrades, Jack Nicholls".

The death did not stop the Costigan juggernaut. For the first nine months it followed the predictable course of investigating the painters and dockers and their criminal associates. But then, opting to follow the money trail using computer techniques, it opened up vast new vistas of infinitely more interesting illegal activity. When it was found that painters and dockers had been enlisted by "tax avoidance" experts to be dummy directors of sham companies which had false addresses, the royal commission began inquiries which in effect took it into the boardrooms of the nation. Costigan's team found that some dockers were deliberately helping in "bottom of the harbour" tax schemes, but the real villainy was being perpetrated by people who were quite unused to physical labour and might never have had a fist-fight.

The tax avoidance schemes, it was found, had cost the country hundreds of millions of dollars. The commission, which went for four years, gathered, in round figures: three million documents, 20,000 exhibits, 1,000 witness interviews and 80,000 names for entry into its computer. It was responsible for the launching of some 1,000 prosecutions.

The commission split the legal community. Some lawyers thought it was the only way to expose crime and corruption in Australia, others thought it a massive invasion of civil liberties. But there could be little doubting its value as a lid-lifting exercise. The *Sydney Morning Herald* editorialised in September 1982: "A thread pulled from the Ship Painters and Dockers' Union has led to the Victorian Government land deals in 1973 and 1974 and in turn to bottom-of-the-harbour tax evasion schemes, to the Nugan Hand Bank, to drug-running, and to the Deputy Crown Solicitor's Office in Perth—and the unravelling continues. Where Mr Costigan's search will finally lead is anyone's guess".

In his final report, delivered in November 1984, Costigan was scathing of the FSPDU. "The union has attracted to its ranks large numbers of men who have been convicted of, and who continue to commit, serious crimes", he said. "They treat the law with contempt, and are scornful of its punishments. They treat law enforcement agencies as their enemies. They are motivated by greed and are not controlled by any consideration for their victims. Violence is the means by which they control the members of their group. They do not hesitate to kill ..."

But it was obvious to all that the villainy went well beyond the painters and dockers. The Federal Government's response to the royal commission was to establish the National Crime Authority, one of the most important innovations in law enforcement in this country, and ironically the product of the activities of one of the country's most lawless groups. The Dockies had unwittingly forced politicians and police to confront an issue they should have dealt with generations earlier. The full exploration of their actions convinced authorities that organised crime was out of control and that there was a crying need for a national attack on the canker. It was years too late, but at least it was a start.

THE TRURO MURDERS

SEVEN BODIES, ONE MADMAN

Anzac Day, 1978. A man, searching for wild mushrooms in desolate bushland near Truro, 80 kilometres northwest of Adelaide, on the outskirts of South Australia's picturesque Barossa Valley, makes a grim discovery. Spread out before him are the scattered remains of a young woman—and the dreadful saga of the state's Truro Murders begins.

When police arrived to investigate the discovery, the scene had all the hallmarks of a murder. The body, as was the case in scores of incidents all over Australia, had been taken into the bush and dumped. It was to be identified later as the remains of a missing Adelaide teenager, Veronica Knight. There were no obvious clues. It would go into the crime files as a murder inquiry but with no outlandish features. A hitchhiker perhaps? Someone lured to a stranger's home after a night at the disco? Happens all the time.

Later that year, the skeletal remains of another young woman were found near Murray Bridge, east of Adelaide. They were identified as those of Maria Dickinson, 20, who had been missing for eight months. She had been shot in the head. This discovery was followed in March 1978 by the abduction and murder of another young Adelaide woman, Lina Marciano, 20, who was severely bashed and stabbed numerous times. Her body was found at a rubbish tip in a northern suburb of Adelaide.

For South Australia's police there was a distinct possibility that the three murders were connected. They were all of young women who had disappeared in the space of two months, and they had all apparently taken place in the northern suburbs or north of Adelaide. The head of the SA Police Major Crime Squad, Detective Superintendent Ken Thorsen, assigned Sergeant Bob "Hugger" Giles to look at any possible connection between the cases.

Thorsen and Giles were veterans. They had worked together for many years. Giles came into Thorsen's office for a meeting which, in terms of great Australian crimes, was historic. "I can remember, to this day, him coming into my office with a bundle of papers", Thorsen said in retirement years later. "He told me he had not had any luck with anything similar on the Marciano or Dickinson cases, but that he would show me what he had come up with".

Giles handed Thorsen a missing person report. "I read it and Bob told me to read the back, which I did, and it had been recorded as, "Voluntarily missing from home", he said. Giles said, "That's bull ... ", and he then systematically went through another six missing person reports on young women. One of those reports was that of Veronica Knight.

The murders of Maria Dickinson and Lina Marciano might have been related to that of Veronica Knight. But what interested police was the pattern in the reports of young women who were listed as missing between December 1976 and February 1977. As Thorsen reviewed the cases, a disturbing thought emerged. Could they have been picked up by a maniac on some "killing spree"?

Thorsen again looked at the reports, which disclosed: Veronica Knight, vanished from Rundle Mall, Adelaide City, about 9.20 pm on 23 December 1976; Tania Kenny, 15, vanished from an Adelaide street about midday on 12 January 1977; Julie Mykyta, 16, last seen getting into a white Valiant station wagon in King William Street, Adelaide, about 10.30 pm on 21 January 1977.

The reports also disclosed the disappearances of: Vicki Howell, 26, last seen near the City about 7 pm on 2 February 1977; Sylvia Pittman, 16, last seen near her suburban Taperoo home about 7 pm on 6 February 1977; Connie Iordanides, 16, last seen near her suburban Brooklyn Park home about 7 pm on 9 February 1977; and Deborah Lamb, 20, who was last seen in the City about 6 pm on 12 February 1977.

The similarities were far too obvious to be ignored. Staring from the picture board, beaming out upon the world, with all the exuberance of youth, the missing girls were screaming out in their very silence that they were gone.

"We were both of the opinion that the others, like Veronica Knight, were probably dead also", Thorsen said later. He had told Giles to continue his inquiries. "I wanted the families to understand we were still making inquiries, I wanted Giles to get every bit of background information possible and I told him to work alone with no leaks to the press and to be discreet with what he told the victims' families".

Thorsen had a number of serious concerns. He did not want the suspected serial killer to be alerted to the fact that police were becoming aware of what he was doing. He wanted responsibility for the investigation to pass quietly to the Major Crime Squad who would set about their job discreetly and professionally. He knew that if media publicity blew up that the disappearances had been categorised as "missing persons" rather than suspected murders, it would be embarrassing to the Police Department. He could see as a future headline that a life could have been spared had police woken up earlier to the fact that a serial killer was on the loose.

Days later, Thorsen presented a comprehensive report for the Police Commissioner, Laurie Draper, outlining the "serial killer" theory. Draper went along with Thorsen's recommendations. He directed that the Major Crime Squad investigate, and that the operation be kept secret.

Thorsen was confronted with a manpower problem. Most of the experienced investigators were on other major inquiries. The two who were not got the job—Sergeant Glen Lawrie, a somewhat bohemian character but a talented detective, and Senior Constable Peter Foster, a younger detective who had impressed superiors with his hard work and versatility. They needed those qualities, because the task was daunting. They had only one body from this series of seven apparently connected disappearances and no suspects.

It was open to Lawrie and Foster to examine the circumstances of the seven disappearances and to note similarities among the victims. If the seven victims were in fact part of a killing spree by a single deranged individual, it was important to note the timings, anything at all, that could produce a pattern. Once a pattern was established, it was necessary to ask what was significant about discrepancies in that pattern? If their theory was correct, why had the "killings" stopped after the seventh victim?

The investigators also attempted to build up a "psychological profile" of the suspected serial killer—a technique which could only ever produce a guide, but which was certainly better than nothing. What Lawrie and Foster came up with was this: the offender was likely to be a local man, a sex offender, likely to have been released from gaol just before the first murder, and that he was likely to have been returned to prison for some reason after the seventh apparent murder. Lawrie and Foster concentrated on lists of known sex offenders and people who had been released from prison in that period.

It really was not much to go on. Lawrie and Foster laboured on, impeded by the fact that they had to maintain such secrecy. The year passed with no progress. Then on Easter Sunday, 1979, the remains of Sylvia Pittman were discovered near Truro, two kilometres from where the body of Veronica Knight had been found. Sylvia had been on the list of missing girls. Thorsen's theory was looking more and more to be true—and his worst fears to be confirmed. The bushland east of Truro looked as though it was the dumping ground for the victims of a serial killer. The news broke.

It was necessary to search the Truro area. The task was not made any easier when Thorsen discovered that the SA Police's newly-created "STAR Force" was about to do a training exercise in the Flinders Ranges. Thorsen exploded. "I [told] my boss that I would not accept that, as we were confronted with possibly the greatest homicide investigation in South Australian history, [and] I was being denied use of our specialist section because of a training exercise!", he said later. The logic looked compelling, even without the anger, and the police force gave way. Thorsen got the services of the STAR Force and anything else he required.

The media went into overdrive. Publicity spread around the nation. The names of the two apparent murder victims and the other five missing women were publicised. The State Government announced a reward of $20,000 for information leading to the conviction of the offender or offenders. The *Advertiser*, Adelaide's morning newspaper, offered a reward of its own—$10,000. The Government increased its offer to $30,000.

The reward offer brought results, though the information that came to the police was kept confidential. A man approached police saying that a woman friend of his had had a conversation with one James William Miller (born 1937), in which Miller had made statements incriminating of himself and another man, Christopher Robin Worrell (born 1954). Miller's statements to the woman had been made on 22 February 1977, two days after the death of Worrell in a car smash in the southeast of the state. The woman had told her sister about the conversation. The sister had told her husband, and he had decided to go to the police.

The date of the alleged statements was from the very outset significant to the police. Worrell's death occurred eight days after the disappearance of the last girl on the list, Deborah Lamb.

When interviewed by police, the woman Miller had allegedly spoken to made a formal statement. In part, it said: "About two days after the accident in which Chris was killed I was at a friend's ... place talking to Jamie [Miller] in the backyard, he kept on talking about Chris, he was crying and talking about committing suicide, we talked for some time.

"Jamie started talking about what he and Chris used to do together. He said they used to con these "camp" guys by leading them up the garden path, they would take them back to the camp guy's place and tell them that if they didn't give them money they would let everyone know what they were like. The conversation then changed from camp guys and Jamie said to me that I didn't really know what Chris was like.

"I was unable to recall the exact conversation but he said that he and Chris used to pick girls up and kill them. He did not use the word "kill", it was some form of Australian slang. I am unable to recall the exact words he used but he made it quite clear that they had killed girls. I saw that he was serious about what he was saying so I questioned him further. He said that he couldn't stop Chris from doing this, that he would just pick them up and rape them and strangle them. Jamie said that he just drove the vehicle for Chris.

"I questioned him further about this and Jamie said that if I didn't believe him he would take me up to Blanchetown [near Truro] and show me the bodies of the girls that they had killed. I got the impression of what he said that there were about six victims. Jamie said that one of them had been strangled with a guitar string. Jamie said he couldn't stop Chris from raping and killing these girls. They were not his exact words but that was the meaning conveyed to me. He [Miller] said that just before Chris died he got worse and really went mad and killed a number of them.

"At the time of Jamie telling me this he was serious about it and I have no doubt in my mind he was telling the truth. I thought about it for some time and decided that I would not say anything because if it was as Jamie said it was Chris who done it, then nothing could be done and Chris was dead anyway".

The information on Worrell fitted perfectly with the offender profile Lawrie and Foster had initially drawn up. Worrell had been convicted and gaoled for attempted rape. He had been released from Adelaide's Yatala Prison in October 1976, just a few weeks before the first disappearance, that of Veronica Knight. If he was the offender, then his death in the car smash accounted completely for the halt to the disappearances. In one fell swoop, so it seemed, the police had identified both the principal offender—Worrell—and his willing accomplice, Miller. Thorsen reacted cautiously. He did not want Miller tipped off that they were on to him. But he had to be located. A Social Security check revealed that he was on the dole and that welfare cheques were being sent to an address in inner Adelaide. They were cashed, but irregularly. Police set up surveillance on the address.

Commissioner Draper returned from holidays. He summoned Thorsen to his office and asked how the operation was going. Thorsen said: "We are not without a chance ..." Draper asked Thorsen who else knew about it. Thorsen replied: "Lawrie, Foster, myself and now you". Draper told him to keep it that way.

On 26 April 1979, soon after the surveillance operation had started, searchers at Truro found two more skeletons, the remains of Vicki Howell and Connie Iordanides. They were found in the same paddock, a kilometre from where the skeleton of Veronica Knight had been found. Further searching revealed nothing more; the other three young women on the list—Tania Kenny, Julie Mykyta and Deborah Lamb—remained unaccounted for.

The *Australian* reported: "Mass killer is on loose, say police". Across the country police turned up files on unsolved murders of young women.

The search of the Truro area was exhaustive and when nothing further was found, it was called off. A few days later, on 23 May 1979, the police surveillance team spotted Miller, in Gouger Street in inner Adelaide. Lawrie and Foster were alerted, hurried to the scene and approached Miller, just opposite Adelaide's central market. They asked him to go to Police Headquarters for a talk. He agreed, arriving there with Lawrie and Foster just after 4 pm, and was taken to the Major Crime Squad offices.

Lawrie and Foster interviewed Miller for several hours, while Thorsen listened in an adjoining room. Miller made no admissions. Thorsen called Lawrie out. Later, he said: "It was my opinion Miller was unlikely to make any admissions and to continue the interrogation too long would cause any judge to rule it inadmissible. Lawrie agreed with me. He went back into the interview room to wind up the interview and take Miller to the charge room".

Lawrie, Foster and Miller left the interview room. There was enough evidence to charge Miller, but without an admission the process of justice would take longer. Thorsen rang Draper to tell him what had happened. He had just put down the telephone when Lawrie rushed in. "Guess what!", Lawrie said. "We took him to the charge room and started the system and he [Miller] said he would take us and show us where the other bodies are. What do we do now?"

Thorsen was faced with a difficult legal and procedural problem. It was 8 pm. According to the law, it was necessary now to charge Miller and to either grant him bail or take him before a court. Bail was out of the question. Leaving Miller in the cells overnight might have rebounded on them because he might have changed his mind about showing them where the bodies were. It was possible to take him before a night court but if they did that Miller, who till then had not asked for a lawyer, might ask for legal representation. If that happened, the legal advice and representation might be that he was not obliged to cooperate with the police and this opportunity would be lost.

Thorsen said later: "It was a decision that had to be made and we knew if he showed us the other bodies we would have had a case he would not get out of. I made the decision to take him to Truro to show us the bodies and have him back for court by 10 am the next day".

It took several hours for Thorsen to organise a night time search near Truro. The forensic team was recalled, a pathologist located and other detectives briefed. Thorsen left a message with the operations sergeant to say that if the media called that night about any developments in the case, he was simply to say that detectives were making further inquiries and a statement would be issued in the morning. Somehow the news leaked out, and when Thorsen, Lawrie and Foster arrived at Truro with Miller, two reporters from the *Advertiser* were already there. They were briefed by police on what was happening and asked to remain in the background.

The cold, pitch-black country night came to life as Miller directed the detectives through Truro and out past the paddocks where the first four bodies had been found. Thorsen said later: "He [Miller] directed us to a track running off the Sturt Highway in a northerly direction. After about 500 metres we stopped and got out of the vehicles and Miller led us about 300 metres into the scrub to a large bush. He then told us he thought that was the one". With the aid of a large torch the detectives could see a skeleton, curled up under the branch of a bush. The skeleton was Julie Mykyta. Miller then directed the detectives to Port Gawler beach, 50 kilometres north of Adelaide, to search for another victim. At the beach, the police were confronted by darkness and a maze of tracks. "He had little difficulty finding the place to tell us where to dig", Thorsen said. "It was just getting light when we eventually located the body of Deborah Lamb".

The discoveries were absolutely dreadful, the sort of discoveries that live with even the most hardened police till the end of their careers and forever after—the stark evidence of human bestiality. Deborah's body had been buried in a makeshift grave and the grave covered with timber and iron. A pathologist who examined the body said that, of all the findings, the remains of this victim showed most signs of violent physical attack. Her ankles and wrists had been bound with nylon cord. Her pantyhose had been wrapped around her neck and mouth. Sand and shellgrit were found in her lungs—an indication that in all probability she had been buried alive.

Miller told the police that the remaining victim was buried at Gillman, an isolated area on the outskirts of Adelaide. Police searched where he told them to but could find no body. Miller was taken back to Adelaide and put before a court. Police continued to search the area. Later in the day, as they were getting the assistance of a council grader operator to unearth an area around a new road construction site, they would find the skeleton of Tania Kenny. They had them all. All seven young women. All accounted for. All dead.

Miller appeared in Adelaide Magistrate's Court on Friday, 24 May. He was charged with the murders of Veronica Knight, Sylvia Pittman, Vicki Howell and Connie Iordanides, whose bodies had been positively identified. Miller was remanded in custody. Later, he was charged with the murders of Tania Kenny, Julie Mykyta and Deborah Lamb. The public glimpsed for a time some of the agony. Rhonda Evelyn Lamb, mother of Debbie Lamb, gave evidence, began weeping and collapsed as she left the witness box. Andreas Pittman rose to his feet in the court on another occasion and shouted: "Miller—damn you! I shall never forget your face!".

The horror for a time fixed the attention of the nation—on Adelaide. Sydney journalist Tony Stevens wrote in the *Sydney Sun-Herald*: "Adelaide is sometimes known as the city of churches. There also remains a quaint pride that, unlike Sydney, Melbourne or Brisbane, Colonel William Light's city was never a penal colony. There is a feeling that the most horrific aspects of life are best left to places like Sydney. Yet South Australia has its share of weirdness..."

Miller was committed for trial in the South Australian Supreme Court. On 12 March 1980, after a six-week trial, he was found guilty of six counts of murder and acquitted on one—that of Veronica Knight. Miller was gaoled for life. A subsequent appeal was dismissed and he was refused leave to appeal to the High Court.

Serious questions were raised as to how such horror could have occurred and how it could have going unnoticed for so long. The *National Times* said: "There is an underlying question about the Truro murder case: how could seven young women disappear from the streets of Adelaide, within a period of two months in the summer of 1976–77, and no trace be found of their fate until a bushwalker accidentally tripped over a skeleton 80 kilometres away, 16 months later?". Veteran Melbourne crime reporter Bill Hitchings, writing in the *Sydney Morning Herald*, indicated that as far as serial killings went it might have been just another case of Australia catching up with the rest of the world. The United Kingdom had its Christie and its Yorkshire Ripper, the United States its Bundy.

Miller himself attempted to tell the world how, in his case, it all came about. In 1984 he published a book, *Don't Call Me a Killer*. Claiming innocence and seeking a retrial, he said he had been infatuated with the much younger and more handsome Worrell, and it was this that had prevented him from telling authorities about Worrell's perverse sexual habits and horrible murder techniques. Going on a hunger strike to try to force the issue of his innocence, he said: "I am doing Chris's time. I am not a murderer". Miller did not get a retrial and in March 1993, when the question of parole was considered, the full horror of the events was revived. The director of the SA Victims of Crime Service, Andrew Paterson, thought of the safety of society when he said: "There's no indication from Miller that he is showing remorse".

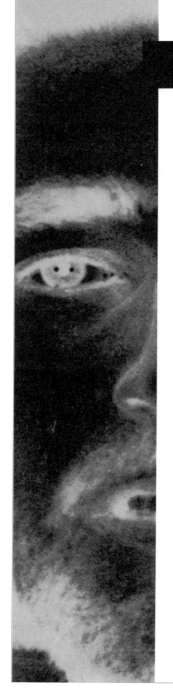

DRUGS, GANGSTERS AND GRANNIES

The period that was the 80s could really be called the drug era. Not that narcotics were unknown before that. Experimenting with LSD had in all probability cost Dr Bogle and Mrs Chandler their lives on New Years Day, 1963. But by the late 1970s illicit drugs had become a problem so huge it threatened to break down the traditional structures of law enforcement. A point where that threat might be said to have acquired crisis proportions can be precisely dated—15 July 1977—when Donald Bruce Mackay, a businessman from Griffith in southern New South Wales, was murdered.

In the immediate aftermath of the Mackay killing, marijuana was the issue. But it later became evident that the crime syndicate responsible for Mackay's death had been flirting with heavier stuff, heroin. The Clark syndicate, which combined fabulous profits with brutal murder, had come onto the scene. The fact that the marijuana industry had become so big in the Riverina was due partly to the complicity of local police. This raised larger questions about law enforcement—the performance of the NSW Police in investigating the murder was not beyond criticism.

The Barlow and Chambers saga was always tragic. The Malaysians insisted on imposing a penalty that would not have been enacted in this country. Australians were torn between condemnation of heroin trafficking and intense sympathy for the condemned men whose home country had long dispensed with capital punishment. But the extraordinary financial rewards—so much money, as the international trafficker Terry Clark once said, that he could not spend the interest—meant that however high the risks, others were prepared to have a go.

In our third chapter in this section we return to traditional gangland, this time with the vicious Walsh Street shootings in Melbourne and the subsequent shootings by police. The underworld was cynical about the actions of police which resulted in the deaths of two men, whatever the police might have said by way of justification. There is little doubt that, as with the unintended shooting in Sydney in 1989 of an innocent Aboriginal man, David Gundy, the police hunt for people who attack and kill their own number is thorough and at times ruthless. But it is a natural reaction of those who guard the thin blue line between law and order and chaos, and who are bound together for mutual protection.

The career of Arthur Stanley "Neddy" Smith probably marries these two strands of Australia's criminal history—traditional gangsterism and drugs. His world, as revealed in evidence before the NSW Independent Commission Against Corruption, has been one of gunshops, molls and fellow gangsters, with a handful of crooked police thrown in. The real question that emerged from his evidence was how easily it appeared Smith had been able to obtain heroin and how easily he had been able to market it, apparently without fear of arrest. When he was nabbed, it was for murder.

The final chapter is devoted to John Wayne Glover, the English immigrant with the wretchedly unhappy up-bringing, who was given the best possible start in adult life by marrying a competent and loyal wife who encouraged him to make the best of himself. She took him to live in the comfortable environs of her parents' home in Sydney's Mosman. Glover rewarded that faith by murdering some of society's most vulnerable citizens—elderly women. When he went on trial, there was an attempt to prove some sort of mental illness. But the jury preferred more pedestrian logic and put the killer away.

With Glover gone, the elderly continue to trudge slowly along the streets of Mosman, as they have a perfect right to do, protected by a society which is mercifully deficient in those who would prey on them. But children also play in the parks and accept lifts from strangers, and there are far more deviants on the watch for them than for old women. Young people still go hitchhiking, despite all the warnings—the bodies found in bush graves, and the cases like that of Trudie Adams, a girl who left a hotel on impulse in 1978 on Sydney's northern beaches peninsula, caught a ride in a vehicle ... and was never seen again.

THE MURDER OF DONALD MACKAY

HIS DEATH CHANGED THE DRUG WORLD

Few killings in Australia could have generated more profound reaction than that of Donald Bruce Mackay, 43, furniture store proprietor, in a hotel carpark in Griffith, southern New South Wales, on Friday, 15 July 1977. Though Mackay was known only locally as an anti-drug campaigner, news of his death brought the national media flocking. The story was not to disappear for more than a decade. In retrospect, it is easy to see that the "mafia" syndicate, variously referred to in following years as L'Onorata Societa (The Honoured Society) N'Dranghita or La Famiglia, had made its worst mistake.

As a result of the murder, most participants in the syndicate were named. Many ended up before the courts. Some directly involved in the murder were gaoled. Many reputations were destroyed. A royal commission under Justice Phil Woodward held up years of dirty linen to public view. Another royal commission, under Justice Donald Stewart, as well as the New South Wales and Victorian police forces, targeted criminals. The marijuana operation was badly damaged and its principals dispersed.

The speed and thoroughness with which the Woodward Royal Commission gathered its material soon after Mackay's murder, demonstrated that information had been there for the taking. Concern about the local marijuana industry had long been voiced. Albert Jaime Grassby, who until the 1974 Federal election was Federal ALP MP for Murrumbidgee (Grassby lost office in the 1974 double dissolution election), and afterwards Federal Commissioner for Human Rights, sent the town into a state of derision when at a public meeting he said he had heard nothing about it. Local wisdom had it that on certain days you could arrive at Griffith airport and smell the stuff.

Even though huge New South Wales police resources were devoted to the inquiry into Mackay's murder, it was the Victorian police who provided the vital breakthrough.

Griffith, in the heart of the Riverina, had long attracted Italian migrants. The Riverina was fertile and intensively farmed. Italian migrants, many from Calabria in southern Italy, had arrived in Griffith since the beginning of the century. Their beneficial contribution was well recognised. Griffith accountant Giovanni Piazza said: "Out of several thousand Italians who have migrated here since 1913, only a small group have proved stupid enough to let themselves be led by the nose into marijuana growing. The others are hard workers and solid, industrious citizens".

But it was the minority who were the worry. From the time the presence of the mafia (using the term in a generic sense) became apparent in the north Queensland canefields in the 1920s, there had been talk of mafia in Australia. The existence of the Calabrian brand was described in a secret report to the Victorian Government in the mid-1960s.

The Riverina was well supplied with water throughout much of its vast expanse. Marijuana had been grown there since the 1930s. The Society was in a position to control it and take advantage of the Riverina's central location between Sydney and Melbourne.

Between 1974 and 1977, the syndicate ran four marijuana plantations in the Griffith area, supervised by a local winegrower, Antonio Sergi. Distribution and marketing were supervised from Sydney by businessman Robert Trimbole. Trimbole channelled part of the profits through a wholesale fruit and vegetable business, Trimbole, Sergi and Sergi, which had stalls in Melbourne and at the Haymarket in Sydney. The syndicate had cells in Griffith, Woolloomooloo, Leichhardt, Brookvale, Fairfield and Wollongong.

Born in Griffith on 19 March 1931, Trimbole married in Sydney in 1952 and returned to Griffith. The first part of Trimbole's married life was characterised by poverty. He lived in Housing Commission accommodation. Ultimately to father four children, he tried panel beating, spray painting and repairing pinball machines. In 1968 he was declared bankrupt.

At some time after that, Trimbole decided there were easier ways of getting ahead. His change of direction became apparent.

In the early 1970s he had a fleet of cars and was able to shower his children with gifts—worth as much as $25,000—and send them on overseas holidays. In Griffith he set up a restaurant, a butchery and a clothing shop. In Casula, southern Sydney, he set up a food supermarket.

That Trimbole and others were becoming rich through marijuana trafficking was common knowledge. It was a bonanza for all participating. The annual crop for one plantation alone was valued at $30 million. The money flowed into the local economy. On one estimate, 54 per cent of the money flowing through the town's trading banks was coming from marijuana.

Lesley Hicks, author of a book on the case, *The Appalling Silence*, was to write in one of her many newspaper articles: "The well-known beneficiaries of the marijuana bonanza are seen to have unlimited capital for houses and business buildings around Griffith. Parts of East Griffith are like Vaucluse for the opulence of the new houses".

Trimbole, who also used the name "Bruno", was easily able to attract a following. He became, according to his wife Joan, a generous Godfather figure. "He never talked about it, but I know that he helped so many", she said. "He helped people with their businesses. He helped people when they were in trouble. He was always giving. He always took an interest in other people".

In retrospect, there was a suspicion, if not outright proof, that Trimbole's interest in some people was far from benevolent.

On 18 February 1974, Patrick Joseph Keenan, 39, a fruit-fly inspector, went to the farm of Giuseppe Scarfo at Hanwood, near Griffith. He chanced upon several adults, including Antonio Sergi, packing marijuana plants into bags. "All the adults stopped working and talking and I formed the opinion they were surprised to see me", he said later.

Keenan reported what he had seen to Detective Sergeant John Kenneth Ellis and Detectives Borthwick and Robbins at the Griffith police station. "I felt they [the police] were not particularly impressed with my information", he said. "I felt rather let down by their attitude".

On 3 March 1974, the body of another man of exactly the same name, Patrick Joseph Keenan, 63, was found in a local canal. An initial coroner's inquest, at which Ellis gave evidence that there were "no suspicious circumstances", found Keenan had died by misadventure while walking home intoxicated. But the death was later seen in a far more sinister light.

Don Mackay was an aspiring Liberal parliamentarian, standing for election in either the State or Federal Parliament in 1973, 1974 and 1976. According to his wife, Barbara Mackay, several people approached him about the drug problem. They had done so "because they did not know who else to turn to".

Mackay took up the issue with relish. Former Griffith policeman Thomas James Bindon said later he recalled speeches in which Mackay had said Trimbole and his family "spent money like water" and that it came from illegal activities. In 1974, Trimbole, whom Bindon knew to be close to Sergeant Ellis, had come to Griffith police station in "a most irate and upset state", stating that he would "kill" Mackay if his remarks affected his wife and children.

In late 1975, Mackay had received information about marijuana growing at Colleambally, 60 kilometres from Griffith. The inform-ation was contained in two letters signed "Your friend, Nick". They gave accurate descriptions of where a large plantation could be found. Mackay contacted the CIB Drug Squad in Sydney. A member of that squad, Detective Sergeant Ronald Arthur Jenkins, met Mackay on 10 November.

Using a map supplied by Mackay, Jenkins led a police team to a farm at Colleambally. Six or seven men ran into the bushland. Five were arrested. Police found 13 hectares of marijuana in rows, each separately irrigated. Five tonnes of fertiliser were found in a shed. The plants at maturity would have been worth $25 million on the street. Two of the arrested, Luigi Pochi and Pasquale Agresta, were found to be business partners and friends of Trimbole.

Mackay's stirring continued. In early 1977, he wrote to the Griffith *Area News* urging people to complain about the inadequacy of laws on cultivating marijuana. In May he presented a petition on the subject to the NSW Government.

In March 1977, during the trial of the five from Colleambally, before Judge Newton in the Griffith District Court, defence counsel called for police notes and diaries. Jenkins said later he produced those documents but told the judge his diary contained the names of informants. The judge directed that defence counsel be restricted to viewing certain pages. However, Jenkins said, "the diary was freely available and it is clear that Mr Mackay's name [as one of the informants] could have been disclosed".

On 5 March 1977, police raided a property at Mt Diversion, 32 kilometres west of the Riverina town of Euston, and discovered two hectares of marijuana plants. Another four hectares had been harvested. The plantation had drying sheds. Jenkins estimated that the matured plants from the six hectares would have yielded about $16.8 million in drugs. Four people were arrested. Mackay did not give police information about the property. But some people thought he did.

With so many more millions of marijuana dollars in jeopardy, the syndicate became agitated. At one of their meetings it was decided to hire a hit man to silence Mackay—and warn others.

In June 1977, Trimbole contacted Gianfanco Tizzone, an associate from his pinball machine repair days who, in 1971, had followed him into marijuana. They met in Melbourne, in Park Hill Road behind Kew Cemetery. According to Tizzone, Trimbole said: "Donald Mackay is causing trouble and disruption. There is too much at stake and too many people in danger and Mackay will have to go". Tizzone contacted a friend, George Joseph, a Melbourne gun dealer. Joseph put him in touch with James Frederick Bazley, "a man prepared to commit violent offences".

Bazley was a Melbourne painter and docker who had been involved in the vicious power struggle of the early 70s and had survived two attempts on his life. He asked for $10,000 for the hit. Tizzone told Bazley he was not to use a shotgun, as it would reflect on the Italian community. The body was never to be found. According to Tizzone, Bazley said: "I will have to cut out his guts good". Bazley had a Unique .22 calibre pistol, which he had bought from Joseph in 1971.

Bazley made his first move on Monday, 11 July 1977. He rang Mackay, gave his name as "Ray Adams" and said he wanted to buy furniture. He asked to meet Mackay outside the Flag Inn at Jerilderie, 140 kilometres south of Griffith. Mackay agreed. On Tuesday, 12 July 1977 he found he had other things to do and asked an employee, Harold Bruce Pursehouse, to go. Pursehouse drove to Jerilderie, using Mackay's car, accompanied by his father-in-law Patrick Gaynor, 83.

When they got there, Bazley drove up beside them. Pursehouse, Gaynor and Bazley looked at each other without saying anything. Bazley left.

Though he had no indications of imminent danger, Mackay was tense. He had read a report in the *Area News* that Francesco Sergi, who had been charged with growing marijuana, had been no-billed by the Attorney-General and was free. Mackay reportedly said: "Now I am worried".

Other developments were ominous, and not just for Mackay. Martin Johnstone, a leading figure in the Mr Asia international drug syndicate—with which Trimbole was having increasing association—had come to Griffith early in 1977 ostensibly to buy property. That syndicate, headed by Terrence Clark, dealt in heroin and murder. Evidently it was eyeing Trimbole's distribution network. Don Mackay was standing in the way of enormously wealthy, powerful, ruthless interests.

At 5.20 pm on the evening of 15 July, Mackay phoned his wife that he would be home at 7 pm, then went to the Griffith Hotel Motel to drink with friends. He left the lounge at 6.20 pm, bought some wine and went into the car park. A woman conducting a raffle in the hotel noticed another man, short and heavily built, leave the hotel straight after him.

Outside, the car park was in darkness. In all probability Bazley had smashed the lights. When Mackay got to his car three shots rang out, sounding to an accountant working in a nearby building like the cracks of a whip. At 8 pm, Barbara Mackay reported her husband missing. At 1.30 am that same night, Mackay's lawyer, Ian Salmon, found Mackay's car still behind the hotel. He saw bloodstains and three spent cartridges. Marks on the ground indicated there had been a scuffle.

On the following day, Bazley met Tizzone at Kew. According to Tizzone, Bazley said, "I killed him last night", and produced a driver's licence belonging to Mackay as well as what appeared to be a doctor's bill. Tizzone paid Bazley $10,000.

At Griffith, the search for Mackay's body was intensive. Local police, reinforced from Sydney, searched the countryside, inquired house to house, even dug up the foundations of a new building.

People were talking openly of an organised crime hit. On 18 July, the Sydney *Daily Mirror* said: "All Australians must feel a deep sense of outrage at what appears to be a mafia-type slaying in Griffith ... Mr Mackay's sinister disappearance reinforces the need for a royal commission to investigate and expose the extent of the illegal drug industry in this state".

Significantly, police—and in particular the leader of the inquiry, Detective Sergeant Joe Parrington—already had information about the phone call to Mackay's business arranging the trip to Jerilderie. On 20 July, Ced Culbert, the doyen at the time of Sydney crime reporters, wrote in the Sydney *Daily Telegraph* about the Pursehouse visit.

Local people had their suspects. Antonio Sergi, the local winegrower who was linked to the syndicate, complained that 17 shots had been fired at his home. As well, his winery had been bombed. Communal resentment extended to local police. On 25 July, the then New South Wales Country Party leader, Mr Leon Punch, said police inquiries into Mackay's disappearance were hampered by suspicion of corruption.

The NSW Government appointed the Woodward Royal Commission on 5 August 1977. Very quickly, people never called to account found themselves before the public gaze. Counsel assisting, Bill Fisher, QC, asked Antonio Sergi why Trimbole had given him a $40,000 loan without security. Sergi said it was because Trimbole had wanted to help him with his winery.

Fisher: "It looked like Mr Trimbole needs to pay you very large sums of money. Mr Trimbole is sending you the money for a good reason and that reason is that you and he were growing marijuana in Griffith and selling it in Sydney".

Sergi: "I have not grown any marijuana".

Various residents of the Griffith district dissembled, some feigning not to be able to speak English. But Woodward was not to be deterred, slipping off one afternoon to look at the "grass castles"—palatial homes—of the suspected drug traffickers. Fisher told journalists the royal commission was a "carpet operation", starting with the small fry and rolling it up till they reached the heavyweights.

In his final report of 6 November 1979, Woodward found that Mackay had been murdered by a Griffith-based drug organisation. He described Trimbole as the practical, if not the titular, head of the organisation.

As well as Trimbole, the commission identified as members of the Honoured Society: Antonio Sergi, Giuseppe Scarfo, Francesco Barbaro, Leonardo Gambarcorta, Vincenzo Ciccarello, Francesco Sergi, Giovanni Sergi, Rocco Sergi, Domenico Sergi, Giuseppe Sergi, Pasquale Agresta, Giuseppe Agresta, John Trimbole, Antonio Velardi and Domenico Velardi. The list, the commission said, was not complete.

The commission said Detectives Ellis, Borthwick and Robbins had close ties with the marijuana activities. It recommended that an internal police inquiry be conducted into Sergeant Ellis and be extended to Borthwick and Robbins. Ellis, it said, was "either an active participant in a conspiracy to cultivate cannabis or in order to aid Sergi in his involvement in that crime".

The three were to be charged with conspiracy to pervert the course of justice, convicted and gaoled.

There was no direct evidence at that time to link Trimbole with the murder. Trimbole for his part was not inclined to take the royal commission as a warning. According to Tizzone, Trimbole told him in 1978 that there was now a chance to move into the heroin scene. In July 1979, Trimbole met Terrence Clark in London. On Clark's behalf, Trimbole utilised the services of Tizzone (and through him Bazley) to murder two drug couriers, Douglas and Isobel Wilson.

While this was happening, the Italian community in Griffith, devastated by the inquiry and the shattering of their reputation, were not prepared to take it all lying down. The community found a sympathetic ear in Al Grassby, who from the beginning had vigorously opposed statements implicating the Italian community in Mackay's disappearance.

Some criminal elements within the Italian community appear to have taken advantage of the man and his attitude. As a result of representations made to him, Grassby in 1980 gave two parliamentarians and a Sydney newspaper a scurrilously defamatory document which implicated Mackay's widow Barbara, his son and Ian Salmon in the murder. There was no substance in what was suggested. Grassby was later convicted of criminal defamation but the conviction was overturned on appeal.

The breakthrough in the police inquiries came after Victorian police, investigating the murders of Douglas and Isobel Wilson, got to Tizzone. In 1981, Tizzone disclosed his involvement in the Mackay murder and turned informer. Police arrested Bazley and the gun dealer, Joseph. Trimbole, due to appear before the Stewart Royal Commission on Drug Trafficking, skipped the country on 7 May that year. His daughter, Glenda, met him in a waterfront unit on the French Riviera at the time he should have been giving evidence. Other members of the family holidayed with him in the French coastal resort of Nice.

The Stewart Royal Commission found in February 1983 that Trimbole was "an active member, if not a principal, of the Clark organisation, particularly in its later stages of operation in both Australia and the United Kingdom".

Tizzone, Bazley and Joseph were all convicted in Victoria of conspiring between themselves and with others to murder Mackay. But it was never formally established that Bazley had murdered Mackay. Nor what happened to Mackay's body.

The citizens of Griffith set about trying to restore their town's shattered image. But marijuana growing continued in the Riverina. On 10 May 1984, the bodies of Rocco Medici and his brother-in-law, Giuseppe Furina, both from the Melbourne suburb of East Keilor, were found in the Murrumbidgee River at Darlington Point. Griffith civic leaders said the bodies were found outside Griffith's boundaries, so it had nothing to do with them. A group, Concerned Citizens of Griffith, led by scientist Dr Richard Smith, and including Barbara Mackay, knew it was not as simple as that. But the murders were never solved.

For his own part, Trimbole eluded international attempts to return him to Australia. In 1985, he was detained by Irish police. The Irish courts found that the grounds for detaining him were unacceptable and let him go. Trimbole skipped Ireland.

In Australia, agitation over the NSW Police performance in the Mackay investigation forced the hand of the State Government. In 1986, Justice John Nagle conducted a Special Commission of Inquiry into the matter. He pursued the serious questions that had been raised about what Joe Parrington—by then an executive chief superintendent of police—had been doing. Parrington had already caught public flak for failing to present a full account of Pursehouse's testimony to the coroner's inquest held into Mackay's death in 1984. The transcript of evidence given before Justice Woodward, containing Pursehouse's full testimony, was available to the coroner but it was suggested Parrington's omission had significance.

Nagle found that Parrington had not pursued the Jerilderie connection with any vigour. He said there was enough evidence to justify charging him with attempting to pervert the course of justice and that he should at least be charged departmentally.

Nagle was also critical of a former Assistant Commissioner (Crime), Cec Abbot, for not following up the question of the authorship of the document circulated by Al Grassby.

Parrington was charged departmentally with neglecting to ensure that police interviewed Patrick Gaynor, and failing to record details of his interview with Pursehouse in his official diary. Parrington was found guilty, and on 26 March 1987 Police Commissioner John Avery fined him $1,000 and removed him for 12 months as manager of criminal investigations. Avery added that he had found Parrington's actions were a result of unsound judgement rather than a desire to conceal, mislead, pervert or impede the course of justice. Parrington's fall from grace was temporary, though he was to retire without being further promoted.

Trimbole, rumoured to be suffering from cancer, was living in Spain. His course was run, and fate sealed the matter when he died of a heart attack. At Trimbole's funeral at St Benedict's Shrine at Smithfield, in Sydney's outer west, on 27 May 1987, friends and associates took it on themselves to violently assault the media. Police prosecuted the assailants.

BARLOW AND CHAMBERS

Brian Geoffrey Chambers, who grew up in Perth and was one day to make world headlines before departing his temporal existence, had always dreamed about making the big time. As a small child, he started believing something was going to happen in his life. He did not know when he was going to "make it". All he had to do was wait and it would happen. School was a bore for him. He had the ability, plenty of it, but not the temperament.

Chambers' life of crime started when, as a juvenile, he stole lawnmowers and sold them. He went on to alcohol at an early age, and marijuana. Leaving school at 15, Chambers started working with his father in the building industry. But his income was coming too slowly, especially after he started a heroin habit. He was impatient, thinking of the good times that would somehow be his—girls, cars, travel.

By 1977, Chambers had established himself as a small-time dealer in marijuana, LSD and heroin. He moved through the pubs and clubs, dealing and making contacts. He also sold around local schools, to children of all ages. He took money from a lot of them, and was prepared to accept sexual favours from girls who wanted his drugs. "One of the perks", he told his friends.

Chambers was using heroin himself, and it was becoming a problem, though he kept reassuring himself that he was not addicted. In the meantime, his activities spread further. He was getting high-quality heroin from Thailand and using contacts in established drug syndicates to spread it across Australia.

Perth became too small for him, especially when local police started taking a keen interest in him. He moved to Darwin and took up with a Thai prostitute who had good contacts in her own country. In Perth, Chambers' father started realising what sort of a son he had. Among other things, he had to pay off a finance company which had lent Chambers money to buy a car. In

Darwin, Chambers was making good money from drug deals and robberies. He bought an MG sports car and headed for Sydney with his girlfriend. In Sydney, his top-level contacts gave him easy access to the Kings Cross drug scene.

Chambers returned to Perth, in April 1978, to celebrate his 21st birthday. His parents banned his girlfriend from entering the house. Needing money, Chambers quickly re-established his drug network from a flat near Fremantle, developing a relationship with a criminal who was later regarded as a good operator in the burgeoning local drug scene. The police had not forgotten Chambers. In early 1979, they arrested him and charged him with a number of burglaries in the Fremantle area. Somehow, Chambers escaped conviction. His girlfriend did not fare as well. She was found to be an illegal immigrant and was deported to Thailand, where she kept up a connection with Chambers and became a good contact.

The Perth police continued their inquiries about Chambers. Not caring for the attention, he returned to Sydney, where he met an attractive blonde trainee nurse, Sue. Chambers introduced her to drugs. Following that, Chambers and Sue returned to Perth and set up house in upmarket Cottesloe, overlooking the ocean. At least Chambers' parents approved of Sue, even if they did not know what their son's relationship with her entailed. Chambers and Sue got deeply into drug-smuggling, making frequent trips to Asia and bringing drugs back. The drug was stuffed into condoms which were concealed in Chambers' rectum and Sue's vagina. As well as enjoying the good money, the two enjoyed the trips, where they were able to freely feed their own heroin habits. Chambers was also able to indulge his taste for Asian prostitutes, something that apparently did not worry Sue, who still loved him and enjoyed the diet of drugs and sex.

The trips were usually to Singapore, and to Penang in Malaysia. They became more frequent. Chambers sometimes travelled with Sue, sometimes not. He sometimes travelled on false passports. The money, after the drugs were distributed throughout Australia, came to millions. Chambers and his associates began to recruit more couriers, whom they referred to as "mules", to carry drugs for generous fees. Chambers would buy the drugs in an Asian country, ensure they were top quality, pass them to the mules in hotels and restaurants, and then return to Australia at his leisure.

But it was only a matter of time before this seemingly trouble-free existence was to be disrupted. In early 1983, Chambers and Sue were stopped at Singapore airport and asked to undergo a body search for drugs. They bribed their way out of being searched. In Perth, they were robbed at gunpoint. A little later, their house was ransacked. Nobody was arrested for any of these offences. It is possible that Chambers had attracted suspicion from other criminals, who thought he could take a bit of ripping-off. Perhaps corrupt police had been responsible. Whatever the truth, the incidents convinced Chambers that Perth was too "hot". Chambers and Sue decided to travel by car to Sydney. They did not make it. On the way, Chambers, full of alcohol and heroin, rolled his car, killing Sue.

The accident had a profound effect on Chambers. He became morose and sank deeper into the pain-numbing world of drugs. He lost confidence. Constant depression saw him using heroin just to get from one day to the next. He returned to his family, who did the "fatted calf" bit and took him in. That lasted until the day Chambers' father discovered, hidden in the toilet, some of the pure heroin Chambers was using. Chambers was obliged to leave home. He returned to the only trade he knew, which was drugs.

In August 1983, Chambers and his drug syndicate bosses, in particular the brains of the outfit, businessman and drug-dealer Paul Musarri, arranged a heroin run from Penang to Perth. The mule was to be one Glenys Bennett, 42. She had done it before for a fee of $20,000, strapping more than a kilogram of pure heroin to her body and flying back to Perth. On her previous trip, she had been accompanied by one of Musarri's associates, Gerry Maio. Taking a companion was a device intended to make the trip look like a lovers' holiday. But Maio, a dealer in his own right, was not entirely trusted by Musarri and associates. For the run from Penang to Perth, it was decided that Bennett should be accompanied by another syndicate member, Giovanni Garoffolo. Chambers would meet them in Penang, take $30,000 from them, buy the heroin and hand it over.

Bennett and Garoffolo's trip was anything but loving. They had to spend more than a week together in Malaysia before making the connection with Chambers. Bennett's refusal to have sex with Garoffolo created tension. The day before Bennett and Garoffolo were to meet Chambers they had a chance meeting with Maio, who was on a drug excursion of his own. Maio reacted badly to the fact that Musarri had apparently cut him out of the deal.

That, however, was to be the least of the worries facing the Musarri syndicate. Word had got back to narcotics authorities in Australia that a deal was on, and moves were under way to trap the participants.

Chambers liked Penang's Batu Ferringhi strip, with its fine hotels, fine beaches and even finer girls. He liked to stay at the swanky Rasa Sayang. It was there, unaware of the tip-off to narcotics agencies, that Chambers met Bennett and Garoffolo on 26 August 1983. Although Chambers was high on heroin, the deal was transacted quickly. Bennett and Garoffolo went back to their hotel with more than two kilograms of heroin. What they did not know was that Chambers had retained about a third of the consignment, burying it near the hotel, for the purpose of running a little side trade together with Musarri. After a dozen or so runs from Southeast Asia, Chambers and Musarri had become quite relaxed about cheating their backers and partners.

Police were waiting when Bennett and Garoffolo arrived at Perth airport in the pre-dawn hours of 27 August. The two separated in the customs hall and left the airport in separate taxis, but they were under surveillance. Back in her home in Perth's Victoria Park, Bennett stripped the heroin from her body and waited for a phone call from Musarri or Garoffolo. She did not want the heroin in the house any longer than she could help. No telephone call came. She started to panic. She rang Musarri, who answered the call and said angrily that he would collect Garoffolo and come for the drugs. Something was wrong, Musarri sensed it.

Musarri and Garoffolo arrived at Bennett's home, and left with the heroin. That was when police swooped. Musarri accelerated away in his car, pursued at high speed through the empty streets of the city. The chase ended when Musarri's car skidded out of control and hit a wall. Musarri and Garoffolo were arrested on the spot and Bennett a little later in the day. All three were charged with importing 2.4 kilograms of heroin. It was Perth's biggest heroin seizure. Chambers, aware of the arrests, flew into Sydney the following day, travelled to Perth and slipped quietly into his routine of drugs and indolence.

Enter John Asciak, a mad-dog immigrant with a long criminal record heavily punctuated with violence. Orphaned in Malta soon after World War 2, Asciak, as a 10-year-old street kid, was taken in hand by the Catholic Church and sent to Western Australia under a migration scheme for displaced children. In the early 1960s, after five years in schools and institutions, Asciak was fostered to a Melbourne family. By the mid-1960s, he had started a life of crime which saw him spending most of his time in gaol for offences such as assault, breaking and entering, consorting and false pretences. Not blessed with outstanding intelligence, Asciak usually solved personal difficulties with his fists. Built like a bull, he earned a legitimate dollar for a time in a sideshow boxing troupe. In Perth in the early 1970s, Asciak came into contact with Musarri in the city's illegal gambling clubs where Musarri was a big—and very bad—better. In the mid-1970s, Asciak was managing a team of prostitutes in Coober Pedy. Then he caught his wife in bed with another man. He responded by pouring aftershave lotion and gin into her vagina, leaving her screaming.

Back in Perth briefly in 1978, Asciak resumed his acquaintance with Musarri. He made an appearance on television in which he spoke about violence and corruption in the Western Australian prison system. Asciak received a visit from the police. With his new wife, Jill, Asciak beat a hasty retreat from Perth. But after three tempestuous years with Jill—during which time he was questioned over the brutal murder of a Catholic priest in Melbourne—Asciak split with her. Jill opted to do part-time prostitution in Perth. In August 1983, Asciak followed her there to try to win her back. He arrived just before Musarri, Garoffolo and Bennett were arrested on the heroin charges. Musarri got bail and employed Asciak as a minder. Asciak's duties included taking Musarri's children to school in the morning and keeping an eye on the beautiful young prostitute Musarri maintained for his personal use.

The stress of the impending trial and the pressure from constant police surveillance turned Musarri into an even more reckless gambler. The betting and big lawyers' fees quickly destroyed his large cash reserves. It became a matter of utmost importance to retrieve the bundle of heroin Chambers had buried in Penang. The desire for quick money affected his judgement. Chambers, depressed and drug-addled, agreed to make the run to get it. But he needed a mule. Asciak at this time was having an affair with a young separated mother, Debbie. To help make ends meet at her suburban Balcatta home, Debbie had recently taken in a young boarder, Kevin John Barlow.

Barlow had come to Australia from England at the age of 13 with his working-class family. They settled in Adelaide. It was obvious at school that he was no great intellect. After a brush with the law, Barlow dropped out of school and started a short working career. By the time he arrived in Perth in 1979, he had a reputation as a bludger and a no-hoper. He liked a drink and a joint of marijuana, but did not care too much for work. When he moved into Debbie's house as a boarder in September 1983, he was unemployed and his car was on the point of being repossessed. He had had a relationship with a woman that had not gone well. Asciak had scant regard for Barlow. But when Musarri said he was looking for someone to go to Penang with Chambers, Asciak saw him in a different light.

Asciak befriended Barlow by giving him marijuana, which Barlow was able to sell and thus make a bit of money. One morning, when Barlow brought Asciak and Debbie a cup of tea in bed, Asciak lightheartedly raised the matter of the trip to Malaysia. Barlow said he would think it over. In the next week or so, Asciak started applying the pressure. In the end, very worried about the possibility of losing his car and depressed after being dumped by his girlfriend, Barlow agreed to make the run with Chambers for $6,000.

A few days later, on 13 October 1983, Asciak brought Chambers to Debbie's house to meet Barlow. "Charlie [Chambers' code-name], meet Kevin", he said.

"G'day, I'm Geoff Chambers".

"Hi, I'm Kevin Barlow".

After the initial meeting, Asciak took Barlow to East Fremantle several times to see Chambers and finalise arrangements for the run. Chambers did Barlow a personal service in the process. He introduced him to heroin, which Barlow found to his liking. The two talked. Unbeknownst to Asciak and Musarri, they decided to break the rules to make money for themselves on the side by withholding some of the heroin they were to bring back. That money they planned to use on cheap Asian drugs and sex.

Despite his nervousness about the trip, and Debbie's urging that he not go, Barlow committed himself to Chambers' plan. The lure of drugs, sex and a good time clouded his mind even without the reassuring note of what Chambers was saying to him. On 27 October, Barlow flew out of Perth for Singapore. Musarri had borrowed $6,000 to cover fares and expenses but, to save money for their own use, Chambers and Barlow decided to buy only one-way tickets. They would also share hotel rooms during their week or so in Asia. If they ran out of money, they would simply sell some of the heroin.

Their plan was to travel together. That was against the specific instructions of the experienced Musarri. The arrangement also was counter to Chambers' proven modus operandi. Drugs and depression had made him careless. Chambers left Australia through Sydney and met Barlow in Singapore on 28 October. They missed a flight to Kuala Lumpur and spent the night in Singapore, drinking and whoring. That was a curtain-raiser for the week they spent—drug-taking, drinking and whoring virtually around the clock—after they got to Kuala Lumpur. Then they caught the train north to Penang, tired and anxious.

Contact with Perth was sporadic. When Chambers rang Asciak from Penang, he told him he and Barlow were having such a good time they were staying an extra week; selling some of the drug to pay for the holiday, and using some as well. Musarri was furious, but there was nothing he could do. He needed the heroin badly, and fast, because people were beating at his door for money. He vowed that Chambers and Barlow would pay for what they were doing.

Retrieving the buried parcel from the beach in front of Rasa Sayang was easy. But Barlow was becoming increasingly nervous. Now that the fun was over and the business end of the trip had arrived, his feet were getting cold. Drugs and booze did not help the fear growing within him. It was his first sortie into the field. Perhaps he sensed something was wrong.

As it turned out, Barlow's fear was well justified. In Perth, Debbie had had enough of the brutish Asciak. She had met another man, and copped a fist in the face for it. To get Asciak out of her life, she went to her brother-in-law with information. The brother-in-law in turn went to the police. He gave them sketchy details about the Malaysian drug run and Asciak's role in recruiting Barlow. Police informed the National Crime Authority. But Australian drug enforcement authorities were already on to Chambers and Barlow. The Malaysian drug run had been doomed from the start. Chambers and Barlow were not making it any easier for themselves. Drunk and drugged, they did little to disguise their presence in Malaysia. It is probable that their scheme would have been detected even if the authorities at home had not been alerted.

The initial plan for smuggling the heroin back to Australia involved Chambers swallowing half the drug in condoms and Barlow consenting to the other half being shoved, in condoms, into his anal passage. But Barlow was now in a bad way. Whatever else did or did not happen, a drug smuggler needed a cool nerve. To the immense chagrin of Chambers, Barlow was terrified. The nonstop indulgence in drugs and alcohol had taken its toll on them. They were not thinking straight any more. Caution was thrown to the wind. Chambers relented on secreting the drugs inside their bodies.

When Chambers and Barlow arrived at Penang airport, the heroin was in three packages in their luggage and the Malaysian police were waiting. At the check-in counter, Chambers and Barlow were approached by the airport's anti-narcotics chief. After inspecting their passports, he led them away for questioning and a drug search. Barlow was shaking visibly. Surrounded by police, he was sweating freely and could hardly talk. It is likely that his nervous and erratic behaviour would have attracted police attention even if they had not known in advance what he and Chambers were up to.

The luggage search produced more than 450 grams of "smack", containing almost 180 grams of pure heroin. It was easy to establish that the men were traffickers under Malaysian law. Inevitably came the words that burned into Chambers' and Barlow's ears: "You're under arrest". In Malaysia, a conviction for drug trafficking carried a mandatory death penalty.

Chambers and Barlow spent the next two years in a squalid, overcrowded Penang prison. They helped pass the time by injecting themselves with cheap heroin, supplied by warders. Their high-priced lawyers tried every possible avenue to have them set free and, when that failed, to have their death sentences commuted. The prospect of execution horrified Australian government authorities, who made representations on their behalf. The story received worldwide coverage. But the Malaysian Government and the country's legal system remained unmoved.

When hope started to fade, Chambers and Barlow started to blame each other. Their lawyers also attacked each other. Curiously, there was no attempt by Chambers to inform on the "Mr Bigs" in Australia who had planned and financed the drug run and many undetected runs in previous years.

Despite conflicting evidence, it became evident that Chambers was an experienced and skilful drugrunner who had become careless and was now paying the price. There was more sympathy for Barlow. He was a weak pathetic creature who was going to die for his one and only excursion into the international drug scene—and that only because he had been depressed and needed $6,000 to save his car from repossession.

In Australia, neither Musarri nor Asciak offered any assistance to lawyers or Australian government officials trying to save Chambers and Barlow. But they did have troubles of their own. The mule, Glenys Bennett, had been gaoled for ten years in March 1984 for importing heroin. In June, Asciak was arrested for stabbing a policeman. A search of his car revealed a quantity of cannabis. He was gaoled for 18 months. Musarri pleaded guilty for his part in the previous drug run, and on 3 September was gaoled, along with Garoffolo, for 15 years.

On his release in 1985, Asciak started dealing in heroin and was arrested after police raided a Perth motel. In May 1986, still to stand trial on the heroin charge, Asciak was gaoled for assaulting a woman. Just weeks before Chambers and Barlow were due to swing, a National Crime Authority officer visited Asciak in Fremantle Prison to try to get evidence from him which would show that Chambers and Barlow were simply pawns in a bigger game—and so should be spared the rope. Asciak refused to cooperate. His attitude was brutal and callous. "They're mugs", he said. "If you can't do the time, don't do the crime". Asciak was to be gaoled for ten years for conspiring with Chambers and Barlow to import heroin.

At dawn on 7 July 1986, with the world media gathered outside, Chambers and Barlow were led blindfolded from their cells on death row in a Kuala Lumpur prison. With their arms and legs bound, they were bundled onto the gallows platform. The noose was roughly fitted around their necks. Within minutes of leaving their cells, they were dead. While their families grieved in a nearby church; the media clambered to tell the world that the first

Europeans had been executed under Malaysia's drug law. The saga became the subject of a television mini-series.

For Geoffrey Chambers, who had dreamed as a schoolboy of hitting the big time and being someone to take notice of, his day had arrived—on the last day of his life.

THE WALSH STREET SHOOTINGS

THE POLICE VERSUS THE MELBOURNE UNDERWORLD

At about 3.20 pm on 11 October 1988, Graeme Jensen, a 33-year-old criminal, walked from a hardware store in Narre Warren, an outer eastern suburb of Melbourne, carrying a spark plug he had just bought for his lawnmower. He walked towards his Holden Commodore sedan, climbed in and started the ignition. Suddenly, a group of detectives from the Victoria Police Armed Robbery Squad appeared, pointed shotguns and revolvers, and told him not to move. Jensen's response was to accelerate at high speed. He did not get far. Two police opened fire. A shotgun blast went though the back window of the car and hit Jensen in the back of the skull. When the car, out of control, crashed into a power pole, Jensen was dead.

An official police inquiry followed into the circumstances of the shooting, and a coroner's inquest. The police involved in the incident said Jensen had picked up a weapon from inside the car and they had been in fear of their lives. A sawn-off bolt-action .22 rifle was produced as evidence. The police said it had been found in the car. Jensen's family and friends denied Jensen had been in possession of the weapon.

It was the start of an appalling feud between police and the underworld that was to leave two policemen and two more criminals dead. The police killings traumatised the state. The police investigation ultimately produced a series of convictions on a variety of charges, including as drugs and firearms offences. The police also laid a series of charges over the shootings of the police. But the charges over the shootings did not lead to convictions. In the washup, the saga of violence that followed the death of Jensen brought out the deepest cynicism and hostility that always exists among some elements of any community towards the police.

According to friends, Graeme Jensen was funny, intelligent and loyal. Dark-haired and fit, he was something of a ladykiller. To police, he was hardened and vicious. He had seen the inside of boys' homes as a youth. At 15, he had robbed a bank, been arrested and sent to a juvenile detention centre. At 18, he had been convicted of housebreaking and sent to gaol. In 1978, aged 23, he had been convicted and gaoled on three armed-holdup charges. He had escaped from custody and robbed a bank. Arrested again, he had been gaoled and not released till 1987. According to police evidence, he had lost little time getting back to bank robbery.

Jensen appears to have joined a gang that raided a number of banks, mostly in the inner western suburbs of Melbourne. Most holdups were done by three members of the gang, with a fourth acting as getaway driver. During the robberies, a particular weapon, a rare Japanese-made slide action shotgun, was used. It was fired during one robbery, in March 1988. The plastic shell casings were ejected and not picked up. Police retrieved the shells and gave them to their ballistics experts. Distinctive marks made by the weapon on the shells were noted. Police identified the weapon from the bank security photographs, confirmed how many had been imported into the country, and traced them. They located all but one.

Anxious to bust the gang's activities, police kept suspected members under surveillance. The suspects were seen apparently casing banks during deliveries by Armaguard vans. But it was not sufficient to justify any arrests. One of the robberies they were investigating intensively was that of an Armaguard van on 11 July 1988 in which a security guard had been shot dead and $33,000 in supermarket takings stolen. Police came across information that pointed to Graeme Jensen as a culprit. They decided on his arrest. It was when the Armed Robbery Squad located Jensen and made their move that he was shot dead.

It later became apparent that Jensen had nothing to do with the Armaguard robbery, that it had been committed by another gang altogether. Jensen's friends had no doubts that Jensen was innocent of that offence. They also had no doubts that police had "planted" the weapon said to have been discovered in his car. To them, the weapon had been, in underworld terms, "a throw-down", an untraceable weapon that was held in an unofficial police armoury for just such occasions as this, when a criminal is killed and the police have to find a reason why they shot him.

Prahran, a busy inner Melbourne police district covering an area from the wealth of South Yarra to the drug dealing and prostitution of St Kilda, was usually quiet during the week. At weekends, policing could be hectic. On 11 October 1988, less than eight hours after Jensen was killed, Constables Tynan and Eyre began an 11 pm to 7 am shift. They were in a police van, code-named "Prahran 311" for the purposes of police communications. Tynan, 22, had been a policeman for three years. Eyre, 20, had been in the force for less than a year.

Like most Tuesday nights, it was relatively quiet. There was an alarm at a furniture shop, followed by a complaint that a woman had been bashed by her husband. There was a noisy party, a drunk at St Kilda, an assault in a pub, a smashed shop window and two more security alarms. Then came their ninth call of the night. A newsagent on his way to work some time after 4 am had spotted a Holden Commodore parked in the middle of quiet, leafy Walsh Street, South Yarra. It was empty, its lights were on, its doors open and it had been vandalised. He telephoned police. The police taking the call relayed the information to Sergeant Ron Beaton, operator at Melbourne's police communications centre, known as D-24. Beaton noted it down as a suspect vehicle. He called Prahran 311 to attend, saying: "If you can slip down to Walsh Street ... Mr Ellis of 222 Walsh Street states there's a white Holden sedan. Not known what the rego is. It's got the lights on and smashed windows in the middle of the road".

At 4.39 am, Damian Eyre, in the passenger's seat, acknowledged the call. Minutes later Tynan and Eyre drove from Domain Road into Walsh Street and parked some metres behind the Commodore. They got out and inspected the vehicle. Tynan climbed into the driver's seat to examine the inside with Eyre squatting on the road beside him. It was 4.47 am. Then they were attacked. Tynan turned his head towards the attackers. He was hit once in the head by a blast of heavy calibre SG ammunition from a shotgun, pointed at him about a metre away. The shot was lethal. Each of the nine pellets was the size of a .38 calibre bullet. He had no chance. Eyre rose from his squatting position but was hit in the back by another shotgun blast. Despite his injuries, he turned and grappled with the gunman, who fired twice more but missed. One blast went into the wall of a house. A second assailant reached for Eyre's holster, pulled out the .38 calibre revolver, put it to Eyre's head and fired. Eyre fell to the ground. The second assailant fired another shot from the revolver into his back. The attackers fled.

Residents, blasted into consciousness by the shots, rang police. At 4.51 am, Sergeant Beaton began calling Prahran 311. There was no response. More calls came from the public. Beaton became more alarmed. The recorded calls between Beaton and other police are as follows:

D-24 (Sergeant Beaton): VKC to Prahran 311 [pause] VKC to Prahran 311 [pause] VKC to South Melbourne 250, any unit clear near Walsh Street, South Yarra [pause] VKC to 311, South Melbourne 250, any unit clear near Walsh Street, South Yarra.

Police car (the duty inspector, at South Melbourne police station): South Melbourne 150.

D-24: South Melbourne 150.

Police car: South 150, I'm in the area near South Yarra.

D-24: South Melbourne 150. I sent Prahran 311 down to Walsh Street. There's a car, a white Holden sedan parked in the middle of the road with lights on and smashed windows. Since then I've had about three or four cards [information given by callers to a police emergency number] come down saying that they've heard shots fired in the street and I can't get 311 at this stage.

Police car: South Melbourne 150. I'm on my way.

D-24: Roger. Is there any other unit?

Police car: Russell Street 621 [we] can head that way.

D-24: 621 Roger.

Police car: St Kilda 311. Do you want us to go down?

D-24: Affirmative.

Police car: 650. Would you like us to assist?

D-24: 650. You can if you want.

Police car: [unintelligible]

D-24: Unit calling?

Police car: 650. What is the location of the last?

D-24: Walsh Street in South Yarra.

Police car: Roger that.

Police car: South Melbourne 250. We're clear of South [South Melbourne police station] heading for that one in Prahran.

D-24: Roger. And the first unit down there give us a SITREP

[Situation Report] thanks, and take care. I sent Prahran 311 down there and haven't heard from him since [pause] South Melbourne 250. There's one complainant, a Mrs Borg from Walsh Street. Says she heard approximately three or four shots. She saw a male run into a lane behind the flats there and into Airlie Street and then into Punt Road. She also saw a white car in the street and another man chasing after him.

D-24: Russell Street 650.

Police car: 650.

D-24: Can you come down Punt Road and have a look around there?

Police car: 650. Roger that.

Police car: St Kilda 350.

D-24: St Kilda 350.

Police car: En route to your last. What's the address again thanks?

D-24: It's 220 Walsh Street in South Yarra and the last we've heard was a person running up into Punt Road with another man chasing after him.

Police car: South 250, urgent. South 250, urgent.

D-24: Unit calling?

Police car: South Melbourne 250. Two members down, urgent.

D-24: Roger. Need an ambulance?

Police car: 250 urgent. Yes, an ambulance please. Two members down.

Police car: City West 250, do you need any assistance?

D-24: City West 250, affirmative.

Police car: South Melbourne 250, for God's sake get an ambulance.

D-24: Yeah, we're getting one now.

Police car: South Melbourne 250. We've got two members down with gunshot wounds outside 222 Walsh Street, 222 Walsh Street.

D-24: All members take care.

Police car: [unintelligible]

D-24: Unit calling?

Police car: South Melbourne 250. Hurry up. We'll need a Mica [Mobile Intensive Car] ambulance for these two ...

The first police team on the scene, Unit 250 from South Melbourne, found Eyre lying by the back wheel of the car, blood gushing from his head. Tynan was slumped across the front seat. Both were unconscious. Ambulance teams worked on them at the scene for 20 minutes before attempting the trip to hospital. Both were dead on arrival. There was little trace of the robbers. They had not thrown away their weapon, although the plastic shells ejected by the weapon lay on the ground. Ballistics experts later found the same distinctive marks as had been found on the shells used in the bank robberies they had been investigating.

It would be difficult to adequately gauge the impact of these murders on the public and on the police force. Not since 1878, when members of the Kelly gang gunned down three police near Mansfield, northeast of Melbourne, had there been a multiple murder of police. The police force had already been attacked in a dramatic and outrageous way by criminals. In March 1986, a gang of robbers had left a stolen car packed with high explosives outside Russell Street police headquarters. When the explosives went off, more than a dozen people had been injured, including a young policewoman, Angela Taylor, who received fatal injuries. After Walsh Street, police rage was fuelled not just by the fact that two policemen had been killed, but because they had been lured into an ambush. Like any force of people living under constant threat of violence, they banded together. Many police suspected that the Walsh Street shootings were an underworld payback for the killing of Jensen. That was picked up by the media and reported within 24 hours of the shootings.

The scale of the police hunt for the culprits was unprecedented in the state's history. In the first weeks, more than 100 police were assigned to the task force to find the killers. In the months that followed, hundreds of homes were raided. Police entered pubs, nightclubs, illegal casinos. Informants were pressured. Police had names of dozens of suspects, including criminals known specially to hate police, cranks, escapees—and friends of Graeme Jensen. Suspected members of Jensen's gang, who had been under surveillance a few weeks earlier, went to the top of the suspect list. The Victorian government posted a $200,000 reward. It also proclaimed, quietly, legislation making telephone intercepts legal. Police on the task force took advantage of the legislation and tapped the phones of suspects. One result of the huge police operation was that crime dropped sharply. Criminals cancelled plans for holdups and major burglaries. Melbourne was too hot.

Police were particularly interested in Jedd Houghton, 23, who had grown up in the Flemington area. He had become a close friend of Jensen after Jensen's release from gaol. Houghton had allegedly been casing banks with Jensen weeks earlier. Police, pursuing the "payback" angle, were looking closely at Jensen's associates. They traced Houghton to Bendigo, where he was staying in a caravan park with a girlfriend, followed his movements and bugged a house where he had spent some time.

Early one morning, five weeks after the Walsh Street killings, and only a few days after police had located him, Houghton found one of the listening devices. He was furious. The police listening in realised their cover was blown so they decided to arrest him. Several hours later, while Houghton was in the cabin at the caravan park, members of the police Special Operations Group crashed through the door. Two policeman opened fire with shotguns. Houghton was hit by blasts in the chest and arm. He died instantly. The raiding police said Houghton had pointed a pistol at them and refused to drop it.

As tension increased, police changed their procedure for attending calls. They would only respond to a call if there were at least two cars available. People needing help had to wait longer. In the early hours of one morning, a package was left outside Prahran police station, the station that Tynan and Eyre had operated from. It was not a bomb. But tension increased further. Friends of Jedd Houghton were spotted one night near the entrance to the Police Club in Russell Street. The police raids were hard and uncompromising. Some addresses were raided four or five times. Numerous people complained they had been bashed or threatened.

The underworld was cynical. Criminals said Houghton had been shot dead in revenge for Walsh Street. Gary Abdallah, 24, who had been an associate of Houghton, heard what had happened to Houghton and was told by friends that the police wanted to get him as well. It had got around that they were looking for him. Abdallah had indeed been named by one Jason Ryan, 17 years old at the time of the shootings. Ryan was to be described in court proceedings as an experienced criminal, even at that age, familiar with burglaries and robberies. He had been charged and convicted of an offence relating to drug running and had decided that the best chance of securing his future lay in becoming a police informant. Part of his information was that Abdallah may have supplied a getaway car used by the killers at Walsh Street. There was virtually nothing to support this story but it focused the police spotlight on Abdallah. Abdallah went to ground in Melbourne, with a network of friends protecting him.

Several raids were aimed at finding Abdallah. On 22 February 1989, Abdallah went with his solicitor to see police. He said he had been in fear of his life. Police replied that that was based just on rumours. Abdallah replied: "It'd get you worried!" Six weeks later, detectives—who were not part of the Walsh Street task force—arrested Abdallah on a charge of assault and took him to his flat. In the flat, police shot him seven times. The police involved said Abdallah had threatened them with a firearm. They presented as evidence an imitation firearm which they said Abdallah had drawn. Abdallah spent 40 days in a coma before dying. His death prompted the State Government to call a major inquiry into police shootings and tactics. It also served to reinforce the belief in the underworld that police were still exacting revenge for Walsh Street.

The police claimed to have done a thorough and objective investigation into the murders of Constables Tynan and Eyre. They said they had identified six people who had taken part in the attack. These included Jedd Houghton, deceased, and Jason Ryan. They also included two uncles of Ryan, Victor George Peirce and Trevor Pettingill, Ryan's best friend Anthony Leigh Farrell, and a lodger at the house of Ryan's mother, Peter David McEvoy. Ryan, having decided to turn Crown witness, informed on the four surviving accused. On his account the four, together with Houghton, left a South Yarra flat shortly before the killings, stole the white Commodore, dumped it in Walsh Street and waited for the police to investigate. Ryan said he stayed behind at the flat. According to Ryan, Farrell returned, saying he had shot two police.

The police had another witness whose evidence appeared to be conclusive. Wendy Peirce, wife of Victor Peirce, had entered the witness protection program and had given a series of interviews to police. Police arrested Peirce, McEvoy and Farrell on charges of murdering Constables Tynan and Eyre.

The three went before magistrate Hugh Adams on 31 October 1989, amid intense security. Special Operations Group police escorted the accused to court along a circuitous route that turned what should have been a ten-minute trip from Melbourne's remand centre to an endurance test of one hour.

Giving evidence, Wendy Peirce said she recognised in a series of bank security photographs several men committing armed holdups. These were her husband, Graeme Jensen, along with Jedd Houghton and Peter McEvoy. She said she recognised their clothing and shoes, their features and their stance. She said she had seen her husband and Jensen wearing the balaclavas as a joke, so she knew what they looked like wearing them. Asked about the Japanese-made shotgun in the bank photographs, she said she had seen her husband with the shotgun twice, once when he was sawing off the barrel in a shed. On the night of the Walsh Street murders, she said, her husband and children had gone to a motel at Tullamarine. Victor Peirce had left about 11.30 pm saying: "Don't worry, I won't be late. I'm going to kill the jacks that knocked Graeme". The next morning, her husband had returned and said: "They're dead". After 59 sitting days, magistrate Hugh Adams committed the three men to stand trial in the Victorian Supreme Court.

Adams explained it was up to the Victorian Director of Public Prosecutions to decide whether there was enough evidence to lay charges against Pettingill. Murder charges were layed against him and he was directed to stand trial without a committal proceeding.

But before the trial of the four began, Mrs Peirce's testimony, which seemed so persuasive as to guarantee convictions, came unstuck. In January 1991, a few days before the trial began, and after more than 18 months under 24-hour guard, she walked out of the witness protection program. She ended up not giving evidence at the trial. She was later convicted of perjury and gaoled. The trial went ahead, but now the Crown was entirely reliant on Ryan, and major and deadly flaws started to appear in what he was trying to say. He kept changing his account of events. He admitted to numerous lies in his video interviews, especially the "re-enactments". He admitted to so many lies that defence counsel asked him to mark his interview transcripts with coloured pens to show which sections were true and which false.

The Crown case had other deficiencies. There were no eye-witnesses. Nor were there fingerprints or any other scientific evidence that could link any of the accused with the murders, or the murder scene.

Ryan's final version of what had actually happened had little resemblance to what he had said in his initial interview with police. Numerous changes he had made to his account were seized on by the defence. The attack on Ryan's credibility was devastating. David Ross, QC, counsel for Farrell, said of Ryan: "A psychologist or psychiatrist could have a birthday party on such a person. It defies description that there are so many lies told about so many subjects on so many occasions!". The trial lasted seven weeks, the jury took six days to consider the evidence, and came back on 26 March 1991 with verdicts of acquittal.

At the time of writing, a man has been arrested in Victoria. Strongly suspected of having committed the Armaguard robbery in 1988 that began the trail of events—including the shooting of Graeme Jensen—he was being closely questioned by police.

NEDDY SMITH
IN THE SPOTLIGHT

THUG, THIEF, RAPIST, MURDERER, INFORMANT

On 31 October 1987, more than 20 New South Wales and Federal Police gathered in the carpark of the Belfield Pizza Hut in Sydney's western suburbs. Wearing bullet-proof vests and armed with high-powered rifles, they moved carefully towards the home of Arthur Stanley "Neddy" Smith, in Burwood Road. Their caution was justified. Smith was a tough fighter, a known armed robber ... and wanted for murder.

But when police burst in, Smith sat calmly in the kitchen, his hands resting on the table to show he had no weapon. He gave up without a fight.

Twenty years earlier, a young mother in Sydney's inner western suburb of Petersham put up a fight when Smith and three mates burst into her home intent on rape. Alone with her six-week-old daughter, she screamed for mercy. Smith turned off the light, pulled off her nightdress and pushed her on to the bed. He threatened to drop the baby girl on the floor if she kept screaming, spat at her face, raped her and sat watching while his mates took their turn. Smith was 22 years of age and a wharf labourer. The viciousness of the attack prompted a judge to remark that the men had behaved like "arrogant gangsters". The judge said Smith's violent actions were "an indication of the warped and perverted mind underneath".

In the years to come, many would come to know that mind and many would regret the association. Several police would lose their jobs, many businesses would lose their payrolls, dozens would feel the might of his fist and the terror of his temper. A thug, standover man, SP bookie, rapist, street fighter, pimp, car thief, housebreaker, drug dealer and murderer, Neddy Smith came, in the words of one experienced New South Wales detective, "in the top two of the lowest people I have ever known".

But for all the crimes, for all the arrests in his lifetime, Smith's record contained surprisingly few convictions. He has claimed his charmed career was due to dozens of corrupt police who not only took cash to keep him out of court but also took an active part in his "work" by supplying police uniforms, badges and guns, suggesting potential payroll hits and sometimes keeping lookout.

Arthur Stanley Smith was born on 27 November 1944 and grew up running on the streets of inner-city Sydney. One of four sons of the same mother but different fathers, he first ran foul of the law when he was 11 years old. Stealing earned Smith a stint in a boys' home. At the age of 14 he was arrested for attempted break and enter and possessing housebreaking implements. In the juvenile institution he was uncontrollable and after hitting a prison officer over the head Smith was sent to a tougher lock-up at Tamworth, in the state's north.

The institution at Tamworth was, by many accounts, a breeding ground for young thugs. One of Smith's old mates from childhood days reckons his bad ways began there. Although still a teenager, Smith was a strong lad and took on the role of "dingo" for the warders, chasing and catching inmates who tried to escape. He also kept offending. Before he turned 18, Smith had been charged seven times. Growing to about 190 centimetres and weighing 98 kilograms, Smith was formidable. It was said he could fight like a threshing machine. He once tried to bite the ears off a man in a pub brawl. On another occasion he king-hit a Sydney solicitor. He was a massive drinker who could consume 33 middies of beer in an evening. Such binges could be dangerous if Neddy's infamous temper was aroused. One of his brothers, Edwin, said that when Smith came home drunk, everyone cleared out.

Smith was also a great womaniser. In 1967 he had a daughter, Nicole, with his then de facto, Dorothy Traynor. Two years later he had a son, Anthony, with Deanna Kelly but abandoned them.

The pack rape of the young mother earned Smith a 12-year term, most of it spent in Parramatta Gaol where his "leadership" qualities flourished. He served seven years before he was paroled, and by that time was virtually running the place, intimidating anyone who got in his way. Some inmates begged to be transferred elsewhere; one even injured himself to get away.

Back on the streets in 1975, Smith took up with Debra Bell, then a 19-year-old with a young son. The two married and were to have two children. Within a year of his release from gaol, Smith met the man who had one of the greatest impacts on his life. Detective Roger Rogerson was with the Armed Hold-Up Squad in November 1976 when he arrested Neddy and charged him with shooting with intent to murder, assault with intent to rob, attempted armed robbery and possessing an unlicensed pistol (the first three charges were dismissed at local court level; Smith's conviction over the pistol was later quashed on appeal). Smith became Rogerson's informer.

Smith's association with heroin probably began during the 70s, too. He was to be named in several royal commission reports. By 1978, he was obviously making big money. He and his wife moved into a house in St Peters, in inner Sydney, and spent a fortune on security doors and windows, an intercom system, a spotlight, closed-circuit TV to check on visitors and walls 2.5 metres high. To police, it had all the hallmarks of an electronic fortress erected to prevent anyone ripping-off Smith's valuables—his drugs or his money.

Smith's brother, Edwin, told the Woodward Royal Commission into Drug Trafficking that Smith boasted he would be one of the only "cash" millionaires around. Edwin said he would watch Smith breaking up lumps of glucose powder which he would mix with heroin to increase his financial cut. Smith made connections with William Sinclair, an Australian expatriate who ran a bar in Bangkok, Sydney travel consultant Warren Fellows, and Paul Hayward, a promising fullback for the Newtown Rugby League Club. According to Justice Woodward, the four were involved in massive heroin importation, with Smith handling the distribution and sales in Sydney.

On 11 October 1978, Fellows and Hayward were arrested in a Bangkok hotel where Thai police found 8.4 kilograms of heroin. Sinclair was implicated as the financier. In Sydney two days later, Smith's St Peters fortress was raided by police who found $39,360 in a wardrobe. The police, spotting a receipt for a locked steel box at a Marrickville bank, later discovered $90,100 in cash, $10,000 worth of diamonds, a manual explaining how to get a container past Customs and a passport with Smith's picture in the name of Douglas Keith Richmond. Smith and his wife were charged.

A day later, Fellows's wife, Janet, was arrested at her Manly home where $185,990 was found. She, too, was charged. Edwin Smith pleaded guilty to possession and then decided to talk. He gave damning evidence to the Woodward Royal Commission about seeing his brother dancing around a suitcase containing bags of white powder exclaiming "I'm rich, I'm rich". By the time Smith went to court, however, Edwin Smith had retracted his allegations (possibly something to do with the fact that Neddy Smith had twice threatened to kill him) and on day two of the trial, the judge directed the jury to acquit on the charge of conspiring to import heroin. Neddy Smith ultimately got six months for possession of goods suspected of having been unlawfully obtained.

Another of Smith's "associates" was Warren Lanfranchi. As a 17-year-old in 1976, Lanfranchi had been sentenced to five years for stealing colour television sets. While in gaol, he learnt about drug dealing. He also met Smith. On his release, Lanfranchi put his drug-dealing knowledge into practice but was soon in strife. One Tuesday afternoon in late June 1981, Lanfranchi met Smith at the Broadway Hotel in Chippendale, inner Sydney, to seek help. According to Smith, Lanfranchi had heard that Rogerson was going to arrest him for ripping off a fellow dealer and was willing to offer up to $50,000 to have the investigation dropped. Smith himself would pocket $5,000 if he acted as go-between. Smith agreed to see what he could do.

It transpired that Lanfranchi was wanted not for any drug deal but for the attempted murder of a policeman and for armed robbery. Rogerson laughed off the bribe but said he would meet Lanfranchi. Smith arranged it for the following Saturday. After he and Lanfranchi had checked out a suitable site nearby, Dangar Place, they repaired to the Broadway Hotel where Smith bought Lanfranchi several bourbons to calm his nerves. Smith stayed in the pub while Lanfranchi went to the rendezvous. Eighteen police waited. Rogerson kept the appointment. Lanfranchi was shot dead. A jury at the coroner's inquest concluded Rogerson had shot Lanfranchi while trying to arrest him. Significantly, the jury declined to add a rider that Rogerson had shot Lanfranchi in self-defence or in the execution of his duty.

By this time, Smith and Rogerson were seeing a fair bit of each other. Rogerson helped him prepare a statement for the Lanfranchi inquest and delivered it to the St Peters "fortress" the night before Smith was to give evidence. He stayed a while and had a few drinks. Smith was drinking with other police, too, in pubs or at weekend barbecues with respective families. One time in the mid-80s, Smith and Murray Stewart Riley (convicted over a massive cannabis importation) staged a joint celebration for their wives' birthdays in the Coachmen Restaurant in inner city Redfern. Guests included Rogerson, Detectives Bill Duff and John Openshaw, Smith's solicitor Val Bellamy, and two of Smith's good crim mates, Glen Roderick Flack and Graham "Abo" Henry, who was to be gaoled for stabbing a police prosecutor.

In 1986, things went bad for several participants in that gathering. Sydney's "gang war" had been on in earnest for more than a year and at least four criminal figures had been gunned down. It did Smith no good that Rogerson in a rare television appearance told the world that Smith was an informer. Mid-morning on 2 April 1986, Smith strolled along McEvoy Street, Alexandria, in Sydney's inner southeastern suburbs, planning to visit his daughter. Suddenly, a green Holden burst out from behind some trees, veered across to the wrong side of the road, mounted the footpath and careered into Smith. He was thrown into the air and then just managed to roll out of the way as the driver tried to reverse over him. With six fractured ribs, a broken leg and spinal injuries, Smith crawled into the Iron Duke Hotel. He was rushed to Royal South Sydney Hospital but didn't waste much time there. He discharged himself that afternoon and went into hiding.

Smith claimed in a television interview that police and the underworld had teamed up to have him knocked off. He said word had gone around that the hit-and-run tactic used in the attempt on him had been chosen because the six "Mr Bigs" of organised crime in Sydney had issued an edict that there were to be no more shootings. Smith was not impressed by what Rogerson had said about him on television. "It's a good way to get someone killed", he said.

Duff, who had worked in the Homicide Squad, was found guilty by the NSW Police Tribunal in March 1986 of misconduct over his "improper relationships" with Smith and several other criminals, notably Leonard Arthur Macpherson and the missing hitman, Christopher Dale Flannery. At the hearing, Smith was described as "an active criminal well-known as an assailant, gunman and standover man ... who is feared by other criminals. He is considered to be a major distributor of heroin and an organised crime figure". Duff went on to become licensee of the Iron Duke Hotel, the pub at Alexandria which Smith apparently owned and the same establishment into which he had crawled after being shot.

Rogerson was thrown out of the police force in July 1986 after the NSW Police Tribunal accepted that he had had an improper association with Smith. Whatever rift there was between Rogerson and Smith appeared to have healed by that time. Smith asked Rogerson to join him in a drink. Rogerson needed some comfort, because he was a long way from being out of the woods. He was later convicted and sentenced to eight years' gaol for conspiring with three other men to pervert the course of justice.

John Openshaw, at one time a distinguished detective, was dismissed from the police force in October 1986 for bringing discredit on the force by his dealings with Smith. Depressed, unable to find permanent work, suffering from the breakdown of his marriage, he was gaoled in 1992 for trying to extort protection money from the madam of a brothel at Hornsby, in Sydney's north.

Smith in the meantime was having other problems, unrelated to his criminal behaviour. He had been afflicted since 1980 with Parkinson's Disease and it was getting worse. He drank more and more because of it. Alcohol helped overcome the embarrassment of a man who once stood back-to-back with a mate in the pub offering to take on all comers but was being slowly reduced to a quivering mess. It was probably making him even more short-tempered, and that was to bring him down.

One Friday in October 1987, Smith and Flack started drinking early in the day. By 9 pm, they decided to go to the Coogee Sports Club. Outside the fish and chip shop on Coogee Bay Road, Flack pulled out in front of a tow-truck and then inexplicably stopped. The truck driver flashed his headlights a couple of times before turning back to chat to his passenger and partner, Ronnie Flavell. A furious and irrational Flack got out of the car and rushed to the tow-truck driver's window. "How dare you flash your lights at me!" he yelled. Flavell was a solid man, part-Maori, married with four children. He was in regular training at the time and very fit. The driver said later: "Smith was going to get out of the car and

Ronnie stepped in to stop him getting at me and thumped the sh.. out of Smith, absolutely belted him. Dropped him like a maggot, two or three times".

Flack ran to the rescue, armed with a long-handled screwdriver. The tow-truck driver grabbed an iron bar from the back of the truck and went to help Flavell. Before he got there, Smith, according to later evidence, stabbed Flavell in the stomach. Flavell clutched his midriff in agony and rolled over the bonnet of a parked car. Flack allegedly rammed the screwdriver into his chest, then left him lying in the gutter before getting back into the car with Smith and driving off at speed. The car was found abandoned later that night. Police arrested them the following day.

Smith and Flack were charged with murder. In February 1988, a mysterious break-in occurred at Randwick police station, in which police diaries and other documents relating to the case against the two were stolen. Nothing else was taken. It was a setback which put the entire case against Smith and Flack in jeopardy. Magistrate Greg Glass heard evidence against the two in June that year and was not persuaded that the loss of the documentary evidence should prevent him from committing them for trial. Smith and Flack were given bail.

Smith and Flack had the luxury at least of not having to prepare their defence from the inside of a prison cell. But they had more creative uses for their freedom. They decided to rob Botany Municipal Council of its big pre-Christmas payroll. They did a reconnaissance of the council premises on 21 December 1988, the day before the payroll was due. They were spotted and police dropped to it what they had in mind. On the morning of 22 December 1988, police were in place in the council chambers, a nearby fire station and other buildings. Smith and Flack were seen in a van parked near the council chambers. As police moved in, Smith emerged, a radio scanner clipped to his belt tuned to police frequency, and said: "Why don't you shoot me—I would be better off dead". Charged with conspiracy to commit armed robbery, Smith decided to plead guilty and was sentenced to 13 years' gaol.

But he still had the murder charge hanging over his head and Smith's one-time bodyguard, Graham "Abo" Henry, felt there might be an opportunity to arrange something. Henry was a real hard case. His first conviction—for carnal knowledge—came at the tender age of 14. His criminal career continued. In December

1988 he went to the Lord Wolseley Hotel in Ultimo, inner Sydney, for the purpose, he said later, of arranging the case against Smith by giving $50,000 to a police prosecutor, Sergeant Mal Spence, to "fix" the murder trial. Something went wrong and Spence ended up being stabbed. Henry was convicted of the attempted murder of Spence and gaoled. According to Smith's later evidence, he and Spence had met regularly in the King Arthur Court Hotel, Kings Cross, and Spence had been involved with him in fixing court cases. Spence denied all suggestions that he was corrupt. He said he had gone to the hotel just to listen to jazz.

Ironically, Smith and his son Anthony Kelly were reunited in 1990 when they shared the same wing in Sydney's Long Bay Gaol. Anthony, a proper chip off the old block, got seven years for stabbing and robbing a taxi driver in Maroubra. He had been drinking heavily by the age of 14, was in and out of child welfare institutions and eventually gaoled in 1988 for kidnapping and robbery. District Court Judge Rod Madgwick said that Kelly's upbringing had almost guaranteed the young man would find it hard to adjust to a "lawful, hard-working, non-violent way of life".

Smith went on trial for Flavell's murder in 1990. The jury took two hours to find him guilty. Justice McInerney sentenced him to life imprisonment. The same day, the NSW Court of Appeal fined him $60,000 for contempt after he refused to give evidence at Flack's trial (at which Flack was later no-billed). Smith continued to deny that he had murdered Flavell. He conceded he had been in a fight with him but had not stabbed him. After an unsuccessful appeal in the NSW Supreme Court, he was given special leave to appeal to the High Court. At the time of writing, his case had not yet been heard.

Smith found life in Long Bay Gaol somewhat uncomfortable. He told a newspaper reporter in 1991: "Hell, it's hot in here. The place is crowded and I'd fancy some of those new drugs for my disease". He said he was taking a virtual overdose of tablets to stop him shaking.

Spurred on by discomfort or revenge or a chance to die in freedom, Smith started talking. In January 1991, while in Long Bay's Central Industrial Prison, Neddy got a fellow prisoner, Roy Thurgar (since murdered outside his self-service laundry in Randwick), to write to the Independent Commission Against Corruption (ICAC). The message was that Smith wanted to be heard. Smith said he was ready to tell all about crooked cops. The ICAC was interested, interviewed him and checked out his information by referring to police records. It appeared to ICAC investigators that Smith, despite the obvious difficulties with his credibility, was telling the truth. The ICAC launched an Inquiry into the Relationship between Police and Criminals, beginning its hearings in November 1992. The NSW Attorney-General gave Smith immunity from prosecution for all crimes except murder. Smith was free to talk.

On the first day of Smith's appearance as witness, the public queue to get into the hearing room stretched all the way through the foyer and out into the street. When Smith's evidence started, it was sensational. He alleged, amongst many things, that police had organised hit-men to murder criminals and that they set up armed robberies with criminals, getting their own bagman to collect up to 25 per cent of the takings. In an attempt to corroborate his claims, he confessed to involvement in 14 armed robberies since the early 1980s.

At ICAC, Smith refused to name criminal associates, though directed to by the ICAC commissioner, Ian Temby, QC. Temby conceded that because Smith was serving a life sentence there was not much the ICAC could do, short of "turning on the thumb screws", to force Smith to name those associates. When asked the difference between naming a fellow criminal and naming a police officer, Smith said: "It's just the way I was brought up. You look after your own. You don't tell on your own. And I thought that way about police, too, until they tried to kill me on several occasions and eventually set me up when they thought I'd run out of usefulness". But Smith's stand left the entire ICAC inquiry open to criticism and was a factor in the decision by Justice Cole in the NSW Supreme Court in January 1993 to order the hearings closed to the media and the public. (The ruling was later overturned after ICAC appealed.)

Smith's motives in coming forward were savagely attacked. What deals had he made? What scores was he settling? Was he lashing back at the police who had insisted on doing their job and whom he hated? Was he being manipulated? Or was this the first real look the public was having at the seamy world of double-dealing by corrupt police? Was Smith, after a lifetime inflicting suffering, one way or another, on others, finally going straight? At the time of writing, none of those questions had been resolved and there was a chance they never would be. One could go on what Smith himself had to say about his motives. In an interview telecast the night before the ICAC sittings began, Smith solemnly told a reporter: "I think I'm doing the right thing for the first time in me life".

THE GRANNY KILLER

THE MAN WHO PREYED ON ELDERLY WOMEN

Mosman, on Sydney's north shore, with its harbour views, sun-dappled streets and gracious Federation homes was not the setting for violent murder. Among the residents of this upper-middle-class enclave were Cluedoesque characters—the likes of Colonel Mustard and Professor Plum—owners of houses large enough to contain libraries and drawing rooms. Such people and places might have fitted some type of genteel Agatha Christie scenario. But a felonious slaying was rare indeed. And the vicious, brutal battering murders of six elderly women in and around Mosman over a 12-month period unthinkable.

Until it happened.

Elderly women had been for many years a virtual trademark of Mosman. One in five of Mosman residents were elderly. Seventy per cent of the population were 50 and over and 12 per cent more than 70. Widows for the most part, the elderly women lived in the multitude of units and retirement villages in the area. On any day they could be seen walking slowly down Mosman's main street, Military Road: Mosman's grey brigade, veterans of two world wars and the Great Depression, pushing shopping trolleys, leaning on walking sticks, sometimes bent double with arthritis, fiercely independent. Their frailty was immediately apparent. But who would have been concerned?

There were no immediate answers when, shortly before 4 pm on 1 March 1989, 84-year-old Gwendoline Mitchelhill was fatally bludgeoned about the head outside the foyer of her units in Camellia Gardens, Military Road. At first glance, the bashing looked as though it had been part of a robbery that had gone wrong. Her purse was missing. She was wealthy, the widow of a man who had run a successful hardware business. She did not trust banks and it was nothing for her to carry $1,500–$2,000. Police surmised her assailant had followed her from the shops and attacked her.

Dr Jo Duflou, NSW Government forensic pathologist, showing normal professional caution, initially questioned whether Mrs Mitchelhill had been murdered at all. She might have just fallen. At least some of the injuries were consistent with that. But the nature and extent of the wounds indicated otherwise. They included severe bruising to the right eye, severe bruising to the right shoulder, two wounds to the back of the skull, an extensive fracture to the rear of the skull and seven broken ribs, that were consistent with punching.

A peculiar feature of the scene was that Mrs Mitchelhill's shoes had been taken off and placed neatly beside the body. What could be made of that? Had the killer, committing this appalling crime when people were about, lingered? In fact the likelihood of the killer being spotted had been very high. The attack had occurred less than 15 metres from Military Road in a peak traffic period, and there were builders working on a shopping complex which overlooked Camellia Gardens.

For the NSW Police North Region Homicide Squad, the most likely type of offender was a juvenile out for money or perhaps a juvenile who hated his grandmother, taking out his rage on another elderly woman. Detective Inspector Mike Hagan, in charge of the murder investigation, was perplexed. Some weeks passed. A flow chart had been compiled of Gwendoline Mitchelhill's last movements, neighbours had been canvassed. Nobody had seen anything.

On Wednesday night, 26 April 1989, Raymond Roper, a technician at the Special Broadcasting Service (SBS) television station, was walking along Raglan Street which ran off Military Road. Dressed in a long overcoat and wearing a floppy straw hat, he was going to his unit in Musgrave Street, about a kilometre from where Gwendoline Mitchelhill was murdered. From the back, he looked almost feminine. He was hit from behind. When the first blow fell, he raised his hands to protect himself. His hat lessened the second blow and he turned to face his attacker, who fled.

Roper told police his assailant appeared to have been about 30 years old, of slim build, 180 centimetres tall, with a great mop of blonde hair with a yellowish tinge. The attacker had been wearing a sleeveless, white or cream cableknit sweater and light coloured trousers. Because of the similarities with the way in which Mrs Mitchelhill had been attacked, police believed they now had a positive sighting of the murderer to work from. They were to look for a young man.

Thirteen days later, in Raglan Street, metres from where Roper had been attacked, Lady Winifreda Isabelle Ashton, 84, was bashed and strangled in the bin room of her unit block. Lady Ashton's murder had special poignancy. She was the widow of Sir William Ashton, one of Sydney's most famous landscape painters. Her unit was full of priceless antiques. But the killer, who had obviously followed her, had not waited for her to get there.

Lady Ashton's body, bleeding from the mouth, lay with her hat and handbag lying beside it, her black, buckled, velvet low-heeled pump shoes neatly placed in the corner of the room with her walking stick. A resident found the body hours later. When police arrived, they noted that her red raincoat had been pulled up by the killer to hide her face and that the pantyhose ligature had been knotted so tightly around her neck it had become embedded into her skin. A bloodied gas bill bearing her name lay next to her head. Her pantyhose and underpants had been removed and her bare legs were crossed.

Detective Paul Mayger, investigating the murder, was sure the same killer was involved. This time the police canvass extended further. Fifty police were assigned to knock on doors and ask who resided at the premises and whether the occupants had noticed anything unusual. Two months after the murder, Lady Ashton's red wallet turned up in her letterbox. After that, in a nearby park, her bank book, two purses and bus tickets dated the day of the murder were found.

Six months further on, police had a list of suspects and information gained from extensive surveillance. Local residents had nominated an array of misfits. They included an 18-year-old boy with pink and red hair and a rat tattooed on his left upper arm. Another suspect was a transsexual who had two sessions a week at the Kings Cross medical centre. A third was a Canadian man in his early twenties who told everyone he had an Olympic gold medal for ice skating, and who engaged in seducing men in Mosman bars and ripping them off. But none of these suspects fitted the sort of person police felt would commit such crimes.

More information flowed to Mosman police. People telephoned or wrote giving information, sometimes about relatives or about enemies. For police, the "youthful offender" theory was strongest.

The two killings had been just before 4 pm, which was after school had finished for the day. Could the killer in fact have been a schoolboy? The United States Federal Bureau of Investigations sent a theoretical profile indicating the offender was likely to be "young and black". The "young" part of it fitted the local model. Detectives focused on the local high school which sat plumb in the middle of the area where the attacks had occurred.

On 18 October 1989, Doris Cox, 86, was viciously attacked at The Garrison retirement village, Spit Road, Mosman. Her head was repeatedly bashed into a wall and her purse stolen. Mrs Cox survived, probably because her mental state—she was suffering from Alzheimer's Disease—stopped her from going into shock. But it also ruled her out of being of any help to the police. Her face, puffed and bloodied from the force of the assault, greeted police as they questioned her at her hospital bedside. When asked what had happened she said: "Nothing's happened".

That might have been the end of that line of inquiry, but police had what they thought was a stroke of good fortune. An independent witness, who came across Mrs Cox's opened handbag after it had been abandoned by the attacker, told police that at about the time Mrs Cox was attacked, and near where the attack had occurred, she was startled by a young skateboard rider flying out of the bushes on to the main road. The witness gave police a description of the youth's appearance. It was converted into a photo-fit depiction of the suspect which was circulated to the media. Newspapers and television stations labelled the picture: "The Face of the Killer".

How different the reality was! Far from being a stranger in their midst, the real killer was someone nobody suspected, a longtime Mosman resident who was able to discuss the murders with neighbours, join in conversations at parties and chat to his wife and acquaintances, saying more than once that he hoped police would "catch the bastard". John Wayne Glover did not match the photo-fit description at all. He was 58 years of age, a salesman, long-married and a father of two girls.

Born in England, Glover had been dominated by women from childhood. He had had a peculiar relationship with his mother, Freda, who with four husbands and a number of other men in her life was hardly a stabilising influence. Glover believed she had abandoned him at the age of nine to move in with her second husband, taking instead his younger brother, Barrie, with her and leaving John with Walter, his father. In his early teenage years, Glover spent time going back and forth from mother to father, always favouring Freda over Walter whom he considered "weak". Freda and John were always close. He partnered her in ballroom dancing competitions. He admired her and was greatly influenced by her views on life, particularly her ability to survive.

Glover left school at 14. He also began stealing. Freda never asked how he came by the items he brought home from the houses where he worked as an electrical apprentice. She, in turn, asked and got his help when she set fire to the sweet shop she owned to collect the insurance money. Freda looked after John by sharing the spoils of the blackmarket with him during the war. But whenever there was a new man on the horizon, and that was frequently, John always had to take second place. John's feelings for Freda, a psychiatrist was to say, were "ambivalent".

Glover arrived in Australia in 1956, changing his middle name from Walter to Wayne as he did so. Settling in Melbourne, he took a job as a tram conductor. But even in those early years there were signs of the trouble to come. He was arrested for peeping and prying and assaulting two women, one a younger woman of 35, the other more elderly. Then he met Gai Rolls, from all accounts an intelligent, hardworking woman who had a job as a medical records secretary. The two apparently fell in love. They married, and Gai told Glover he had the potential to better himself. Glover, increasingly embittered as he grew older about his lack of educational opportunities, made no protest. Meeting Gai Rolls gave Glover an entry into the class he coveted. For a while he managed to avoid getting into trouble.

The couple moved to Sydney where they settled in with Gai's parents, John and Essie Rolls, in Wyong Road, Mosman. The Rolls built another storey to accommodate the couple, and the resulting dwelling could command some impressive views. Glover and his wife were to stay there for more than 20 years. Glover was later to say: "My life in Mosman was superb. I had no worries about homes or debts or anything like that. I was well accepted in the community. I belonged to clubs". He took a solid if unspectacular job, as a pie company representative—specifically for Four and Twenty Pies—calling himself the "area manager". He also insisted in giving both his daughters a private education, describing that as "everything I should have had".

There were peculiar pressures brought on Glover through the presence of elderly women in his life. One of these women was his mother, Freda, who in 1976 came to Australia to settle. The other was Glover's mother-in-law, with whom he never got on. Essie Rolls saw Glover as a fortune seeker. She made it clear to him that the house he was occupying did not belong to him. Glover had to give way. He was relegated to the role of handyman, and spent time pottering in the garden and tinkering in his aluminium garden shed where he kept, amongst other things, his Stanley Hercules hammer and some hydrochloric acid, an item useful for cleaning away stains.

Glover's job as pie company representative gave him the ability to frequent nursing homes and retirement villages on Sydney's north shore, and that gave him access to elderly women. His deviant urgings began to take over. Whenever asked by concerned staff as to why he was creeping along corridors in the nursing home, he would pretend he had come to visit the chef about ordering some of his wares.

Somewhere around mid-1988 Glover formed a liaison with another woman, a 60-year-old divorcee named Joan Sinclair who lived in Pindari Avenue at Beauty Point, near Mosman. Glover told her at the outset that he was a married man. She agreed to maintain the liaison with him, and to allow him to visit her house, though her family is understood not to have approved. From time to time, Glover dropped in to see her and she locked the security door of her unit for privacy.

In September 1988, Essie Rolls was admitted to a nursing home. Glover visited her. After his visits began, Glover was reported for molesting old women. Essie died in January 1989. That month, not far from where he was to assault Doris Cox, Glover attacked Margaret Todhunter, 84, a Queensland widow who was visiting Mosman. Mrs Todhunter, who received a head wound requiring eight stitches, gave a remarkably accurate description of her attacker: well dressed, about 170 centimetres tall, wearing a clean, white, long-sleeved business shirt with a tie. His cream trousers were clean and pressed, and she thought she noticed hair spray on his thick grey hair. He was cleanshaven, had broad strong shoulders and an ample stomach.

In early 1989, Freda, Glover's mother, died of breast cancer in a nursing home. In March, Glover killed Gwendoline Mitchelhill, following it up in May with the murder of Lady Ashton. On 25 August 1989, Glover attacked Euphemia Carnie, 82, of Lindfield, on the upper north shore of Sydney. Mrs Carnie described her attacker as being a man with grey hair, cleanshaven, well built and in smart casual dress. His height was about the same as the estimate given by Mrs Todhunter—160 to 170 centimetres. Glover kept up his attacks, bashing Doris Cox in October.

On 2 November 1989, Glover saw 85-year-old Margaret Frances Pahud walking from shops along Longueville Road, Lane Cove, another suburb on Sydney's north side, ten kilometres from Mosman. Carefully taking a hammer from his car—as he had when he decided to attack Mrs Mitchelhill—Glover followed her as she turned down a walkway to go to her home unit. He bashed her on the pathway and left her dying.

On 3 November, NSW Police formed a Task Force, comprising the state's 35 most experienced investigators, dedicated to solving the murders and bashings. Still mistakenly working on the theory that their killer was a youth, they began a massive check of retirement villages, bus routes and timetables to try to find anyone who had noticed a youth fitting the description given after the Doris Cox attack.

Hardly had the task force begun to get its bearings when Glover struck again—in fact the very day the task force was set up, he waylaid 81-year-old Olive Cleveland at the Wesley Gardens retirement village in Belrose, on the northern beach peninsula. Her battered body was found on a concrete path with her pantyhose tied several times around her neck. Her spectacles and shoes lay neatly nearby. Before scientific experts could examine the scene a hose had been turned on to it to wash away the blood, something that had happened at two of the other murder scenes; probably wiping out what traces police might have been able to get.

The NSW Government announced a reward of $200,000 for information leading to the arrest of the offender. The news of the Cleveland killing brought more than 2,000 calls from the public. Police also made a thorough review of their information. A week after the Cleveland murder, they looked again at the description of the "grey-haired man" as given by Todhunter and Carnie. For the first time, police doubted the picture they had built up of the youthful offender. The grey-haired man was quickly climbing to the top of the suspect list. But there was an extraordinary lack of witnesses and clues.

On 23 November 1989, Glover struck once more, this time following 93-year-old Muriel Falconer to her home in Muston Street from Military Road, Mosman. He battered her to death inside her own hallway after she turned the key to her front door, rifled through her purse for money, tied her pantyhose around her neck and pulled her dress and petticoat over her head. Her shopping bags strewn with groceries lay next to her body. The difference with this murder was that Glover left a strong clue—a footprint in the blood around the body. Inspector Mike Hagan said that that footprint turned the murder into "the best crime scene we have".

That was not, as it turned out, much comfort to the public. With five elderly women dead, three others and a man bashed, Mosman was in near-hysteria. Council rangers and soldiers from the nearby Army base began escorting elderly women to and from their homes. Security guards were placed at retirement villages and nursing homes. It said something about the spirit of some of the old people that they did not seek the protection. Many said they would not be made to stay indoors and spurned offers of help. Joan Sinclair, who was still continuing her relationship with Glover, was not one to take chances. She had a security gate fitted and a night light installed.

In early January 1990, Glover went to the Greenwich Hospital in his capacity as travelling pie salesman. Carrying a clip board, he went into a ward and indecently assaulted an elderly woman, Daisy Roberts, who pressed the alarm button. A nurse called police and from the call they identified Glover as the offender. Two young constables from the Chatswood police station made arrangements to interview him at his home. Glover made an apparent suicide attempt by drinking Scotch and getting into a bath. He left a note for his family, bidding farewell, saying there would be no more of his boss, and "no more grannies".

In what turned out to be a serious omission the constables took possession of the note but, not realising its significance, kept the information to themselves. Glover was, however, on the list of suspects and a surveillance team was put on to him. It was also clear to Glover that the baying of the hounds was much, much closer.

There was nothing positive to tie Glover to the killings. Police were being cautious. Perhaps the caning the police service had received over the premature arrest and charging of an innocent former police superintendent, Harry Blackburn, in 1989, on a series of sexual offence and robbery charges, restrained their hand. Hagan's instructions to his surveillance team were that if Glover started stalking an elderly woman, he was to be followed till the woman got to her home. Once the woman entered her home, the police were to grab Glover and seize any weapon he was carrying. But Glover, frustratingly, did nothing remarkable.

It is a tragic irony that police had Glover under surveillance when he went to visit Joan Sinclair on 19 March. The surveillance team initially thought he was calling on his solicitor, because he had told his manager at work that he would not be working that day as he had a legal appointment. The facts fitted as he was being questioned about the Daisy Roberts assault. So they waited in Medusa Street, which intersects Pindari Avenue, watching the premises, expecting that when Glover came out they would resume shadowing him.

When Glover entered Joan Sinclair's home he had, as he later told police, confused feelings about committing suicide. It was almost exactly 12 months since he had claimed his first victim. Mrs Sinclair invited Glover in as a friend; he came with a claw hammer. Glover waited until the opportune moment when Joan Sinclair was showing him a leak in her ceiling. He removed his hammer from his briefcase and struck her on the back of the head, viciously and repeatedly. Leaving her body at the top of a staircase, in a position where an intimate view of the body could be gained from a certain position, he took an assortment of pills and Scotch and got into her bath. It was an apparent suicide attempt.

The police remained waiting in Medusa Street for almost eight hours. They formed the belief that Glover was having a "liaison" with a woman in the house and felt there was no cause to go knocking at the door. But when nothing happened, two uniformed police were ordered to knock on the door, with the excuse that neighbours were complaining about a dog barking. When the door was not opened they forced their way in, only to discover Joan Sinclair's body. They called for help. Members of the task force found Glover still in the bath, his mouth just above water, and unconscious.

There was an attempt at Glover's trial to prove diminished responsibility due to an abnormality of the mind, which would have justified a finding of manslaughter. But the evidence of Crown forensic psychiatrist Dr Rod Milton was damning to him, particularly when he spoke about Glover arranging the apparel on the bodies of the murder victims to allow intimate viewing of them. Glover was convicted three days after his 59th birthday on all six counts of murder. Justice Wood expressed no sympathy for him and ordered that he was never to be released. Glover was sent to protective custody at Goulburn gaol, and it was to be a long and lonely time. His wife Gai, concerned only for the welfare of their two daughters, never went to see him. The family have effectively disowned him and in November 1992 Mrs Glover was quoted as saying: "He'd be better off dead".

ABOUT THE EDITOR

Malcolm Brown began as a cadet journalist on the *Daily Liberal* in Dubbo, NSW, after completing an Arts degree at Sydney University. In 1969 he entered the National Service, graduating as a second lieutenant in the Australian infantry and commanding a platoon in a training unit until his demobilisation in 1971, when he entered journalism.

He has been with the *Sydney Morning Herald* since 1972, working on police rounds, inquiries, royal commissions and general reporting, which has taken him around the world, including the Fiji coup in 1987 and the Gulf War in 1991.

He is principally known for his 10-year coverage of the Azaria Chamberlain case, and he was in the vanguard of the campaign for a judicial review.

He is co-author of *Justice and Nightmare*, published in 1992, about the contribution of forensic science to the resolution of innocence and guilt.

General editor of *Australian Crime*, he also contributed the chapters *The Bank of Australia Robbery*, *The Life and Times of Thunderbolt* and *The Murder of Donald Mackay*.

CONTRIBUTING AUTHORS

Tim Atkinson (*Eric Cooke, Random Killer*) started his journalistic career in Brisbane in the mid-1960s. He has travelled extensively, working throughout Australia and Asia. He has written and edited such national magazines as *Prime Time* and written on a broad range of political, social and human interest subjects for major newspapers and magazines. He was the daily columnist of the *West Australian* newspaper for two years. Today, the proprietor of a successful media and contract publishing firm in Perth, Linchpin Communications Pty Ltd, Atkinson is also the special correspondent in WA for *WHO Weekly*.

Jennifer Cooke (*Abe Saffron*) is the winner of two consecutive Law Society of NSW Golden Gavel awards for legal reporting and a former chief court reporter for *The Sydney Morning Herald*. Following a three year stint in Hong Kong as chief reporter for the *South China Morning Post*, she returned to *The Sydney Morning Herald* in 1992 and now writes about crime.

Jennie Curtin (*Neddy Smith in the Spotlight*) joined *The Sydney Morning Herald* as a journalist in 1985. She has been covering courts for the paper since 1990 and has been chief court reporter for the past 18 months.

Andrew Darby (*Terror in Van Diemen's Land*) is a Hobart-based journalist, specialising in Tasmania and Antarctica. His work has been published mainly in *The Age* and *The Sydney Morning Herald*.

Nigel Hunt (*The Rainbird and Other Murders, The Dark Side of Adelaide, The Truro Murders*) has been reporting on police and crime stories in Adelaide since 1982. He has been chief police reporter of *The News* from 1982 till early last year when the paper ceased publication. He was then hired by *The Advertiser* as chief police reporter. He is working on an extended book on the Family (von Einem) murders on the late 1970s and early 1980s, expected to be published in 1994.

Tony Koch (*The Pressler Case, The Whiskey au Go Go Outrage*), the son of a Queensland country policeman, turned to journalism in 1975 after working as an official court reporter. Since then he has won a Walkly award, three Dalgety Australia awards and an Australia-Japan Fellowship and has covered assignments in more than 20 countries. He is the first journalist in Australia to be trained by his employer as a pilot. He is co-author of *JO's KO* (Boolarong Press, 1983) on Queensland politics.

Chips Mackinolty (*The Hunt for Larry Boy*) is a Darwin-based graphic artist and journalist, currently freelancing for *The Sydney Morning Herald, The Age* and other publications. Over the last 13 years he has worked as a writer and researcher for a number of Aboriginal organisations in the Northern Territory, particularly in the areas of the arts, copyright, land rights and economic development, as well as collecting oral history.

David McKnight (*The Croation Bombings*) is a journalist working on ABC TV's *Four Corners*. He worked on the *University of Sydney News* before joining *The Sydney Morning Herald* where he worked from 1985 to 1990, as a feature writer and as a reporter on education and the professions. He edited a collection of essays, *Moving Left*, published by Pluto Press in 1986, and has also worked on the left-wing newspaper, *Tribune*. He is presently working on a history the Australian Security Intelligence Organisation (ASIO) from 1949 to 1980.

Jerry Maher (*Barlow and Chambers*) is a Perth-based journalist and media consultant. He started his career with *The West Australian* newspaper in 1969. He is now director of Maher Durack Media, of West Perth. Most of his work is concentrated in the political and commercial arena but he is writing a cooking book designed for, as he describes it, bachelors and victims of the Family Court.

Tom Noble (*Squizzy Taylor, Gangster, The Walsh Street Shootings*) has been a journalist for 11 years and is a former chief police reporter for *The Age* in Melbourne. He is the author of the bestsellers, *Untold Violence—Crime in Melbourne Today* (John Kerr, 1989) and *Walsh Street* (John Kerr, 1991) about the killings in Melbourne in October 1988.

Tom Prior (*The Plight of the Defenceless*) has been a walk-up reporter specialising in crime, sport and difficult interviews in Australia and overseas for more than 40 years. He has written nine books, including the bestsellers *Plundering Sons* (1966) with Bill Wannan, *The Footballer Who Laughed* (1981) with Lou Richards,

A Knockabout Priest (1985) which is a biography of Father John Brosnan, the famous prison priest, and *Bolte by Bolte*, a biography of the controversial premier. Prior's most recent book, *The Sinners' Club*, reflections on 40 years as a newspaperman, was published by Penguin in July 1993.

John Sylvester (*The Great Bookie Robbery, Battle for the Waterfront*) has been a Melbourne-based crime reporter since 1978. In 1990 he worked for the famous *Sunday Times* Insight Team in London. He has studied crime and corruption in Australia, Asia and Britain. He has been called as a witness at royal commissions in Melbourne and Sydney. He is co-author of *Inside Victoria: A Chronicle of Scandal*, and co-editor of *Chopper: From the Inside* and *Chopper 2: Hits and Memories*, the two best-selling memoirs from underworld standover man, Mark Brandon Read. He is currently an investigative crime reporter for the *Melbourne Herald-Sun*.

Lindsay Simpson (*The Granny Killer*) is co-author of two books, *Brothers in Arms* (1989) about the 1984 Milperra bikie massacre and *My Husband, My Killer* (1992) about the murder of Meagan Kalajzich. Lindsay, a senior journalist with *The Sydney Morning Herald*, is co-authoring two more books: one on the life and times of Granny Killer John Wayne Glover and the other on bringing up twins, a subject dear to her heart because she has had them.

ACKNOWLEDGEMENTS

In the writing of the chapters for this book, the contributing authors are indebted to:

Jimmy Conway, Peter Cooke, Amy Dirngayg, Arnold Goode, Jessie Garalnganjag, Lesley Hicks, Judy King, Jonathon Lumley, Joe McDonald, Doris Rahner, Therese Ritchie, Glenys Simpson, Kerry Smith, Ken Taylor, Dennis Watt, Graham Wilson, the New South Wales Archives, the Archives Office of Tasmania, the archives of the University of New England, the State Library of New South Wales and the libraries of *The Advertiser, The Age, The Courier Mail, The Northern Territory News, The Sydney Morning Herald, The West Australian* and Queensland Newspapers.

INDEX

Abbot, Assistant Commissioner Cec
200—1
Abdallah, Gary 218
Aborigines
Larry Boy Janba manhunt 109—17
Rainbird murder 36
Adams, Hugh 219—20
Adelaide
kidnap 73—7
sexually motivated murders 141—50
Adriatic Trade and Travel Centre,
Sydney 137, 138
Agresta, Giuseppe 198
Agresta, Pasquale 195, 198
Aiton, Paul Leslie 78
alcohol, illicit sale of 58—9
Allard, Victor Frederick 175—6
Allen, Isaac 26
Allen, Police Commissioner William
"Bill" 95, 98
Anderson, Alan "Buckets" 164, 166
Anderson, Hugh 62
Anderson, James 95—7, 98
Anderson, Rosemary 88
Andric, Adolf 133—4, 138
Andric brothers 138
Angilletta, Vincenzo 101—2
Arena, Giuseppe 105—6
armed robbery of Melbourne
bookmakers 161—9
arson: Whiskey au Go Go 151—60
Arthur, Lieutenant Governor George
20—1
Asciak, Jill 206
Asciak, John 205—10
Ashton, Lady Winifreda Isabelle
234, 238
ASIO 132—40
August, Nicholas 80—1
Australian Security Intelligence
Organisation 132—40
Avery, Police Commissioner John 201

Bank of Australia (Sydney) robbery
26—35
bank robberies
Bank of Australia (Sydney) 26—35
Squizzy Taylor 63
Barbara, Antonio 101
Barbaro, Francesco 198
Barbour, Peter 137
Barker, Ian 97
Barlow, Kevin John 207—11
Barnes, Alan 145, 147, 148
Bastard Society 102
Batman, John 22
Bazley, James Frederick 174, 196—7,
199—200
Beamish, Darryl 88
Beaton, Sergeant Ron 214—16
Beaumont, Jim 73—7
Beaumont, Nancy 73—7
Beaumont children 73—6, 147, 148—9
Bejedic, Mr (Yugoslav Prime Minister)
139—40
Bell, Debra 224
Bellamy, Val 226
Bennett (tracker) 113, 115—16
Bennett, Glenys 204—5, 210
Bennett, Raymond Patrick "Chuck"
161—7
Benvenuto, Liboria 103—6
Berkman, Patricia 87
Berriman, Thomas 63
Bindon, Thomas James 195
Biyang, Marjorie 109—10
Black Hand; see Honoured Society
Black Mary (Howe's mistress) 19
Blackburn, Harry 240
blackmail 60
Blackstone, William 28—35
Blanch, Eliza 54—5
Blanch, John 54—5
Blay, Solomon 24
Bolton, Brian 154, 157

bombings, Croatian terrorist 132—40
Bonwick, James 21, 22
bookmakers: Great Bookie Robbery
    161—9
Boreham, Mr (solicitor) 123
Borthwick, Detective 194, 199
"Bourke Street Rats" 57
Bowditch, Jim 117
Bradley, Stephen Leslie 71—3
Brady, Matthew 20—3
Brewer, Jillian 87
bribery 96, 98
Brisbane: Whiskey au Go Go
    firebombing 151—60
Britten, Frederick 49—50
Buckley, Richard 65
Buggy, Hugh 58, 62
Bundaberg, Qld: Pressler murders
    118—27
Burns, William 42
bushrangers
    Captain Thunderbolt 46—55
    Van Diemen's Land 16—25
Button, John 88

Campbelltown, SA 77
Canberra bombings 136, 138
cannabis 105, 192—211
Cannott, Alfred Leslie 175—77
Cappusotto, Giovanni 54—5
Carnie, Euphemia 238
Carroll, Ian Revell 162, 168
Carton, Detective Inspector Kevin 174
Casey, Dan 121, 122, 125—6
Cash, Martin 23—5
Cawley, Detective Francis 142, 145
Chambers, Brian Geoffrey 202—11
Chamings, Lawrence Richard
    173, 174—5
child abuse 78
Chipp, Senator Don 91, 97
Chuck, Ray (Raymond Bennett) 161—7
Ciccarello, Vincenzo 198
Clark, Terrence 197, 199
Clayton (bank robber) 29—30, 33
Clayton, Detective Michael 142, 145
Cleland, R.E. 142
Cleveland, Olive 238
Cockatoo Island 34, 48, 49

Cole, Justice 230
Cole, Cheryl 159—60
Coles—Myer group 107—8
Collarenebri, NSW 52
Commonwealth Police role in Croatian
    bombings 133—9
Conau, Bill 126
convicts
    Sydney 26—8
    Van Diemen's Land 16
Conway, Jimmy 114
Cooke, Eric 80—9
Cooke, Sally 84, 85
corporal punishment 26
Costello, Desmond St Bernard
    "Cossie" 173
Costigan, Francis Xavier 177—8
Cottesloe, WA 82
Cox, Doris 235, 238
Croatian Liberation Movement 135
Croatian Revolutionary Brotherhood
    132—6, 138
Croatian terrorists 132—40
Croiset, Gerard 76
Cronau, Inspector Bill 120—2
Crotty, Robert John 172
Culbert, Ced 198
Culgoa River, NSW 51
Cusack, John T. 102—3, 108
Cutmore, John "Snowy" 64—5

Dalkeith, WA 83
Davey, Thomas 18
David Jones store, Canberra 136
Davidson, Detective Superintendent
Graham "Slippery" 161
Davie, Jennifer Denise 157
Davies, Chief Justice Sir Richard 39
Davis, George 51
death penalty
    bushrangers 17, 20, 22
    drug-running 210—11
    murder 36, 38, 39, 41—4, 63
    robbery 26—7
Delianis, Paul 162, 169
Delltones 154—5
Demarte, Domenico 101—2, 104
Denison Diggings mining camp,
    NSW 52—3

Devlin, Thomas 26
Dickinson, Maria 179—80
Dingle, James 28—33
Dirngayg, Amy 109
Donnegan, Jimmy 172
Dowd, Carl 83
Dowd, Wendy 83
Dowling Justice James Sheen 33—4
Draper, Police Commissioner Laurie
    181, 184
drugs
    Barlow and Chambers 202—11
    Melbourne mafia 105
    murder of Donald Mackay 192—201
Duff, Detective Bill 226—7
Duffy, Frederick John 104
Duflou, Dr Jo 233
Duggan, Justice 149
Duncan, Attorney-General 94
Duncan, Dr George 141—5
Duncan, Peter 91

Ellis, Dr J. 87
Ellis, Detective Sergeant John Kenneth
    194, 199
Elsey Station, NT 109—17
execution; see death penalty
extortion 101
    Brisbane nightclubs 152—4
    kidnap of Graeme Thorne 71—3
    Melbourne mafia 100—8
Eyre, Constable Damian 214—17, 219

Fagan, Hugh 42
Falconer, Muriel 239
Famiglia, La; see Honoured Society
"Family" murders, Adelaide 145—50
Farrell, Anthony Leigh 219
Farrell, George 26, 28—33
Federated Ship Painters and Dockers'
    Union 170—9
Fellows, Janet 225
Fellows, Warren 224
Finch, James Richard 151—60
firebombing of Whiskey au Go Go,
    Brisbane 151—60
Fisher, Bill 198
"Fitzroy Vendetta" (Melbourne) 59
Flack, Glen Roderick 226, 227—8

Flannery, Christopher Dale 226
Flavell, Ronnie 227—9
Fook, Tommy Ah 43—4
Forbes, Chief Justice Francis 33—4
forgery 125
Foster, Senior Constable Peter 181—2,
    184—5
Foster, William 33—4
Fraser, Malcolm 177
Frew, Barry 113
Furina, Giuseppe 105, 200

Gambarcorta, Leonardo 198
gambling 59—60
gangsters
    Neddy Smith 222—31
    Painters and Dockers' Union 170—9
    Raymond Bennett 166—8
    Squizzy Taylor 56—65
    see also mafia
Garalnganjag, Jessie 109, 111, 113
Gardiner, Frank 48
Garoffolo, Giovanni 204—5
Gaynor, Patrick 196, 201
"Ghosting" 176—7
Gibbs, Roger 116
Giles, Sergeant Bob "Hugger" 179—80
Glenelg, SA 73—6
Glover, Freda 235—6, 237—8
Glover, Gai 236, 241
Glover, John Wayne 235—41
Golchert, Clifford 118—20, 123—4
Golchert, Marjorie 118—20, 123—4
Goode, Arnold 54
Gordon, Kirsty 77, 147, 148—9
Gordon, Terry 170
Grainger, Sergeant 49—50
"Granny Killer" 232—41
Grassby, Albert Jaime "Al" 192, 199
Great Bookie Robbery 161—9
Greenwood, Ivor 138—40
Grey, Dolly 59
Griffith, NSW: marijuana growing
    104—5, 192—201
Gurry, David 147

Hagan, Detective Inspector Mike 233,
    239—40

Hagenfelds, Biruta Aina 93
Haines, William 57
Hall, Sergeant Major James 37
Hamilton, Ian 153, 155—6
Hamilton, Ronald "Joey" 174
hanging; see death penalty
Harding, Gary, Leslie 175—7
Hardy, Frank 58
Harrison, Freddie "The Frog" 170—1
Harvey, Roy "Bluey" 111—17
Hatfield, K.W. 87
Hayward, Paul 224
Henry, Graham "Abo" 226, 228—9
heroin 202—11, 224—5
Hicks, Lesley 194
hit-and-run 63—4
Hitchings, Bill 187
homosexuals
    murders by known 145—50
    murders of 141—5
Honoured Society
    Melbourne mafia 100—8
    murder of Danald Mackay 192
HOP (Croatian Liberation Movement)
    135
Hope Royal Commission 140
horse-stealing 48, 49, 53—4
Houghton, Jedd 218, 219—20
Houseley, Ann 32
Howe, Michael 17—20
Howell, Vicki 180, 184, 186
HRB (Croatian Revolutionary
    Brotherhood) 132—6, 138
Hub Theatre, Sydney 138
Hudson, Detective Brian 142, 145
Hughes, Sir Walter 40
Hurst, Jennifer 83

Independent Commission Against
    Corruption 229—30
insanity plea 87—8
Iordanides, Connie 180, 184, 186
Italian immigrants 100—8, 193, 199
Italiano, Domenico 100—1

Jackson, Detective Bob 112
Jackson, David 110, 117
James, Dr Ian 87
James, Roger 141, 144—5

Janba, Larry Boy 109—17
Jenkins, Detective Sergeant Ronald
    Arthur 195
Jensen, Graeme 212—14, 220
Jents, Beril 92
Jilks, Senior Constable George 31
Johnson, Robert 43
Johnstone, Martin 197
Jones, George 23, 24
Joseph, George 196, 199—200
Jurjevic, Marjan 134
jury fixing 62

Kable, Barry "The Bear" 175
Kalkie, Qld 118—19
Kane, Brian 166—8
Kane, Les 166—7
Kapunda, SA 36—8
Kavanagh, Lawrence 23, 24
Keehner, Mr and Mrs (of Adelaide) 84
Keenan, Patrick Joseph 194—5
Kelly, Anthony 223, 229
Kelly, Deanna 223
Kelly, Osmond James "Hoppy" 173
Kelly, Patrick John 52
Kelvin, Richard 146, 147
Kenny, Tania 180, 186
Kentucky Creek, NSW 55
Kerr (Van Diemen's land landholder) 24
kidnap of children 71—7
Kingston, SA 43
Kipling, Detective Sergeant Trevor 146
Knight, Veronica 179—80, 182, 186—7
Knopwood, Rev Robert 16, 19, 21, 22, 24
Kolvorat, Zlatko 174—5

Lamb, Deborah 180, 182, 186
Lamb, Rhonda Evelyn 186
Lanfranchi, Warren 225
Langley, Mark 146, 147
Lawrie, Sergeant Glen 181—2, 184—5
Lee, Norman 163, 165—6, 169
Lee, Way 43
Lehmann, Chief Superintendent Col 142
Lesic, Tom 132, 138
liquor license infringements 92—3
Little, Brian 155
Lloyd, Pat 157

Longley, Billy "The Texan" 172, 174, 175—7
Lucas, Justice 158

McCabe (bushranger) 21, 22
McCracken, Peter 109—15
McDonald, Joe 112, 114, 116
McDonald, Wilson 116
McEvoy, Peter David 219—20
McGowan, Chief Superintendent Bob 142
McGrath, Constable David 58
McGuire (bushranger) 18
McInerney, Justice 229
Mackay, Barbara 195, 197, 199, 200
Mackay, Donald Bruce 104, 192—201
McLeod, Norman 167
McLeod, Shirley Martha 83
McMahon, Sir William 136—7
Macmenimen, Jane 39
McNamara, Anthony Paul 162, 168
Macpherson, Leonard Arthur 226
Macquarie, Governor Lachlan 17
Macquarie Harbour penal settlement, Tas 20
McVitie, Thomas 27, 31
McWilliam, Scott 81
Maddox, Janice 156
Madgwick, Judge Rod 229
Madrill, Constance Lucy 83, 85
mafia
    Melbourne 100—8
    murder of Donald Mackay 192—201
Mahoney, Constable James 122
Maio, Gerry 204—5
manhunt for Larry Boy Janba 109—17
Manoa, Chief Magistrate Nick 143—5
Mansfield, Sir Alan 126
Marciano, Lina 179—81
Maric, Jure 135
marijuana 105, 192—211
"Market Murders" (Melbourne) 102—3
"Market Wars" (Melbourne) 102
Martin, Brian 147
Martin, Malachi 38—9
Mary Ann (Ward's companion) 48—53
Mason, Thomas 52—3
Maxwell, Justice Victor 92
Mayger, Detective Paul 234

Medici, Rocco 105, 200
Melbourne
    bombing 137
    Great Bookie Robbery 161—9
    mafia 100—8
    Painters & Dockers' Union 170—9
    Squizzy Taylor 56—65
    Walsh Street shootings 212—21
Melbourne Mail Exchange 134
Melbourne Market 100—8
Melbourne Trades Hall 58
Melville, Constable Robert 30
Menzies, Prime Minister 133
mercury poisoning 41
Merredin, WA 82
Mikkelsen, Vincent Francis William 167
Miller, James William 182—7
Milte, Inspector Kerry 137
Milton, Dr Rod 241
Mitchelhill, Gwendoline 232—3, 238
Moffitt Royal Commission 93
Molloy, Sergeant Warren 95, 98
Monckton, Will 52
money-laundering 106, 164—65
Moonta mines, SA 40—1
Morehant, Mr (solicitor) 124
Morisset, Lieutenant Colonel 32
Morris, David 32
Morris, Sergeant Robert 43
Mosman, NSW, "granny killer" 232—41
Mt Diversion, NSW 195—6
Mr Asia international drug syndicate 197
Muir, Neil 145
Mulhall, Constable 49—50, 55
Muratore, Alfonso 105, 106—8
Muratore, Vincenzo 101—2
murders
    by Larry Boy Janba 109—10
    by police 141—5, 217—21
    by Pressler family 118—27
    of Donald Mackay 192—201
    of police 42—3, 212—17
    sexual abuse 145—50
    South Australia 36—46
    Walsh Street shootings, Melbourne 212—17
    see also gangsters; serial killings
Murdock, Robert Arthur 158

Murphy, Edward 26
Murphy, Lionel 133, 139—40
Murray, Angus 63
Murray, Robert 24
Musarri, Paul 204—10
Mykyta, Julie 180, 186

Nagle, Justice John 200—1
narcotics; see drugs
National Crime Authority 97—8, 178
N'Dranghita; see Honoured Society
Nedlands, WA 81
Neilsen, Detective Sergeant John 85
Nelson, Alfred Desmond "The Ferret"
    172—3
New England district, NSW 46—55
New Norfolk, Tas 18, 23
New South Wales
    Captain Thunderbolt 46—55
    murder of Donald Mackay 192—201
    see also Sydney
Newton, Judge 195
Nicholls, Jack "Putty Nose" 175, 177
Nielsen, Juanita 95
nightclubs
    Abe Saffron 92—7
    Whiskey au Go Go firebombing
        151—60
Noble, Joy 82
Nolan, William David 156
Norfolk Island penal settlement 25, 27
Norris, Constable 52
Northern Territory: Larry Boy Janba
manhunt 109—17
Nugent, Harold 171

Oban, NSW 54
O'Brien, Police Commissioner Les 83
O'Hanlon, Sergeant Charlie 142
Onorata Societa see Honoured Society
Openshaw, John 227
Openshaw, Detective John 226
organised crime
    Abe Saffron 90—9
    see also gangsters
O'Shea, Police Sergeant Lawrence 71
O'Shea, Mick 142—3

Pahud, Margaret Frances 238

Painters & Dockers' Union 170—9
Palethorpe, Lesley Gordon 156
Parramatta Gaol 223
Parrington, Detective Sergeant Joe
    197, 200—1
Pasti, Geza 134
Paterson, Andrew 187
Pavelic, Dr Ante 133
Pearce, Trooper Constable Harry
    Edmond 42
Pedder, Judge 20
Pederson, Don 160
Peirce, Victor George 219—20
Peirce, Wendy 219—20
penal colony at Macquarie Harbour,
    Tas 20
Pendergast, Laurence Joseph 167—8
Perth: Eric Cooke murders 80—9
Pettingil, Trevor 219
Pezzimenti, Domenico 104
Piazza, Giovanni 193
Pittman, Andreas 186
Pittman, Sylvia 180, 182, 186
Pochi, Juigi 195
poisoning 41
police
    early years 27
    killings by 141—5, 217—21
    murders of 42—3, 212—17
Poo, Mah 43—5
Pressler family 118—27
Pressler, Alan 122—3
Pressler, Enid 118—19, 121, 122—6
Pressler, Eric 124
Pressler, Geoffrey 121
Pressler, Henry 122—6
Pressler, Henry Edward 119
Pressler, Neville 119, 125—6
protection money; see extortion
Public Transport Authority 96
Pugh, Private William 20
Punch, Leon 198
Pursehouse, Harold Bruce 196, 200
Pyke, Jacky 37

Queen Victoria Market, Melbourne
    100—8
Queensland
    Pressler murders, Bundaberg 118—27

Whiskey au Go Go firebombing,
    Brisbane 151—60
Quinn, Constable 30

Rainbird murders 36—8
rape 221
Ratcliffe, Joanne 77, 147, 148—9
Ratcliffe, Les 77
Razor Gangs (Sydney) 59
Read, Mark Brandon 162, 164
Reeves, Rowena 80—1, 82
reward for Bank of Australia robbery 31
Reynolds, Constable 49—50
Rice, Paul 143—4
Ridgeway, William 42
Riley, Murray Stewart 226
Rixon, Annie 47
robberies
    Bank of Australia, Sydney 26—35
    Great Bookie Robbery, Melbourne
        161—9
Robbins, Detective 194, 199
Roberts, Daisy 239
Roberts, Ray 156
Robinson (murder victim) 38—9
Rogerson, Detective Roger 224
Rollison, Police Officer William 39
Rolls, Essie 236—7
Rolls, Gai 236, 241
Rook, Val 30, 33
Rooklyn, Jack 95
Roper, Raymond 233
Rosebud, Vic 78
Ross, David 221
Rover, Srecko 137
Roy, Lola 156
Rushdie, Salman 141
Ryan, Jason 218—21

Saffron, Abraham Gilbert "Abe" 90—9
Saffron, Doreen 92—4, 98—9
St George's Free Serbian Orthodox
    Church 137
Salisbury, Police Commissioner
    Harold 142
Salmon, Ian 197, 199
Scarfo, Giuseppe 198
schizophrenia 87
Scriva, Michele 100, 104, 106

Seeny, Thomas 32
Senic, Josip 134, 136
Sergi, Antonio 193, 194, 198
Sergi, Domenico 198
Sergi, Francesco 196—7, 198
Sergi, Giovanni 198
Sergi, Giuseppe 198
Sergi, Rocco 198
serial killings
    Erik Cooke 80—9
    "granny killer", Sydney 232—41
    Truro, SA 179—87
sexual abuse 145—50
Shannon, Pat 172, 174—5
Sheehy, Justice Joe 121—2
Sinclair, Joan 237, 239, 240
Sinclair, William 224
Slater, Harry 59—60
Slater, Sergeant Pat 112
sly grog 58—9
Smith, Arthur Stanley "Neddy" 222—31
Smith, Edwin 223, 224, 225
Smith, James Edward "Jockey" 161
Smith, Kerry 126
Smith, Dr Richard 200
Sorell, William 19
South Australia
    murders 36—46
    Truro murders 179—87
    see also Adelaide
Spence, Sergeant Mal 229
Sproule, Doug 173
STAR Force 182
Stephen, Justice Alfred 33—4
Stevens, Tony 187
Stewart, Justice Donald 192, 199—200
Stewart Royal Commission on Drug
    Trafficking 192, 199—200
Stogneff, Peter 145—6
Stokes, Henry 59—60, 64—5
Strasser, Sir Paul 96
Streitman, Charles 42
Stuart, Dan 152—3, 155, 157, 160
Stuart, John Andrew 152—5, 157—9
Sturkey, John 81, 87—8
Sydney
    Abe Saffron 90—9
    Bank of Australia robbery 26—35
    bombings 134, 136, 137—8, 138—9

"granny killer" 232—41
kidnap 71—3
Neddy Smith 222—31

T. Costa Pty Ltd 107
Tasmanian bushrangers 16—25
tax fraud 97—8, 177—8
Taylor, Angela 217
Taylor, Joseph Leslie Theodore
"Squizzy" 56—65
Taylor, Kevin James 175—7
Temby, Ian 230
terrorism 132—40
theft; see robberies
Thomson,John 51—2
Thorne, Bazil 71
Thorne, Freda 71
Thorne, Graeme 71—3
Thorsen, Detective Superintendent Ken
179—81, 182, 184—5
Threfall, Henry 88
Thunderbolt, Captain (Fred Ward) 46—55
Thurgar, Roy 229
Tizzone, Gianfanco 196—7, 199—200
Todhunter, Margaret 237
"Toecutters" (gang) 165
Torino nightclub, Brisbane 152
Traynor, Dorothy 223
Trimbole, Joan 194
Trimbole, John 198
Trimbole, Robert 193—201
Truro, SA, murders 179—87
Turner, Superintendent Paul 142
Turner, Thomas 28—9
Twist, John Eric 171
two-up schools 59
Tynan, Constable 214—17, 219

Union, Painters and Dockers' 170—9
Uralla, NSW 49, 54—5

Valerio, Daniel 78
Van Diemen's Land bushrangers 16—25
Vannon, Patrick 42
Vasilopolous, John 107
Velardi, Antonio 198
Velardi, Domenico 198
Verscace, Guiseppe "Fat Joe" 104
Victoria; see Melbourne

Victorian Club robbery 161—9
Virtue, Justice 88
Vizzard, Fred 72
von Einem, Bevan Spencer 145, 146—50

Walker, Constable Alexander Binne
54—5
Wallace, John 31
Walmsley, George 81
Walmsley, Sandra 81
Walsh Street shootings, Melbourne
212—21
Ward, Fred (Captain Thunderbolt)
46—55
Watt, Dennis 159—60
Weir, Brian 82, 89
Wellingrove, NSW 54
West, John 17—18, 19
Western Australia: Eric Cooke
murders 80—9
Whiskey au Go Go firebombing,
Brisbane 151—60
Whitehead (bushranger) 18
Wilkinson, Constable Reginald
George 171
Wilsen, William 39
Wilson, Douglas 199
Wilson, Isobel 199
witness intimidation 57—8, 62
Woberton, Robert 20
wombats 37, 39, 40
Wood, Justice 241
Wood, James 30
Woodward, Justice Phil 192, 198
Woodward, Thomas 32, 33—4
Woolcock, Elizabeth 40—2
Woolcock, Thomas 40—1
Wootton, Charles Joseph "Charlie"
171, 174
Worrall, Jack 20
Worrell, Christopher Robin 182—4
Wran, Neville 94

Yugoslav Consulate, Melbourne 137
Yugoslav Consulate, Sydney 134, 136
Yugoslav Embassy, Canberra 136
Yugoslav terrorists 132—40
Yung, Willie 43—4

PICTURE CREDITS

TERROR IN VAN DIEMEN'S LAND
Pictures of Matthew Brady and Martin Cash by permission of the Archives Office of Tasmania
Copy of a watercolour by TG Gregson by permission of the Diocesan Officer, Hobart and courtesy of the Mitchell Library, State Library of New South Wales

THE BANK OF AUSTRALIA ROBBERY
All pictures courtesy of the Mitchell Library, State Library of New South Wales

THE RAINBIRD AND OTHER MURDERS
Picture of Elizabeth Woolcock courtesy of Moonta Bay National Trust
Picture of Adelaide Gaol gallows courtesy of *The Advertiser*, Adelaide

THE LIFE AND TIMES OF THUNDERBOLT
Picture of Fred Ward courtesy of the National Library of Australia
Picture of the bushranger in death from a copy of a photograph on loan to the Mitchell Library, State Library of New South Wales

THE PLIGHT OF THE DEFENCELESS
Pictures of Stephen Leslie Bradley, Bazil and Freda Thorne, the cave where Thorne's body was found and police combing the area courtesy of John Fairfax Group Pty Ltd
Pictures of Jim and Nancy Beaumont and sketch courtesy of *The Advertiser*, Adelaide
Picture of replicas printed with permission: *The Courier Mail*
Picture of police cadets searching dump courtesy of *The News*, Adelaide

ERIC COOKE, RANDOM KILLER
All pictures courtesy of *The West Australian*

ABE SAFFRON
Picture from *People* magazine courtesy of ACP Publishing Pty Ltd
Picture of Abe and Doreen Saffron courtesy of John Fairfax Group Pty Ltd

DOMENICO ITALIANO, AUSTRALIAN "GODFATHER"
Pictures of the murder scene and funeral courtesy of The Herald & Weekly Times

THE HUNT FOR LARRY BOY
Pictures of Peter McCracken and Roy Harvey courtesy of *Northern Territory News*
Pictures of Jessie Garalnganjag and Joe McDonald courtesy of Chips Mackinolty

THE PRESSLER CASE
All pictures printed with permission: *The Courier Mail*

THE DARK SIDE OF ADELAIDE
Pictures of the River Torrens scene, Mike O'Shea, the police cordon around Kelvin's body and Bevan von Einem courtesy of *The News*, Adelaide
Pictures of Brian Hudson, Michael Clayton and Francis Cawley courtesy of *The Advertiser*, Adelaide

THE CROATION BOMBINGS
All pictures courtesy of John Fairfax Group Pty Ltd

THE WHISKEY AU GO GO OUTRAGE
All pictures printed with permission: *The Courier Mail*

THE GREAT BOOKIE ROBBERY
All pictures courtesy of The Herald & Weekly Times

BATTLE FOR THE WATERFRONT
Pictures of Patrick Shannon, Billy Longley, Jack Nicholls and Frank Costigan courtesy of The Herald & Weekly Times
Picture of Doug Sproule courtesy of *The Age*, Melbourne

THE TRURO MURDERS
Picture of Peter Foster courtesy of *The News*, Adelaide
Pictures of Julie Mykyta's remains, Tania Kenny's remains and James Miller courtesy of *The Advertiser*, Adelaide

THE MURDER OF DONALD MACKAY
News pictures courtesy of John Fairfax Group Pty Ltd

BARLOW AND CHAMBERS
Pictures of Kevin Barlow and Brian Chambers on 18 December courtesy of Reuter
Pictures of a handcuffed Chambers and Barlow's body courtesy of AP/AAP
Pictures of John Asciak and Debbie Coyler-Long courtesy of *The West Australian*
Picture of Mrs and Mrs Barlow courtesy of *The Advertiser*, Adelaide

THE WALSH STREET SHOOTINGS
News pictures courtesy of *The Age*, Melbourne

NEDDY SMITH IN THE SPOTLIGHT
Picture of Paul Hayward courtesy of Express Newspapers plc
Pictures of Roger Rogerson, Bill Duff and Dangar Place courtesy of John Fairfax Group Pty Ltd

THE GRANNY KILLER
Pictures of Gwendolin Mitchelhill and a police officer accompanying an elderly woman courtesy of John Fairfax Group Pty Ltd
Picture of John Glover courtesy of The National Nine Network News